Frommer's®

Bermuda

17th Edition

by Darwin Porter & Danforth Prince

WILEY

John Wiley & Sons, Inc.

Published by:

JOHN WILEY & SONS, INC.

111 River St.
Hoboken, NJ 07030-5774

ISBN (paper) 978-1-118-28752-1; ISBN (ebk) 978-1-118-33360-0; ISBN (ebk) 978-1-118-33474-4; ISBN (ebk) 978-1-118-33119-4

Editor: Kathleen Warnock
Production Editor: Michael Brumitt
Cartographer: Elizabeth Puhl
Photo Editor: Richard Fox
Production by Wiley Indianapolis Composition Services

Front cover photo: Natural Arches beach © Philip H. Coblentz / Alamy Images
Back cover photo: Colorful local architecture and moped in front, Hamilton, Bermuda © Nancy Tobin / Alamy Images

For information on our other products and services or to obtain technical support, please contact our Customer Care Department within the U.S. at 877/762-2974, outside the U.S. at 317/572-3993 or fax 317/572-4002.

Wiley also publishes its books in a variety of electronic formats. Some content that appears in print may not be available in electronic formats.

Manufactured in the United States of America

5 4 3 2 1

CONTENTS

4 FUN ON & OFF THE BEACH 64

5 SEEING THE SIGHTS 84

6 WHERE TO EAT 110

7 SHOPPING 146

8 BERMUDA AFTER DARK 158

9 WHERE TO STAY 164

10 PLANNING YOUR TRIP TO BERMUDA 188

Index 206

LIST OF MAPS

ABOUT THE AUTHORS

A team of veteran travel writers, **Darwin Porter** and **Danforth Prince** have produced numerous titles for Frommer's, including best-selling guides to Italy, France, the Caribbean, England, and Germany. Porter is also a noted Hollywood biographer, and his recent releases include *Howard Hughes: Hell's Angel and Brando Unzipped*. He is a newspaper columnist on popular culture as well as a radio commentator, with broadcasts heard in all 50 states. Price, formerly of the New York Times Paris bureau, is the president of Blood Moon Productions and other media-related firms.

HOW TO CONTACT US

In researching this book, we discovered many wonderful places—hotels, restaurants, shops, and more. We're sure you'll find others. Please tell us about them, so we can share the information with your fellow travelers in upcoming editions. If you were disappointed with a recommendation, we'd love to know that, too. Please write to:

Frommer's Bermuda, 17th Edition
John Wiley & Sons, Inc. • 111 River St. • Hoboken, NJ 07030-5774
frommersfeedback@wiley.com

ADVISORY & DISCLAIMER

Travel information can change quickly and unexpectedly, and we strongly advise you to confirm important details locally before traveling, including information on visas, health and safety, traffic and transport, accommodation, shopping and eating out. We also encourage you to stay alert while traveling and to remain aware of your surroundings. Avoid civil disturbances, and keep a close eye on cameras, purses, wallets and other valuables.

While we have endeavored to ensure that the information contained within this guide is accurate and up-to-date at the time of publication, we make no representations or warranties with respect to the accuracy or completeness of the contents of this work and specifically disclaim all warranties, including without limitation warranties of fitness for a particular purpose. We accept no responsibility or liability for any inaccuracy or errors or omissions, or for any inconvenience, loss, damage, costs or expenses of any nature whatsoever incurred or suffered by anyone as a result of any advice or information contained in this guide.

The inclusion of a company, organization or Website in this guide as a service provider and/or potential source of further information does not mean that we endorse them or the information they provide. Be aware that information provided through some Websites may be unreliable and can change without notice. Neither the publisher or author shall be liable for any damages arising herefrom.

FROMMER'S STAR RATINGS, ICONS & ABBREVIATIONS

Every hotel, restaurant, and attraction listing in this guide has been ranked for quality, value, service, amenities, and special features using a **star-rating system.** In country, state, and regional guides, we also rate towns and regions to help you narrow down your choices and budget your time accordingly. Hotels and restaurants are rated on a scale of zero (recommended) to three stars (exceptional). Attractions, shopping, nightlife, towns, and regions are rated according to the following scale: zero stars (recommended), one star (highly recommended), two stars (very highly recommended), and three stars (must-see).

In addition to the star-rating system, we also use **seven feature icons** that point you to the great deals, in-the-know advice, and unique experiences that separate travelers from tourists. Throughout the book, look for:

special finds—those places only insiders know about

fun facts—details that make travelers more informed and their trips more fun

kids—best bets for kids and advice for the whole family

special moments—those experiences that memories are made of

overrated—places or experiences not worth your time or money

insider tips—great ways to save time and money

great values—where to get the best deals

The following abbreviations are used for credit cards:

AE   American Express   DISC   Discover   V   Visa

DC   Diners Club   MC   MasterCard

TRAVEL RESOURCES AT FROMMERS.COM

Frommer's travel resources don't end with this guide. Frommer's website, www.frommers.com, has travel information on more than 4,000 destinations. We update features regularly, giving you access to the most current trip-planning information and the best airfare, lodging, and car-rental bargains. You can also listen to podcasts, connect with other Frommers.com members through our active-reader forums, share your travel photos, read blogs from guidebook editors and fellow travelers, and much more.

THE BEST OF BERMUDA

Adrift in its own dreamy archipelago in the balmy Gulf Stream, this rich little oasis of pink-sand beaches and sparkling blue waters is simultaneously slightly British, slightly American, and very Bermudian. Whether you've come to unwind on Elbow Beach, shop among the pretty pastels and whites of historic Hamilton, or discover 400 years of history at Fort St. Catherine in St. George, you'll discover a pleasant mix of formal British culture dressed in a pair of Bermuda shorts.

THINGS TO DO   Sit by the bustling waterfront and take in the capital scene in **Hamilton** or step back in time in **St. George.** Take a morning swim with the kids at sheltered **Tobacco Bay** or a sunset dip at **Elbow Beach.** The clear waters and white coves of **Warwick Parish** are made for scuba diving and **snorkeling.** Marvel at the subterranean beauty of **Crystal Caves.** Away from the beach, discover the **Verdmont Historic House Museum,** with its period furnishings, or walk along the **Bermuda Railway Trail** for a closer look at the island's exotic wildlife.

SHOPPING   All sorts of shops are clustered along **Front Street** in Hamilton. Under the atrium in The Emporium, you can browse boutiques and jewelry stores, or stroll the Royal Naval Dockyard area on Ireland Island for crafts and island pottery. You can watch local artisans at work at the **Bermuda Arts Centre.** Comparison shop at the Somers **Wharf & Branch Stores,** along Water Street, for better prices than their Hamilton counterparts.

NIGHTLIFE & ENTERTAINMENT   Many of Bermuda's bars and clubs hug the busy waterfront at **Front Street** in Hamilton, where Victorian-era balconies offer Atlantic views. The nightlife scene continues in the streets leading uphill from the harbor. Many hotels host steel-drum or calypso bands, or you can head to **LVs Piano Jazz Lounge,** where live jazz is performed nightly. The little port of St. George and adjoining St. David's Island are loaded with pubs. Enjoy a pint at **White Horse Tavern,** the oldest pub in St. George.

RESTAURANTS & DINING   Bermuda embraces a wide swath of American and European cuisines, but fresh seafood is still the default—and best—choice. Savor spiny lobster and wahoo steak in the elegant dining rooms of Sandys Parish or sink your teeth into shark hash and Bermudian rockfish in the restaurants along Hamilton's Front Street. For a cool treat, try the ice cream at island favorite Bailey's Ice Cream & Food D'Lites Restaurant in Hamilton Parish.

THE most UNFORGETTABLE BERMUDA EXPERIENCES

○ **Exploring the Colonial Heritage:** Start with **The Royal Naval Dockyard** (Sandys Parish): Nothing recaptures the maritime spirit of this feisty island colony more than this sprawling complex on Ireland Island. Fearing attacks on its fleet by Napoleon, pirates, or rebellious Americans, Britain began building this massive fortress and dockyard in 1809. The Royal Navy occupied the shipyard for almost 150 years. The Dockyard closed as an official outpost of the British Empire in 1951, and Her Majesty's Navy has little presence today. The Maritime Museum's centerpiece is the spectacularly restored Commissioner's House, which during the mid-1800s was the most potent symbol of British military might in the western Atlantic. Its exhibits on Britain's (and Bermuda's) nautical heritage give you a good feel for a vanished era. See p. 88.

○ **Diving:** If you're happiest under the sea, Bermuda has what you're looking for. That includes the wrecks of countless ships, underwater caves, rich reefs, and, during most of the year, warm, gin-clear waters. All around the island you'll find a kaleidoscope of coral and marine life that's the most varied in this part of the world. Many scuba experts consider Bermuda one of the safest and best places to learn the sport. Seasoned divers will not be disappointed, either—Bermuda has terrific diving areas for experts. Depths begin at 7.5m (25 ft.) or less, but can exceed 24m (79 ft.). Some wrecks are in about 9m (30 ft.) of water, which puts them within the range of snorkelers. See "The Best Dive Sites," below, and "Scuba Diving," in chapter 4.

○ **Honeymooning:** Perhaps you'll head for **Tucker's Point Hotel & Spa** (Hamilton Parish; www.rosewoodtuckerspoint.com; ✆ **866/604-3764** or 441/298-9800): This is the most opulent resort in Bermuda. On 80 private hectares (200 acres) of beautiful seafront, the 88-room resort is a posh pocket of privacy. With four swimming pools, a championship golf course, a state-of-the-art spa, and a private pink-sand beach, lovers will adore this resort's romance and honeymooners will want to return for a second honeymoon. It's that special. See p. 182.

○ **Biking & Hiking:** We recommend **The Bermuda Railway Trail** (Sandys Parish): Stretching for about 34km (21 miles), this unique trail was created along the course of the old Bermuda Railway, which served the island from 1931 to 1948 (automobiles weren't allowed on the island until the late 1940s). Armed with a copy of the *Bermuda Railway Trail Guide,* available at visitor centers, you can follow the route of the train known as "Rattle and Shake." Most of the trail still winds along a car-free route, and you can travel as much of it as your stamina allows. See p. 55 and 80.

○ **Golfing:** **Play a round at Port Royal Golf Course** (Southampton Parish): This public course ranks among the best on the island, public or private; in fact, it's one of the greatest public courses in the world. Jack Nicklaus apparently agrees—he's fond of playing here. Robert Trent Jones, Sr., designed the original ocean-fronting course. One wrong hit from the club and your ball will go flying into the ocean below. See p. 78.

○ **Going Underground:** Explore **Crystal Caves** (Hamilton Parish; www.caves.bm; ✆ **441/293-0640**): Bermuda has the highest concentration of limestone caves in the world, many with echo patterns and sedimentary deposits that some spelunkers consider mystical. Collectively, these caves form one of the island's major natural wonderlands. Their surreal formations took millions of years to come into being, and the great stalactites and stalagmites have a gothic grandeur. Crystal Caves, at Bailey's Bay, are among the best, and also among the few whose tunnels and chambers can be navigated by laypersons as part of a guided tour. Discovered in 1907, these caves house crystal-clear Cahow Lake. See p. 100.

THE best FOOD & DRINK EXPERIENCES

You don't come to Bermuda for grand cuisine. That said, there are quite a few places where you can enjoy a memorable meal.

- **Fourways Inn** (Paget Parish; ✆ 441/236-6517). For a refined continental cuisine in an elegant, even romantic, setting evocative of an English manor house, this inn is almost without equal. Dishes from an imaginative chef are both innovative and classic, many recipes from the classic French repertoire. See p. 122.
- **Tamarisk Dining Room** (Sandys Parish; ✆ 441/234-0331): This is an elegant enclave at the western tip of Bermuda. Housed in one of the island's premier accommodations, Cambridge Beaches, it offers excellent service and a frequently changing menu of impeccably prepared international cuisine. For your main course, you can't do better than juicy tenderloin of beef with grain mustard and blanched garlic sauce. The wine cellar is up to the high standards of the menu. See p. 114.
- **Waterlot Inn** (Southampton Parish; ✆ 441/238-8000): In a historic inn and warehouse that's part of the Fairmont Southampton Princess, this restaurant serves the island's most famous Sunday brunch, but it's also an ideal choice for dinner. Eleanor Roosevelt and Mark Twain praised the cuisine in their day, and it continues to please. See p. 116.
- **Ascots** (City of Hamilton, Pembroke Parish; ✆ 441/295-9644): In the Royal Palms Hotel, this restaurant specializes in a Continental menu that is mostly inspired by France and Italy, and does it exceedingly well. Classic techniques and first-rate ingredients are combined to make this one of the most enduring restaurants on the island. See p. 122.
- **The Harbourfront Restaurant and Komodaru Sushi Lounge** (City of Hamilton, Pembroke Parish; www.diningbermuda.com; ✆ 441/295-4207): The most fashionable restaurant in Bermuda attracts serious gastronomes eager to sample its take on savory Asian and Mediterranean cuisine. Its sushi bar is also one of the best on the island. It's on the ground floor of the Bermuda Underwater Exploration Institute. See p. 125.
- **Silk** (City of Hamilton, Pembroke Parish; www.bermudasbestrestaurants.com; ✆ 441/295-0449): Some critics, including the discriminating readers of *Condé Nast Traveler,* are hailing Silk as the island's finest restaurant. After our most recent feast here, we're inclined to agree. Recipes are inspired by the ancient Kingdom of Siam (think something like Thai, in other words). See p. 130.
- **Tom Moore's Tavern** (Hamilton Parish; www.tommoores.com; ✆ 441/293-8020): The Irish poet Tom Moore reportedly was a frequent visitor to this restaurant, which dates from 1652 and overlooks Walsingham Bay. The menu, however, is no relic—it's quite innovative. Duck is a specialty, as is Bermuda lobster; but who can forget the quail in puff pastry stuffed with foie gras? See p. 138.

3

o **Lobster Pot & Boat House Bar** (City of Hamilton, Pembroke Parish; ℂ **441/292-6898**): If you don't find the local foodies at the restaurants discussed above, they'll surely be at this local favorite, enjoying some of the island's best regional dishes. Black rum and sherry peppers are the not-so-secret ingredients in the fish chowder, and baked fish and lobster are sure to tempt you. See p. 129.

THE best WAY TO SEE BERMUDA LIKE A LOCAL

o **Head for St. David's Island** (St. George's Parish): Though most of Bermuda looks pristine and proper, you'll still find some vestiges of rustic maritime life on St. David's. Some St. David's Islanders never even bother to visit neighboring St. George, and to some locals, a trip to the West End of Bermuda would be like a trip to the moon. St. David's Lighthouse has been a local landmark since 1879. To see how people used to cook and eat, drop by Black Horse Tavern (p. 140).

o **Explore the Back Streets of St. George** (St. George's Parish): Almost every visitor to the island has photographed the 17th-century stocks on King's Square in historic St. George. But it's in the narrow back alleys and cobblestone lanes, such as Shinbone Alley, that you'll really discover the town's old spirit. Arm yourself with a good map and wander at leisure through such places as Silk Alley (also called Petticoat Lane), Barber's Lane Alley (named for a former slave from South Carolina), Printer's Alley (where Bermuda's first newspaper was published), and Nea's Alley (former stomping ground of the Irish poet Tom Moore). Finally, walk through Somers Garden and head up the steps to Blockade Alley. On the hill is the aptly named Unfinished Cathedral. See "Iconic Bermuda in 1 Day," in chapter 3.

o **Go Natural at Spittal Pond Nature Reserve** (Sandys Parish; ℂ **441/236-6483**): Bermuda still has some oases that aren't overrun with visitors. One such place is the **Spittal Pond Nature Reserve,** a sanctuary for migratory birds. It's a true walk through nature, with flowering bushes and citrus orchards. See p. 99.

o **Visit Verdmont** (Smith's Parish): This 1710 mansion is on property once owned by William Sayle, founder and first governor of South Carolina. Filled with portraits, antiques, and china, the house offers a rare glimpse into a long-faded life of old-fashioned style and grace. Resembling a small English manor house, it's the finest historic home in Bermuda. See p. 99.

o **Beachcomb on Somerset Long Bay** (Sandys Parish): The waters off this beach are often unsafe for swimming, but its isolation will appeal to anyone who wants to escape the crowds. With about .4km (¼ mile) of sand, the crescent-shaped beach is ideal for strolling. The undeveloped parkland of Sandys Parish shelters it from the rest of the island. See p. 68.

THE best FAMILY EXPERIENCES

Bermuda is more kid-friendly than any place we know in the Caribbean or The Bahamas. It's a safe, clean environment in a politically stable country. Nearly all Bermuda hotels go the extra mile to welcome families with children.

o **Go Sunning & Swimming at Horseshoe Bay** (Southampton Parish): This is Bermuda's most famous beach, and it's one of the best for families. Unlike most island beaches, Horseshoe Bay has a lifeguard on duty from May to September. The **Horseshoe Bay Beach Cafe** (℡ **441/238-2651**) offers complete facilities, including watersports equipment rental. See p. 67.

o **Book a Stay at the Fairmont Southampton** (Southampton Parish; www.fairmont.com/southampton; ℡ **866/540-4497** in the U.S. and Canada, or 441/238-8000): From June through Labor Day, this hotel features the best children's program in Bermuda. Children 17 and under stay free; and if the parents choose the MAP (breakfast and dinner included in the rates), kids also get free meals. With its many sports facilities, including two freshwater pools and six tennis courts, the Fairmont is definitely for families who enjoy the sporting life. The former Touch Club has been redesigned as Lenny's Loft, a social center for children's activities. From Lenny's Loft, kids are taken on excursions around the island. See p. 167.

o **Outfit the Gang at Pompano Beach Club Watersports Centre** (Southampton Parish; www.pompanobeachclub.com; ℡ **441/234-0222**): Open from May to late October, it offers a variety of equipment, including the O'Brien Windsurfer, a popular sailboard suitable for one person at the intermediate or advanced level. Its fleet also includes vessels that hold one or two people: Dolphin paddle boats, Buddy Boards, Aqua-Eye viewing boards, Aqua Finn sailboats, and kayaks. These can be rented for up to 4 hours. See p. 75.

o **Go Biking:** You can't rent a car on Bermuda, so you might as well hit the road on two wheels. Most of the island isn't great cycling terrain; the roads are narrow and the traffic is heavy. So we suggest that you head for the Railway Trail, the island's premier bike path. The paved trail, which follows the former route of Bermuda's railway line, runs almost the entire length of the island. See "Other Outdoor Pursuits," in chapter 4.

THE best BEACHES

Your first priority on your Bermuda vacation probably will be to kick back at the beach. But which beach? Hotels often have private stretches of sand; if so, we describe the beach in each hotel's review (see chapter 9). There are many fine public beaches as well. Here are our top choices, arranged clockwise around the island, beginning with the south-shore beaches closest to the City of Hamilton. For more details, see chapter 4.

o **Elbow Beach** (Paget Parish): The pale pink sand stretches for almost 1.6km (1 mile) at Elbow Beach, one of the most popular beaches in Bermuda. Three hotels sit on its perimeter. Because protective coral reefs surround it, Elbow Beach is one of the safest beaches on the island for swimming. See p. 64.

o **Warwick Long Bay** (Warwick Parish): This popular beach, on the south side of South Shore Park, features a 1km (½-mile) stretch of sand against a backdrop of scrubland and low grasses. Despite frequent winds, an offshore reef keeps the waves surprisingly small. Less than 60m (200 ft.) offshore, a jagged coral island appears to be floating above the water. There is excellent snorkeling here—the waters are clear and marine life comes in close to shore. See p. 65.

o **Chaplin Bay** (Warwick and Southampton parishes): At the southern extremity of South Shore Park, straddling the boundary of two parishes, this small but secluded beach almost completely disappears during storms and particularly high tides. An open-air coral barrier rises from the water, partially separating one half of the beach from the other. See p. 66.

o **Church Bay** (Southampton Parish): If you like to snorkel, this southwestern beach is for you. The relatively calm waters, sheltered by offshore reefs, harbor a variety of marine life, and a concession stand sells snacks and rents snorkel gear. Sunbathers love the unusually deep pink sands of this beach. See p. 68.

o **Shelly Bay** (Hamilton Parish): On the north shore, you'll discover calm waters and soft, pink sand—and you'll want for nothing else. This beach is well known among beach buffs, but it's rarely overcrowded and there's always a spot in the sun just waiting for you. See p. 68.

o **Tobacco Bay** (St. George's Parish): A popular stretch of pale pink sand, this is the most frequented beach on St. George's Island. It offers lots of facilities, including equipment rentals and a snack bar. See p. 69.

o **John Smith's Bay** (Smith's Parish): The only public beach in Smith's Parish is long and flat. It boasts the pale pink sand for which the south shore is famous. There's usually a lifeguard on duty from May to September—a plus for families. There are toilets and changing facilities on-site. See p. 69.

THE best OUTDOOR PURSUITS

o **Golf:** Known for its outstanding courses, Bermuda attracts the world's leading golfers. Over the years, such luminaries as President Eisenhower, President Truman, and the Duke of Windsor have hit the island's links. Rolling, hummocky fairways characterize the courses. Many avid golfers come to Bermuda to "collect courses." See "The Best Golf Courses," below, for our top picks, and "Where to Play World-Class Golf," in chapter 4.

o **Boating & Sailing:** Yachters around the world agree: Bermuda is one of the world's top boating destinations. Many people forget that Bermuda isn't one island, but an archipelago, with all kinds of nooks and crannies waiting to be discovered. With the fresh wind of the Atlantic blowing in your hair, you can embark on your own voyage of discovery, exploring Great Sound and its islets, including Long Island and Hawkins Island. Tiny, secluded beaches beckon you to put down anchor and relax awhile. If you're a novice, try Mangrove Bay; it's protected and safer than some of the more turbulent seas. See "More Fun in the Water," in chapter 4.

o **Horseback Riding:** Steering a horse through the dune grass and oleander, especially at South Shore Park, is an experience you won't want to miss. Because this sport is restricted to supervised trails on Bermuda, it can be all the more memorable—you'll have the gorgeous seascapes all to yourself. Horseback-riding centers guide you on trails through the best of the countryside and to beautiful hidden spots along the north coast. See "Other Outdoor Pursuits," in chapter 4.

THE best DIVE SITES

The following are some of the most exciting shipwreck and coral-reef dives. See "Scuba Diving," in chapter 4, for information about dive outfitters and for more about the sites described below.

o **The *Constellation*:** This 60m (197-ft.), four-masted schooner, which wrecked en route to Venezuela with a cargo of glassware, drugs, and whiskey in 1943, lies in 9m (30 ft.) of water off the northwest side of the island, about 13km (8 miles) northwest of the Royal Naval Dockyard. The true story of this ship inspired Peter Benchley to write *The Deep*.

- **The *Cristóbal Colón*:** The largest known shipwreck in Bermuda's waters is this 144m (472-ft.) Spanish luxury liner; it ran aground in 1936 on a northern reef between North Rock and North Breaker. It lies in 9 to 17m (30–56 ft.) of water.
- **The *Hermes*:** This 50m (164-ft.) steamer ship rests in some 24m (79 ft.) of water about 1.5km (1 mile) off Warwick Long Bay on the south shore. It foundered in 1985. The *Hermes*, the *Rita Zovetta*, and the *Tauton* (see below) are Bermuda favorites because of the incredible multicolored variety of fish that populate the waters around the ships. You'll have a chance to see grouper, brittle starfish, spiny lobster, crabs, banded coral shrimp, queen angels, tube sponges, and more.
- ***L'Herminie*:** A first-class, 60-gun French frigate, *L'Herminie* was 17 days out of its Cuban port, en route to France, when it sank in 1838. The ship lies in 6 to 9m (20–30 ft.) of water off the west side of the island, with 25 cannons still visible.
- **The *Marie Celeste*:** This paddle-wheeler sank in 1864. Its 4.5m-diameter (15-ft.) paddle wheel, off the southern portion of the island, is overgrown with coral standing about 17m (56 ft.) off the ocean floor.
- **The *North Carolina*:** One of Bermuda's most colorful and well-preserved wrecks, this English sailing barkentine foundered in 1879 and now lies in about 12m (39 ft.) of water off the western portion of the island. The bow, stern, masts, and rigging are all preserved, and all sorts of vibrant marine life call the wreck home.
- **The *Rita Zovetta*:** A 120m (394-ft.) Italian cargo ship, lying in 6 to 21m (20–69 ft.) of water off the south side of the island, the *Rita Zovetta* ran aground off St. David's Island in 1924. It's a favorite with underwater photographers because of the kaleidoscope of fish that inhabit the area.
- **South West Breaker:** This coral-reef dive off the south shore, about 2.5km (1½ miles) off Church Bay, has hard and soft coral decorating sheer walls at depths of 6 to 9m (20–30 ft.).
- **The *Tauton*:** This popular dive site is a Norwegian coastal steamer that sank in 1920. It lies in 3 to 12m (10–39 ft.) of water off the north end of the island and is home to numerous varieties of colorful marine life.
- **Tarpon Hole:** Near Elbow Beach, off the south shore, this dive's proximity to the Elbow Beach Hotel makes it extremely popular. The honeycombed reef—one of the most beautiful off the coast of Bermuda—is known for its varieties of coral: yellow pencil, elkhorn, fire, and star.

THE best GOLF COURSES

- **Belmont Hills Golf & Country Club** (Warwick Parish): California-based designer Algie M. Pulley, Jr., radically reconfigured this par-70, 5,501m (6,017-yd.) course in 2002. Since its reopening, amid justifiable brouhaha surrounding the most extensive golf course rebuilding in the history of Bermuda, there has been endless discussion about the peculiar features of this relatively short but quirkily challenging course. See p. 77.
- **Fairmont Southampton Golf Club** (Southampton Parish): This is a par-54, 2,454m (2,684-yd.) course, with elevated tees, strategically placed bunkers, and an array of water hazards to challenge even the most experienced golfer. One golfer said of this course, "You not only need to be a great player, but have a certain mountaineering agility as well." See p. 77.

THE best SAILING OUTFITTERS

Bermuda is one of the Atlantic's major sailing capitals. Many sail-yourself boats are available for rent to qualified skippers, and kayaks, paddle boats, sailboards, and more are available for everyone. If you'd like to sail on a larger craft, the outfitters will provide you with a captain. Here are some of the best outfitters.

o **Blue Hole Water Sports** (Grotto Bay Beach Hotel, Hamilton Parish; www.blue holewater.bm; ℂ **441-293-2915**): Here you'll find a large selection of watercraft, including Sunfish, sailboards, kayaks, Paddle Cats, and Sun Cats. Rentals are available for up to 8 hours. See p. 75.

o **Somerset Bridge Watersports** (Somerset Parish; www.watersportssomersetbridge. com; ℂ **441/234-3145**): This is the best place to rent a Boston Whaler, a small boat that can hold three or four passengers. It's an ideal craft for exploring the archipelago's uninhabited islands. This outfitter rents 4m (13-ft.) Whalers and a 30-hp, 5m (16-ft.) Open Bowrider, a speed-craft often used to pull water-skiers, which accommodates four. See p. 75.

THE best TENNIS FACILITIES

o **The Fairmont Southampton** (Southampton Parish): This is Bermuda's premier destination for avid players. Its tennis court complex is the largest on the island, and is maintained in state-of-the-art condition. The deluxe hotel, one of the finest on Bermuda, offers six Plexipave (professional color surface) courts. The courts are somewhat protected from the north winds, but swirling breezes may affect your final score. See p. 80.

o **Elbow Beach** (Paget Parish): With the closing of several other tennis courts on the island in recent years, avid tennis players have had to search a bit harder for suitable venues on which to play. With a pedigree dating from the early days of Bermuda tourism, and with a sprawling physical plant that incorporates just about everything, these five tennis courts are open to visitors who phone ahead. Three of them are lit for night play. See p. 80.

o **Government Tennis Stadium** (Pembroke Parish): Although Bermuda has been known as the tennis capital of the Atlantic since 1873, players often complain that the trade winds around the island affect their game, especially near the water. That's why many prefer inland courts, such as those at this government-owned stadium. It offers three clay and five shock-absorbing Plexicushion courts (three illuminated for night play). The facility, which is north of the City of Hamilton, requires players to wear proper tennis attire. A pro shop, a ball machine, and a pro offering private lessons are on-site. See p. 80.

THE best DAY HIKES

o **From the Royal Naval Dockyard to Somerset** (Sandys Parish): A 6.5km (4-mile) walk leads from the dockyard, the former headquarters of the British navy on Bermuda, to Somerset Island. Along the way you'll cross a beautiful nature reserve; explore an old cemetery; view the Royal Naval Hospital, where thousands of yellow-fever victims died in the 19th century; and be rewarded with a sweeping panoramic view of Great Sound. Sandy beaches along the route are perfect for pausing from your hike to stretch out on the sand or take a dip in the ocean. See "Iconic Bermuda in 3 Days," in chapter 3.

○ **Spittal Pond Nature Reserve** (Smith's Parish): This 24-hectare (59-acre) sanctuary is the island's largest nature reserve, home to both resident and migratory waterfowl. You can spot some 25 species of waterfowl from November to May. Scenic trails and footpaths cut through the property. Explore on your own or take a guided hike offered by the Department of Agriculture. See p. 99.

THE best VIEWS

○ **Warwick Long Bay:** This stretch of pristine pink sand is a dream beach of the picture-postcard variety. It backs up to towering cliffs and hills studded with Spanish bayonet and oleander. A 6m-high (20-ft.) coral outcrop, rising some 60m (200 ft.) offshore and resembling a sculpted boulder, adds variety to the stunning beachscape. See p. 65.

○ **Scaur Hill Fort Park:** From Somerset Bridge in Sandys Parish, head for this fort atop the parish's highest hill. Walk the fort's ramparts, enjoying the vistas across Great Sound to Spanish Point. You can also gaze north to the dockyard and take in the fine views of Somerset Island. On a clear day, a look through the telescope reveals St. David's Lighthouse, 23km (14 miles) away on the northeastern tip of the island. After enjoying the fantastic views from the fort, you can stroll through the fort's 9 hectares (22 acres) of beautiful gardens. See p. 88.

○ **Gibbs Hill Lighthouse:** For an even better view than the one enjoyed by Queen Elizabeth II when she visited but did not climb the lighthouse in 1953, hike the 185 spiral steps to the top. Built in 1846, it's the oldest cast-iron lighthouse in the world. From the top, you can relish what islanders consider the single finest view in all of Bermuda—a panorama of the island and its shorelines. In heavy winds, the tower actually sways, so be sure to hang on to the railing when you're up there. See p. 92.

THE best HISTORIC SITES

○ **Scaur Hill Fort Park** (Sandys Parish): Fort Scaur and Fort St. Catherine were part of a ring of fortifications that surrounded Bermuda. Built by the British navy, the fort was supposed to protect the Royal Naval Dockyard from an attack that never materialized. During World War II, U.S. Marines were billeted nearby. Overlooking Great Sound, the fort offers views of some of the island's most dramatic scenery. See p. 88.

○ **St. Peter's Church** (St. George's Parish): This is the oldest Anglican house of worship in the Western Hemisphere. At one time, virtually everyone who died on Bermuda was buried here, from governors to criminals. To the west of the church lies a graveyard of slaves. The present church sits on the site of the original, which colonists built in 1612. A hurricane destroyed the first structure in 1712, but some parts of the interior survived. It was rebuilt on the same site in 1713. See p. 104.

○ **Fort St. Catherine** (St. George's Parish): This fort—with its tunnels, cannons, and ramparts—towers over the beach where the shipwrecked crew of the *Sea Venture* first came ashore in 1609 (becoming Bermuda's first settlers). The fort was completed in 1614, and extensive rebuilding and remodeling continued until the 19th century. The audiovisual presentation on St. George's defense system helps you better understand what you're seeing. See p. 105.

○ **Great Head Park** (St. George's Parish): This memorial to the men and women who died at sea has been cited as one of the genuinely evocative monuments of Bermuda. See p. 103.

BERMUDA IN DEPTH

ven some diehard fans compare Bermuda to certain beauty queens—beautiful but dull. We prefer to think of it as "tranquil." If you're looking for exotic local color or sizzling rum-and reggae-filled nights, look farther south to the Caribbean. But if you need to escape the stress and strain of daily life, go to Bermuda.

This quiet island is one of the best places in the world for a honeymoon or a celebration of any romantic occasion. The joint may not be jumping, but it's the most relaxing—and safest—of the foreign islands, with a relatively hassle-free environment where you can concentrate on your tan, minus the annoyance of aggressive vendors and worries about crime. If you're into sunning and swimming, it doesn't get much better than Bermuda between May and September. Pink sand and turquoise seas—it sounds like a corny travel poster, but it's for real. As Mark Twain said, "Sometimes a dose of Bermuda is just what the doctor ordered."

Frankly, Bermuda is predictable, and its regular visitors wouldn't have it any other way. The tiny island chain has attracted vacationers for decades, and there aren't many secrets left to uncover. But those sandy pink beaches remain just as inviting as ever, no matter how many times you return.

Even to friends of Bermuda who make an annual pilgrimage to the island, the Bermudians can be a bit smug. They know their island is more attractive than Chicago, New York, Los Angeles, or Miami, and they're not above reminding you. Bit of an imperial attitude, isn't it? Exactly.

Some critics claim that Bermuda has become Americanized. That's true of islands much farther south, such as The Bahamas, but not of Bermuda. Indeed, the island and its population steadfastly adhere to British customs, even if, at times, that slavish devotion borders on caricature. (The afternoon tea ritual is pleasant enough, but the lawyers' and judges' powdered wigs are a bit much—those things must get hot in a semitropical climate!) Some visitors find all the British decorum rather silly on a remote island that's closer to Atlanta than to London. But many others find the stalwart commitment to British tradition colorful and quaint, enhancing the unique charm of the lovely, wonderful place that is Bermuda.

If you're looking for some of the best golf in the world, Bermuda is your mecca. It has the scenery, the state-of-the-art courses, and the British tradition of golfing excellence. Even the most demanding player is generally satisfied with the island's offerings.

If you're a sailor, you'll find the waters of Bermuda reason enough for a visit. The farther you go from shore, of course, the greater the visibility. Discovering a hidden cove, away from the cruise-ship crowds, can make your day.

If you hate driving on the left side of the road, that's fine with Bermudians. You *can't* drive here—they won't rent you a car. Bike around, or hop on a scooter and zip from one end of the island to the other.

We could go on and on with reasons for you to come to Bermuda, from exploring its natural wonderlands to playing on choice tennis courts with gentle sea breezes and warm sunshine. But we'll end here with a couple of warnings: Demanding foodies will find better dining on other islands, such as Martinique—although Bermuda has made much culinary progress lately. And if you want nightlife, glittering casinos, and all that jazz, head for San Juan. Though there is some nightlife in Bermuda—if you enjoy nursing a pint in a pub—it's always wise to bring along some good company (or a good book) to ensure a blissful night here.

BERMUDA TODAY

If there's a sore point among Bermudians today, it's their extreme desire to separate themselves from the islands of the Caribbean, particularly from The Bahamas, in the eyes of the world. They often send angry letters to publishers of maps, reference sources, and travel guides, insisting that Bermuda is not in the Caribbean. As one irate Bermudian put it, "You don't claim that Washington, D.C., is part of Dallas, Texas. They're the same distance apart that Bermuda is from the Caribbean."

Bermuda prides itself on its lack of economic, socioeconomic, and racial problems, many of which plague the Caribbean islands. Bermuda does not tolerate unsavory businesses. What the island would really like to be known for is its stellar performance in banking and multinational business.

During the first decade of the millennium, international business positioned itself to overtake tourism as Bermuda's primary source of revenue. Before China's takeover of Hong Kong, Bermuda persuaded some of the biggest names in world business to create official domiciles on the island. The trend began in the 1970s, when some Hong Kong businesspeople formed low-profile shipping, trading, and investment companies in Bermuda—companies that became, in essence, corporate cash cows. That trend continues to affect Bermuda's economy.

Based on the downturn of the world's (and Bermuda's) economy, and a falloff in the numbers of tourists even considering a visit to the island's pink sands, many of the hotels have either closed or reconfigured themselves as semipermanent housing for workers associated with Bermuda's emerging role as a financial and insurance industry center. Adding to the hotel industry's present "crisis" is the fact that the bulk of the island's visitors now arrive by cruise ship, sleep aboard their ship, and never even think about either renting a room or dining locally. Tourism is no longer Bermuda's most beloved child.

Closings of some of the hotels would have been unthinkable even 5 years ago, but we've seen the demise of, among others, such island staples as the Sonesta, Harmony Hall, Sky Top, Ariel Sands, Lantana, and a massive reduction (that is, the closure of its main building) in the size of Elbow Beach. Even Horizons & Cottages, beginning in 2012, was reconfigured as housing for the Bermuda Hospital Association's roster of visiting medical specialists and surgeons, and no longer is open to the general public.

Facing a decline in their own business, the once ultra-aloof, ultra-private, and disdainful of "short stay" holidaymakers, the island's cluster of private clubs has made

Just Where Is Bermuda?

Many visitors are surprised to learn that Bermuda lies closer to Nova Scotia than to any island in the Caribbean.

discreet inquiries into getting listed as hotels with available rooms, when they're available, for "short-stay" casual visitors and nonmembers.

When Britain surrendered Hong Kong to China in 1997, Bermuda became the largest British colony. A local businessman watched the televised ceremonies in which Britain handed over control, and gleefully remarked, "All we can say is: Thank you very much, Hong Kong, because here come the insurance companies and pension funds." By the end of the 20th century, nearly half of the companies listed on the Hong Kong Stock Exchange—and even some of the Chinese government's own holding companies—had established a legal presence in Bermuda, because the island provides such hefty tax breaks. Amazingly, tiny Bermuda has emerged as the biggest and most prosperous of all of Britain's colonies, the bulk of which are now in the Caribbean.

In the 21st century, Bermuda continues to attract a growing number of American companies that are incorporating in Bermuda to lower their taxes without giving up the benefits of doing business in the United States. Insurance companies have led the way, but now manufacturers and other kinds of companies are following. It's been trumpeted in the press as "profits over patriotism." Becoming a Bermudian company is a paper transaction that can save millions annually.

And as aggressively as Bermuda is pursuing business, it's also more aware than ever of its fragile environment. Bermuda's population density is the third highest in the world, after Hong Kong's and Monaco's. Because the number of annual visitors is 10 times higher than the population, Bermuda has had to take strong initiatives to protect its natural resources. Environmental protection takes the form of stiff antilitter laws, annual garbage cleanup campaigns, automobile restrictions, cedar replanting (a blight in the '40s and '50s wiped out the native trees), lead-free gasoline, a strict fishing policy, and other measures.

Along the shaky road to self-government, Bermuda had some ugly racial conflicts. Riots in 1968 built up to the assassination of the British governor in 1973. But that was a long time ago; today, Bermuda has the most harmonious race relations in this part of the world, far better than those in the United States, the Caribbean, or The Bahamas. There's still a long way to go, but Bermudians of African descent have assumed political, administrative, and managerial posts in every aspect of the local economy. Bermuda hasn't quite reached the point where the color of your skin is unimportant, but it has made more significant advancement toward that goal than its neighbors to the south.

Impressions

. . . Bermuda is, without doubt, a success. It is, generally speaking, a peaceful place—more so than many Caribbean islands nearby. [Still, there are critics, from whom] you hear complaints about the Americanization of the place, the suggestion that Bermudianism is merely an anomalous cultural hybrid, a mule of a culture, attractive in its own way but of no lasting value or use. And yet it does seem to work; it is rich, it is as content as any place I know, and it is stable.

—Simon Winchester, *The Sun Never Sets: Travels to the Remaining Outposts of the British Empire* (1985)

Bermuda Shorts: Not Too Far Above the Knee

Most Bermudians consider the winter months too cold for Bermuda shorts; but by May, just about every businessman along Front Street has traded in his trousers for a pair. Bermuda shorts weren't initially Bermudian; they originated when the British army was sent to India. Later, when British troops were stationed in Bermuda, they were issued the shorts as part of the military's tropical kit gear.

By the 1920s and 1930s, the shorts had become quite fashionable, although they were not considered acceptable at dinner parties or at church. Now suitable business attire, the shorts are worn with a blazer, collared shirt, tie, and knee socks. They shouldn't be more than 7.6cm (3 in.) above the knee, and they must have a 7.6cm (3-in.) hem.

In the 21st century, Bermuda's average household income averages $68,500—contrast that with some of the less fortunate islands in the Caribbean, many of which don't even have the budgets to compile such statistics. Compared with residents of Puerto Rico, Jamaica, and certainly Haiti, no one is really poor in Bermuda. On the downside, home prices in Bermuda are at least three times the median cost of a house in the United States or Canada.

As a tourist destination, Bermuda was a resort long before Florida, Hawaii, Mexico, and many other places. Over the years, it has exploited its position in the northwest Atlantic between North America and Europe. It is even working to throw off its image as a staid resort, hoping to project a lively, more with-it atmosphere (although it has a long way to go in that department). The United States remains its largest market—about 80% of visitors are Americans—but in recent years more and more visitors from Europe, the Far East, and the Near East have been seen dining, drinking, and shopping in the City of Hamilton.

Life in the Onion Patch
GETTING TO KNOW THE "ONIONS"

Even though Bermuda isn't in the onion business the way it used to be, a born and bred islander is still called an "Onion." The term dates from the early 20th century, when the export of Bermuda onions and Easter lilies to the U.S. mainland were the island's major sources of income.

The "Onions"—a term that still carries a badge of pride—have their own lifestyle and even their own vocabulary. For example, "Aunt Haggie's children" are frustrating, stupid people; "married by 10 parsons" is a reference to a woman with huge breasts; "backin' up" means gay. You don't vomit in Bermuda, you "Go Europe." "Cockroach killers" (a term you may also hear in the American Southwest) are pointy-toed shoes. Although you'll rarely see it on local menus, the bream fish is called a "shit-bubbler."

Residents of more troubled islands to the south often look with envy upon the "Onions," who have a much higher standard of living than Caribbean islanders do; they also pay no personal income tax and suffer from only a 7% unemployment rate. The literacy rate is high: An estimated 99% of females age 15 and older can read and write, as can 98% of Bermudian males.

Today's 62,000 residents are mostly of African, British, and Portuguese descent. Bermuda's population density, one of the highest in the world, is about 3,210 per 2.5

An Island of Religious Tolerance

About a third of Bermuda's population adheres to the Church of England, which has been historically dominant in the colony. Indeed, the division of Bermuda into nine parishes dates from 1618, when each parish was required by law to have its own Anglican church, to the exclusion of any other. That division still exists today, but more for administrative purposes than for religious ones.

Religious tolerance is now guaranteed by law. There are some 10,000 Catholics, many of them from the Portuguese Azores. There are also many members of Protestant sects whose roots lie within what were originally slave churches, among them the African Methodist Episcopal Church. Established in 1816 by African Americans, the sect was transported to Bermuda from Canada around 1870. Today, the church has about 7,000 members.

Also found in Bermuda are Seventh-day Adventists, Presbyterians, Baptists, Lutherans, and Mormons. Less prevalent are a handful of Jews, Muslims, Rastafarians, and Jehovah's Witnesses.

Bermuda today boasts more than 110 churches, an average of five per 2.5 sq. km (1 sq. mile). They range from the moss-encrusted parish churches established in the earliest days of the colony to modest structures with only a handful of members.

sq. km (1 sq. mile). The population is about 61% black, 39% white. Many ethnic minority groups are represented, the largest and most established being the Portuguese; the majority of inhabitants, however, are islanders from the Caribbean or The Bahamas. Some Bermudians can even trace their ancestry back to the island's first settlers, and some to successful privateers and freed slaves.

Britain's influence in Bermuda is obvious in the predominantly English accents and spelling, police who wear helmets like those of London bobbies, and cars that drive on the left. Schools are run along the lines of the British system and provide a high standard of preparatory education. Children 5 to 16 years of age must attend school. The Bermuda College, which offers academic and technical studies, boasts a renowned hotel and catering program.

WHO'S MINDING THE STORE?

In essence, Bermuda is a self-governing dependency of Britain, which protects its security and stability. The governor, appointed by the queen, represents Her Majesty in the areas of external affairs, defense, and internal security.

By choosing to remain a British dependency, Bermuda rejected the trail that many former colonies in the Caribbean (including Antigua) blazed by declaring their independence. Although they remain under the protection of the British, Bermudians manage their own day-to-day affairs. And ever since the people of Bermuda were granted the right to govern themselves in 1968, they have done so admirably well.

Bermuda has a 12-member cabinet headed by a premier. The elected legislature, referred to as the Legislative Council, consists of a 40-member House of Assembly and an 11-member Senate. Bermuda's oldest political party is the Progressive Labour Party, formed in 1963. In 1964, the United Bermuda Party was established; it stayed in power until it was toppled by the Progressive Labour Party in 1998.

Bermuda's legal system is founded on common law. Judicial responsibility falls to the Supreme Court, headed by a chief justice in a powdered wig and a robe. English

Impressions
You go to heaven if you want to—I'd rather stay here in Bermuda. —Mark Twain, in a letter to Elizabeth Wallace, 1910

law is the fundamental guide, and in court, English customs prevail.

The island consists of nine parishes, each managed by an advisory council. The capital, the City of Hamilton, is in Pembroke Parish. (For details on the individual parishes, see chapter 3.)

TOURIST DOLLARS & NO INCOME TAX

Bermuda's political stability has proved beneficial to the economy, which relies heavily on tourism and foreign investment.

For much of the island's early history, the major industry was shipbuilding, made possible by the abundant cedar forests. In the second half of the 19th century, when wooden ships gave way to steel ones, the island turned to tourism. Today, tourism is the country's leading industry, with annual revenues estimated at $450 million. Approximately 550,000 visitors come to Bermuda each year; an estimated 86% arrive from the United States, 4% from Britain, and 7% from Canada. Bermuda enjoys a 42% repeat-visitor rate.

Because Bermuda has enacted favorable economic measures, more than 6,000 international companies are registered there. The companies engage mostly in investment holding, insurance, commercial trading, consulting services, and shipping—but fewer than 275 companies are actually on the island. The reason for this curious situation? Bermuda has no corporate or income tax, so companies register on Bermuda but conduct business in their home countries, thereby avoiding taxes that their home countries would otherwise deduct.

The island's leading exports are pharmaceuticals, concentrates (primarily black rum and sherry peppers), perfumes, and beverages. Leading imports include foodstuffs, alcoholic beverages, clothing, furniture, fuel, electrical appliances, and motor vehicles. Bermuda's major trading partners are the United States, Great Britain, Canada, the Netherlands, and the Caribbean states.

THE MAKING OF BERMUDA
The Early Years

The discovery of the Bermudas is attributed to the Spanish—probably the navigator Juan Bermúdez—sometime before 1511, because in that year a map published in the *Legatio Babylonica* included "La Bermuda" among the Atlantic islands. A little over a century later, the English staked a claim to Bermuda and began colonization.

In 1609, the flagship of Admiral Sir George Somers, the *Sea Venture,* was wrecked on Bermuda's reefs while en route to the colony at Jamestown, Virginia. The dauntless crew built two pinnaces (small sailing ships) and headed on to the American colony, but three sailors hid out and remained on the island. They were Bermuda's first European settlers. Just 3 years later, the Bermuda islands were included in the charter of the Virginia Company, and 60 colonists were sent there from England. St. George Town was founded soon after.

Bermuda's status as a colony dates from 1620, when the first parliament convened. Bermuda's is the oldest parliament in continuous existence in the British Commonwealth. In 1684, Bermuda became a British Crown Colony under King Charles II, and Sir Robert Robinson was appointed the colony's first governor.

Slavery became a part of life in Bermuda shortly after the official settlement. Although the majority of slaves came from Africa, a few were Native Americans. Later, Scots imprisoned for fighting against Cromwell were sent to the islands, followed in 1651 by Irish slaves. This servitude, however, was not as lengthy as that of plantation slaves in America and the West Indies. The British Emancipation Act of 1834 freed all slaves.

Relations with America

Early on, Bermuda established close links with the American colonies. The islanders set up a thriving mercantile trade on the Eastern Seaboard, especially with southern ports. The major commodity sold by Bermuda's merchant ships was salt from Turks Island.

During the American Revolution, the rebellious colonies cut off trade with Loyalist Bermuda, despite the network of family connections and close friendships that bound them. The cutoff in trade proved a great hardship for the islanders, who, having chosen seafaring over farming, depended heavily on America for their food. Many of them, now deprived of profitable trade routes, turned to privateering, piracy, and "wrecking" (salvaging goods from wrecked or foundered ships).

Britain's loss of its important American colonial ports led to a naval buildup in Bermuda. Ships and troops sailed from Bermuda in 1814 to burn Washington, D.C., and the White House during the War of 1812.

Bermuda got a new lease on economic life during the American Civil War. The island was sympathetic to the Confederacy. With the approval of the British government, Bermuda ran the blockade that the Union had placed on exports, especially of cotton, by the southern states. St. George's Harbour was a principal Atlantic base for the lucrative business of smuggling manufactured goods into Confederate ports and bringing out cargoes of cotton and turpentine.

When the Confederacy fell, so did Bermuda's economy. Seeing no immediate source of income from trading with the eastern states, the islanders turned their attention to agriculture and found that the colony's fertile soil and salubrious climate produced excellent vegetables. Portuguese immigrants arrived to farm the land, and soon celery, potatoes, tomatoes, and especially onions were being shipped to the New York market. So brisk was the onion trade that the City of Hamilton became known as "Onion Town."

During Prohibition, Bermudians again profited from the situation in the United States—they engaged in the lucrative business of rum running (smuggling alcohol to the U.S.). The distance from the island to the East Coast was too great for quick crossings in small booze-laden boats, which worked well from The Bahamas and Cuba. Nevertheless, Bermuda accounted for a good part of the alcoholic beverages transported illegally to the United States before the repeal of Prohibition in 1933.

A Hotbed of Espionage

Bermuda played a key role in World War II counterespionage for the Allies. The story of the "secret war" with Nazi Germany is told dramatically in William Stevenson's *A Man Called Intrepid*.

Beneath the Hamilton Princess Hotel, a carefully trained staff worked to decode radio signals to and from German submarines and other vessels operating in the Atlantic, close to the United States and the islands offshore. Unknown to the Germans, the British, early in the war had broken the Nazi code using a captured German coding machine called "Enigma." The British also intercepted and examined mail between Europe and the United States.

Looking Back at Bermuda

1. **1612** Richard Moore, the first governor, landed at St. George's Harbour.
2. **1809** Royal Engineers began construction on the Royal Naval Dockyard.
3. **1815** Hamilton became the new capital of Bermuda, superseding St. George.
4. **1937** The first scheduled air service to Bermuda from New York landed.
5. **1946** Ian Fleming assigned the Hamilton Princess as a residence for master spy James Bond.
6. **1973** Governor Richard Sharples was assassinated at Government House.

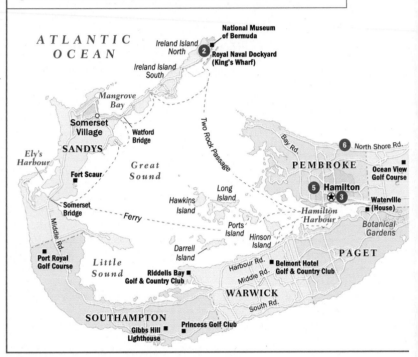

Bermuda served as a refueling stop for airplanes flying between the two continents. While pilots were being entertained at the Yacht Club, the mail would be taken off the carriers and examined by experts. An innocent-looking series of letters from Lisbon, for example, contained messages written in invisible ink. The letters were part of a vast German spy network. The British became skilled at opening sealed envelopes, examining their written contents, and carefully resealing them.

The surreptitious letter readers were called "trappers." Many of them were young women without any previous experience in counterespionage work, yet a number of them performed very well. As Stevenson wrote, it was soon discovered that "by some quirk in the law of averages, the girls who shone in this work had well-turned ankles." A medical officer involved with the project reported it as "fairly certain that a girl with

unshapely legs would make a bad trapper." So, amazingly, the word went out that women seeking recruitment as trappers would have to display their gams.

During the course of their work, the trappers discovered one of the methods by which the Germans were transmitting secret messages: They would shrink a whole page of regularly typed text to the size of a tiny dot, then conceal the dot under an innocuous-looking punctuation mark! The staff likened these messages, with their secret-bearing dots, to the English dessert plum duff, for these "punctuation dots [were] scattered through a letter like raisins in the suet puddings." The term "duff method" came to be applied to the technique that the Germans used to send military and other messages through the mail.

When the United States entered the war, FBI agents joined the British in their intelligence operations in Bermuda.

THE BAFFLING bermuda triangle

The area known as the Bermuda Triangle encompasses 2,414,016 sq. km (932,057 sq. miles) of open sea between Bermuda, Puerto Rico, and the southeastern shoreline of the U.S. This bit of the Atlantic is the source of the most famous, and certainly the most baffling, legend associated with Bermuda.

Tales of the mysterious Bermuda Triangle persist, despite attempts by skeptics to dismiss them as fanciful. Below are three of the most popular.

o In 1881, a British-registered ship, the *Ellen Austin*, encountered an unnamed vessel in good condition sailing aimlessly without a crew. The captain ordered a handful of his best seamen to board the vessel and sail it to Newfoundland. A few days later, the ships encountered each other again on the high seas. But to everyone's alarm, the crewmen who had transferred from the *Ellen Austin* were nowhere to be found—the ship was completely unmanned.

o Another tale concerns the disappearance of a merchant ship, the *Marine Sulphur Queen*, in February 1963. It vanished suddenly without warning, and no one could say why. The weather was calm when the ship set sail from Bermuda, and everything onboard was fine— the crew never sent a distress signal. In looking for explanations, some have theorized that the ship's weakened hull gave way, causing the vessel to descend quickly to the ocean floor. Others attribute the loss to more mysterious forces.

o The most famous of all the legends concerns an incident in 1945. On December 5, five U.S. Navy bombers departed from Fort Lauderdale, Florida, on a routine mission. The weather was fine; no storm of any kind threatened. A short time into the flight, the leader of the squadron radioed that they were lost, and then the radio went silent. All efforts to establish further communication proved fruitless. A rescue plane was dispatched to search for the squadron, but it, too, disappeared. The navy ordered a search that lasted 5 days, but there was no evidence of any wreckage. To this day, the disappearance of the squadron and the rescue plane remains a mystery as deep as the waters of the region.

How do those who believe in the Bermuda Triangle legend account for these phenomena? Some contend that the area is a time warp to another universe; others think the waters off Bermuda are the site of the lost kingdom of Atlantis, whose power sources still function deep beneath the surface. Still others believe that laser rays from outer space are perpetually focused on the region, or that underwater signaling devices are guiding invaders from other planets, and that these aliens have chosen the site for the systematic collection of human beings for scientific observation and experimentation. (Smacks of *The X Files*, doesn't it?) Some, drawing upon the Bible's Book of Revelation, are fully persuaded that the Bermuda Triangle is really one of the gates to Hell (in this version, the other gate lies midway between Japan and the Philippines, in the Devil's Sea).

No matter what your views on these mysteries, you're bound to provoke an excited response by asking residents what they think about it. On Bermuda, almost everyone has an opinion about the island's biggest and most fascinating legend.

Bermuda Comes into Its Own

In 1953, British Prime Minister Winston Churchill chose Bermuda, which he had visited during the war, as the site for a conference with U.S. President Dwight D. Eisenhower and the French premier. Several such high-level gatherings have followed in the decades since; the most recent one, between former British Prime Minister John Major and former U.S. President George H. W. Bush, took place in 1991.

Bermuda's increasing prominence led to changes in its relations with Great Britain and the United States, as well as significant developments on the island itself. In 1957, after nearly 2 centuries of occupation, Britain withdrew its military forces, and decided to grant self-government to its oldest colony. Under the Lend-Lease Agreement signed in 1941, the United States continues to maintain a naval air station at Kindley Field, in St. George's Parish. The agreement is due to expire in 2040.

As Bermudians assumed greater control over their own affairs, they began to adopt significant social changes, but at a pace that did not satisfy some critics. Although racial segregation in hotels and restaurants ceased in 1959, schools were not integrated until 1971. Women received the right to vote in 1944, but the law still restricted suffrage to property holders. That restriction was rescinded in 1963, when voter registration was opened to all citizens.

On the rocky road to self-government, Bermuda was not without its share of problems. Serious rioting broke out in 1968, and British troops were called back to restore order. Then, in 1973, Sir Richard Sharples, the governor, was assassinated.

These events, which occurred when several of the islands in the region and in the Caribbean were experiencing domestic difficulties, proved to be the exception rather than the rule. In the years since, the social and political climate in Bermuda has been markedly calm—all the better for the island's economic well-being, because it encourages the industries on which Bermuda depends, including tourism.

During the 1990s, the political status of the island again became a hot topic among Bermudians. Some people felt it would be advantageous to achieve complete independence from Britain, whereas others believed it was in Bermuda's best interest to maintain its ties to the Crown. In 1995, the majority of voters in an independent referendum rejected a proposal to sever ties with Great Britain.

In 1997, the governing party of Bermuda, the United Bermuda Party, chose the daughter of a well-known civil rights leader as its prime minister. Pamela Gordon, former environment minister, was named to the post at the age of 41, the youngest leader in the island nation's 400-year history and the first woman to be prime minister. David Saul, the reigning prime minister, resigned in favor of this younger and more popular leader. In her first months in office, Gordon, a relative political

---

Impressions

[Many Britons in Bermuda, to their dislike] find that while the colony is supposedly and unquestionably British—nationally, legally, officially—it is in very many senses dominated by the United States, is utterly dependent on the United States and can well be regarded, and not by cynics alone, as the only British colony which is more like an American colony, run by Bermudians, on Britain's behalf, for America's ultimate benefit.

—Simon Winchester, *The Sun Never Sets: Travels to the Remaining Outposts of the British Empire* (1985)

Puritan Justice

Many tales are told about the fate of persons condemned for witchcraft during the 1600s. Anyone suspected of collusion with the devil was thrown into St. George's Harbour; whoever did not sink was adjudged guilty. Many women floated because of their skirts and petticoats. The first woman to be found floating after her trial was Jeanne Gardiner, in 1651. Since her failure to plunge to the depths "proved" that she was a witch, the court ordered her removed from the water; she was then burned at the stake. Not only women were tried for witchcraft; in 1652, a man was condemned to death for having cast a spell over his neighbor's turkeys. Justice in those Puritan times was stern, in Bermuda no less than in the American colonies.

newcomer, pledged to bridge differences between Bermuda's majority black population and its white business elite.

In that stated goal, at least based on subsequent election returns, she did not succeed. In November 1998, the Progressive Labour Party, supported by many of Bermuda's blacks, ended 30 years of conservative rule by sweeping its first victory in general elections. Although Gordon is black, as was most of her cabinet, many locals saw her party as part of the "white establishment."

The Labour Party's leader, Jennifer Smith, became the new prime minister, claiming Bermuda's residents had met their "date with destiny." The Labour Party has moved more from the left to the center in recent years, and Smith sought to reassure the island's white-led business community that it would be "business as usual" with her party in power. The Labour Party made the economy an issue in the campaign, promising higher wages and better benefits to workers, even though Bermuda residents enjoy one of the highest standards of living in the world. In 2003, W. Alexander Scott replaced Smith as the prime minister and head of the party.

Also in 2003, tragedy struck the island in the roaring fury called Hurricane Fabian, Bermuda's worst hurricane in 40 years. For some 12 hours, Fabian pummeled the island with 190 to 225kmph (120–140 mph) winds. This caused small tornadoes to spawn and unleashed a towering surge of ocean that drenched almost all of Bermuda in saltwater, uprooting trees.

In the 21st century, Bermuda faces many problems, including what many see as a declining quality of life. There are environmental concerns—notably overfishing and damage to precious reefs. Traffic jams are now common despite the ban against visitors renting automobiles. Affordable housing becomes scarcer year by year. As more cruise lines launch megaliners, Bermuda is also concerned that its tight harbors will not be able to accommodate the traffic. Nonetheless, the more unfortunate islands to the south still envy Bermuda's standard of living.

In spite of the falloff of the global economy, in late 2008 and in 2009 Bermuda still enjoyed the third highest per capita income in the world, more than 50% higher than that of the U.S.

In 2009, Bermuda celebrated its 400th birthday.

As Bermuda moves into the second decade of the 21st century, the unthinkable seems to be happening. Tourism, mainstay of the island's economy for years, is beginning to play second fiddle to Bermuda's role as a financial and insurance industry center. This has led to a number of hotel closures; many of these former resorts are being taken over by companies for private use by their employees.

BERMUDA ART & ARCHITECTURE

Art

Art in Bermuda has never reached the status enjoyed by such islands as Haiti and Jamaica. A critic once wrote that "Bermuda is the perfect place for the Sunday painter." Some serious art, however, is displayed at such places as the **Masterworks Foundation Gallery** at the Bermuda National Gallery in the City of Hamilton (p. 93). Still, a great deal of Bermudian art is of the watercolor variety, with idyllic landscapes and seascapes sold at various shops around the island.

Bermuda's earliest works of art were portraits painted by itinerant artists for the local gentry. Most of these were by the English-born Joseph Blackburn, whose brief visit to Bermuda in the mid-1700s led to requests by local landowners to have their portraits painted. Many of these portraits can be found today in the **Tucker House Museum** in St. George's (p. 105). A handful of portraits from the same period were done by the American-born artist John Green. Also prized are a series of paintings from the mid–19th century depicting sailing ships; they're signed "Edward James," but the artist's real identity remains unknown.

During the 19th century, the traditions of the English landscape painters, particularly the Romantics, came into vogue in Bermuda. Constable, with his lush and evocative landscapes, became the model for many. Other than a few amateur artists, however, whose works showed great vitality but little sense of perspective, most of Bermuda's landscape paintings were executed by British military officers and their wives. Their body of work includes a blend of true-to-life landscapes with an occasional stylized rendering of the picturesque or Romantic tradition then in vogue in England. Among the most famous of the uniformed artists was Lt. E. G. Hallewell, a member of the Royal Engineers, whose illustrations of the island's topography were used for planning certain naval installations.

Another celebrated landscapist was Thomas Driver, who arrived as a member of the Royal Engineers in 1814 and remained on the island until 1836. Trained to reproduce detailed landscape observations as a means of assisting military and naval strategists, he later modified his style to become more elegant and evocative. He soon abandoned the military and became a full-time painter of Bermuda scenes. Because of Driver's attention to detail, his works are frequently reproduced by scholars and art historians who hope to recapture the aesthetic and architectural elements of the island's earliest buildings.

Later in the 19th century, other artists depicted the flora of Bermuda. Lady Lefroy, whose husband was governor of the island between 1871 and 1877, painted the trees, shrubs, fish, flowers, and animals of the island in much detail. Later, at scattered intervals during their careers, such internationally known artists as Winslow Homer, Andrew Wyeth, George Ault, and French-born Impressionist and cubist Albert Gleizes all painted Bermudian scenes.

Among prominent Bermuda-born artists was Alfred Birdsey, who died in 1996. His watercolors represented some of the most elegiac visual odes to Bermuda ever produced. Birdsey's paintings, as well as those of other artists mentioned above, are on display in galleries around the island.

Today, Bermuda has more artists painting and creating than at any point in its history. Local favorites include Eric Amos, whose illustrations of Bermuda's wild birds are sought by collectors all over the world; Captain Stephen J. Card, who has developed an international reputation by specializing in marine art; Vivienne Gardner, known not just for her paintings but also for her sculpture, stained glass, and mosaics;

and Christine Phillips-Watlington, who has achieved an international reputation for her botanical paintings.

Protecting artworks from climate damage is a constant problem on the island. As the administrator of one major art gallery explained, "Bermuda's climate is unquestionably the worst in the world for the toll it takes on works of art, with three elements—humidity, salt, and ultraviolet light—all playing their part." Some very valuable Bermudian paintings have been totally destroyed. As a result, more and more galleries and exhibition rooms on the island have installed air-conditioning.

In addition to its painters, Bermuda also boasts several noted sculptors, including Chelsey Trott, who produces cedar-wood carvings, and Desmond Hale Fountain, who creates works in bronze. Fountain's life-size statues often show children in the act of reading or snoozing in the shade.

Architecture

Today, Bermuda's unique style is best represented by its architecture: primarily, those little pink cottages that grace postcards. The architecture of the island—a mélange of idiosyncratic building techniques dictated by climate and the types of building materials available—is the archipelago's only truly indigenous art form.

Bermuda's early settlers quickly recognized the virtues of the island's most visible building material, coral stone. A conglomerate of primeval sand packed with crushed bits of coral and shells, this stone has been quarried for generations on Bermuda. Cut into oblong building blocks, it is strong yet porous. However, it would be unusable in any area where the climate has cycles of freezing and thawing, because it would crack. Mortared together with imported cement, the blocks provide solid and durable foundations and walls.

Bermuda's colonial architects ingeniously found a way to deal with a serious problem on the island: the lack of an abundant supply of fresh water. During the construction of a house or any other sort of building, workers excavated a water tank, or **cistern,** first. The cistern was created either as a separate underground cavity away from the house or as a foundation for the building. These cisterns served to collect rainwater funneled from rooftops via specially designed channels and gutters. The design of these roof-to-cellar water conduits led to the development of what is Bermuda's most distinct architectural feature: the gleaming **rooftops** of its houses. Gently sloping, and invariably painted a dazzling white, they are constructed of quarried limestone slabs sawed into "slates" about an inch thick and between 77 and 116 sq. cm (12–18 sq. in.). Roofs are installed over a framework of cedar-wood beams (or, more recently, pitch pine or pressure-treated wood beams), which are interconnected with a series of cedar laths. The slates are joined with cement-based mortar in overlapping rows, then covered with a cement wash and one or several coats of whitewash or synthetic paint. This process corrects the porosity of the coral limestone slates, rendering them watertight. The result is a

A typical roof in Bermuda.

layered effect, since each panel of limestone appears in high relief atop its neighbor. The angular, step-shaped geometry of Bermudian roofs has inspired watercolorists and painters to emphasize the rhythmically graceful shadows that trace the path of the sun across the rooflines.

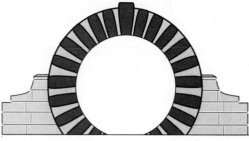
Bermuda moon gate.

Unlike those in the Caribbean, Bermudian houses are designed without amply proportioned hanging eaves. Large eaves may be desirable because of the shade they afford, but smaller ones have proved to be more structurally sound during tropical storms. The interiors of Bermudian houses are usually graced with large windows and doors, and, in the older buildings, floors and moldings crafted from copper-colored planks of the almost-extinct Bermuda cedar. Also common is a feature found in colonial buildings in the Caribbean and other western Atlantic islands as well: **tray ceilings,** so named because of their resemblance to an inverted serving tray. This shape allows ceilings to follow the lines of the inside roof construction to create what would otherwise be unused space. The effect of these ceilings, whether sheathed in plaster or planking, gives Bermudian interiors unusual height and airiness.

Despite the distinctively individualistic nature of Bermuda's architecture, decor remains faithfully—some say rigidly—British, and somewhat more formal than you might expect. Interior designs seem to be a felicitous cross between what you'd find in a New England seaside cottage and how a nautically minded society hostess would accent her drawing room in London. Bermuda homes usually have lots of Chippendale or Queen Anne furniture (sometimes authentic, sometimes reproduction). Whenever possible, decorators love to include any piece of antique furniture crafted from Bermuda cedar. Combine these features with the open windows, gentle climate,

Did You Know?

o More than 25,000 couples honeymoon on Bermuda each year.

o This mysterious island inspired William Shakespeare's 1610 play *The Tempest.*

o Somerset Bridge is the world's smallest drawbridge. At only 56cm (22 in.) wide, the opening is just large enough for a ship's mast to pass through.

o Bermuda has more golf courses per square kilometer than any other place in the world; there are eight of them on the island's approximate 138 sq. km (53 sq. miles).

o Sir Brownlow Gray, the island's former chief justice, played the first game of tennis in the Western Hemisphere on Bermuda in 1873.

o With the arrival of spring comes the blossoming of Bermuda's Easter lilies, first brought to the island from Japan in the 18th century.

o Bermuda has no billboards: There is a ban on outdoor advertising and neon signs.

and carefully tended gardens of the fertile, mid-Atlantic setting, and the result is some very charming and soothing interiors.

No discussion of Bermudian architecture should neglect to mention a garden feature that many visitors consider unique to Bermuda: the **moon gate.** A rounded span of coral blocks arranged in a circular arch above a wooden gate, the moon gate was introduced to Bermuda around 1920 by the Duke of Westminster's landscape architect, who got his inspiration from such gates in China and Japan.

BERMUDA IN POP CULTURE
The Literary Scene

Bermuda has long been a haven for writers, and has figured in many works of literature, beginning with Shakespeare's *The Tempest*. Shakespeare never visited the island himself but was inspired to set his play here by accounts he had read or heard of the island.

The Irish poet Thomas Moore (1779–1852), who visited Bermuda for several months in 1804, was moved by its beauty to write:

> *Oh! could you view the scenery dear*
> *That now beneath my window lies.*

Moore left more memories—literary and romantic—than any other writer who came to Bermuda. He once stayed at Hill Crest Guest House in St. George and soon became enamored of Nea Tucker, the adolescent bride of one of the most prominent men in town. "Sweet Nea! Let us roam no more," he once wrote of his beloved.

It's said that the lovesick poet would gaze for hours upon Nea's veranda, hoping that she'd appear. One day a jealous Mr. Tucker could tolerate this no more and banished the poet from his property. Moore was chased down a street that now bears the name Nea's Alley to commemorate his unrequited romance.

Today, one of the most popular restaurants in Bermuda is **Tom Moore's Tavern** (p. 138). The building was once the home of Samuel Trott, who constructed it in the 17th century. Unlike Tucker, the descendants of Samuel Trott befriended Moore, who often visited the house. Moore immortalized the calabash tree on the Trott estate in his writing; he liked to sit under it and write his verse there.

Following in Moore's footsteps, many famous writers visited Bermuda in later years. None, however, have left their mark on the island like Tom Moore.

For Americans, it was Mark Twain who helped make Bermuda a popular tourist destination. He published his impressions in the *Atlantic Monthly* in 1877 through

Royalty Comes to "Shangri-La"

The Irish poet Thomas Moore and the American humorist Mark Twain publicized the glories of Bermuda, but—for the British, at least—the woman who put Bermuda on the tourist map was Princess Louise. The daughter of Queen Victoria, she spent several months in Bermuda in 1883. Her husband was the governor-general of Canada, so she traveled to Bermuda to escape the fierce northern cold. Although Bermuda hosted many royal visitors in the 20th century, including Queen Elizabeth II, Princess Louise was the first royal personage to set foot in the colony. When she returned to Canada, she told reporters that she'd found the Shangri-La of tourist destinations.

1878, and in his first book, *The Innocents Abroad*. He became so enchanted by the island that, as he wrote many years later to a correspondent, he would happily choose it over heaven.

After Twain, Eugene O'Neill came to Bermuda in 1924, and returned several more times, at least through 1927. While here, he worked on *The Great God Brown, Lazarus Laughed,* and *Strange Interlude*. O'Neill was convinced that cold weather adversely affected his ability to write. He thought that Bermuda would "cure" him of alcoholism. At first, O'Neill and his family rented cottages on what is now Coral Beach Club property. Later, O'Neill bought the house "Spithead," in Warwick. In 1927, however, his marriage ended, and O'Neill left his family—and Bermuda.

During the 1930s, several eminent writers made their way to Bermuda, in hopes of finding idyllic surroundings and perhaps a little inspiration: Sinclair Lewis, who spent all his time cycling around "this gorgeous island"; Hervey Allen, who wrote *Anthony Adverse,* his best-selling novel, at Felicity Hall in Somerset; and James Ramsey Ullman, who wrote *The White Tower* on the island. James Thurber also made several visits to Bermuda during this time.

In 1956, Noël Coward came with his longtime companion, Graham Payn, to escape "the monstrously unjust tax situation in England." He was not, he said, "really mad about the place," yet he purchased "Spithead" in Warwick (O'Neill's former home) and stayed some 2 years, working on *London Mornings,* his only ballet, and the musical *Sail Away*. "Spithead" is now privately owned.

Other well-known authors who visited Bermuda over the years include Rudyard Kipling, C. S. Forester, Hugh Walpole, Edna Ferber, Anita Loos, John O'Hara, E. B. White, and Philip Wylie.

Bermuda's own writers include William S. Zuill—a former director of the Bermuda National Trust who wrote *The Story of Bermuda and Her People,* an excellent historical account—and Nellie Musson, Frank Manning, Eva Hodgson, and Dale Butler, who have written about the lives of African Bermudians.

RECOMMENDED READING

Most of the books listed below have been printed in Bermuda. Thus, while they're readily available on the island, they may be hard to find in the United States and elsewhere. Check with your favorite online bookseller or used bookstore.

The Mysterious Bermuda Triangle

Many writers have attempted to explain the Bermuda Triangle. None has sufficiently done so yet, but all of these books make good reads for those of us intrigued by this tantalizing mystery.

The best of the lot is *The Bermuda Triangle Mystery Solved* (Prometheus Books) by Larry Kusche. It's a good read even though it doesn't actually "solve" the mystery. A mass-market paperback, *Atlantis: Bermuda Triangle* (Berkley Publishing Group), by Greg Donegan, also digs into the puzzle; as does another paperback, *The Mystery of the Bermuda Triangle* (Heineman Library), by Chris Oxlade.

Art & Architecture

For Bermuda style, both inside the house and outside, two books lead the pack: *Bermuda Antique Furniture and Silver,* published by Bermuda National Trust; and *Architecture Bermuda Style,* by David R. Raine, issued by Pompano Publications.

Divers, Hikers & Shipwrecks

Daniel Berg has written the finest book on the shipwrecks of Bermuda—a great choice for a diver to read before actually going under the water. It's called

Bermuda Shipwrecks: A Vacationing Diver's Guide to Bermuda's Shipwrecks (Aqua Explorers).

Divers might also like to pick up a copy of *Marine Fauna and Flora of Bermuda* (John Wiley & Sons, Inc.), edited by Wolfgang Sterrer. Another good book for divers is *Diving Bermuda* (Aqua Quest Publications), part of the Aqua Quest Diving Series, this one authored by Jesse Concelmo and Michael Strohofer. Its second edition is the most up-to-date of all the sports guides to Bermuda.

History

In Bermuda's bookstores, you can find several books devoted to the colorful history of the island. Making for the best reads are the following titles: *The Rich Papers—Letters from Bermuda* by Vernon A. Ives (Bermuda National Trust and the University of Toronto Press); *Biography of a Colonial Town* by Jean de Chantal Kennedy (Bermuda Bookstores Publisher); *A Life on Old St. David's* by Ernest A. McCallan (Bermuda Historical Society); *Chained on the Rock: Slavery in Bermuda* by Cyril O. Packwood (Baxters); and *Bermuda's Story* by Terry Tucker (Bermuda Bookstores Publisher).

Flora & Fauna

If you're a devotee of Mother Nature, seek out *Bermuda Houses and Gardens* by Ann B. Brown and Jean Outerbridge (Garden Club of Bermuda); *Bermuda: Her Plants and Gardens 1609–1850* by Jill Collett (Macmillan Caribbean); and *A Guide to the Reef, Shore, and Game Fish of Bermuda* (self-published) by Louis S. Mowbray.

Fiction

One of the most sensitive portraits, capturing Bermuda of long ago, is *The Back Yard* by Ann Z. Williams (Macmillan), an account of growing up in Bermuda in the 1930s and '40s.

Film

Film buffs may be surprised to discover that Bermuda has an indirect link to the movie *The Wizard of Oz*—Denslow's Island.

The privately owned island is named after W. W. Denslow, who created the original illustrations for the book on which the movie is based, *The Wonderful Wizard of Oz* (1900) by L. Frank Baum, and thus with his pen gave form to many of the characters depicted on the screen. Denslow lived in Bermuda at the turn of the 20th century. The island, however, despite its famous association, is off limits to visitors.

Several films were shot in and around Bermuda. The most famous is *The Deep* (1977), starring Jacqueline Bisset, Nick Nolte, Robert Shaw, and Louis Gossett, Jr., a visually arresting movie about a lost treasure and drugs and, of course, scuba diving off the island's coast. For one of the scenes, a lighthouse near the Grotto Bay Beach Hotel and Tennis Club was blown up.

A movie that was filmed partly in Bermuda is *Chapter Two* (1979), with James Caan and Marsha Mason. Based on the successful Broadway play by Neil Simon, it is the story of a playwright's bumpy romance soon after the death of his wife. The Bermuda scenes were shot at Marley Beach Cottages.

Music

Modern Bermudian music, which you hear today mainly in hotel lounges, is a blend of traditional Bermudian music with sounds from Jamaica, Trinidad, and Puerto Rico, as well as the United States and Britain. However, these aren't the sounds you'll predominantly hear: As elsewhere, American and British rock, modified by local rhythms, has proved the strongest and most lasting influence.

Visitors are often pleased to discover that the island's best-known singers and musicians can be heard at many of the hotels and nightclubs. Inquire about which local artist is performing during the cocktail hour at your hotel; chances are it may be one of the most popular.

GOMBEY DANCING

Despite new pop forms, Bermuda is proud of its original musical idioms. Gombey dancing is the island's premier folk art. Gombey (commonly pronounced *goom*-bee or *gom*-bay) combines West Africa's tribal heritage with the Native American and British colonial influences of the New World. African Caribbeans brought to Bermuda as slaves or convicts introduced the tradition, and its rhythms are similar to Brazilian street samba. Gombey dancers are almost always male; in accordance with tradition, men pass on the rhythms and dance techniques from generation to generation in their family. Dancers outfit themselves in masquerade costumes, whose outlandish lines and glittering colors evoke the brilliant plumage of tropical birds.

Gombey (spelled goombay in some other places, such as The Bahamas) signifies a specific type of African drum, as well as the Bantu word for "rhythm." These rhythms escalate into an ever faster and more hypnotic beat as the movements of the dancers become increasingly uninhibited, and the response of the spectators grows ever more fervent. The most strenuous dances are usually performed during the Christmas season.

Although gombey dancing, with its local rituals and ceremonies, can be seen as one of Bermuda's major cultural contributions, it's not unique to the island. Variations are found elsewhere in the western Atlantic, as well as in the Caribbean. Indeed, during its development, Bermuda's gombey dancing was significantly influenced by some of these other versions. In colonial times, for example, when African Caribbeans were brought to Bermuda as slaves or convicts to help build the British military installations on the island, they carried with them their own gombey traditions, which eventually combined with those that had already taken root in Bermuda. What's unique about the Bermudian version of gombey, however, is its use of the British snare drum, played with wooden sticks, as an accompaniment to the dancing.

A handful of gombey recordings are available, enabling you to hear the sounds of this African-based music, with its rhythmic chanting and rapid drumbeat. Among the recordings, the album *Strictly Gombey Music* (Edmar 1165), performed by four members of the Pickles Spencer Gombey Group, offers a good selection of gombey dances.

Aficionados of this art form, however, will argue that gombey's allure lies not so much in the music as in the feverish—almost trancelike—dancing that accompanies it, as well as in the colorful costumes of the dancers. For that reason, they say, audio recordings can't convey the full mesmerizing power of a gombey dance the way a visual recording can. So, while you're in Bermuda, consider filming a gombey dance to show when you get back home.

Regrettably, there's no one place in Bermuda where you can always see gombey. Your best bet is to inquire at your hotel to see what events and performances might be staged during your visit. Sometimes hotels present gombey shows, but they don't follow a fixed schedule.

THE BALLADEER TRADITION

Bermuda also has a strong balladeer tradition. Although its exponents are fewer than they used to be, local balladeers continue to enjoy considerable popularity among islanders and visitors alike. A wry, self-deprecating humor has always distinguished their compositions, and balladeers can strum a song for any occasion on their guitars. Today, many of their songs have to do with Bermuda's changing way of life.

By virtually everyone's estimate, the musical patriarch of Bermuda was **Hubert Smith,** who was the island's official greeter in song. A balladeer of formidable talent and originality, Smith composed and performed songs for the visits of nearly all the foreign heads of state who graced Bermuda's shores in recent memory. His performances for members of the British royal family included one of the most famous songs ever written about the island: *Bermuda Is Another World.* The song is now the island's unofficial national anthem; it's included in the best-selling album *Bermuda Is Another World* (Edmar 1025).

RECORDINGS

In the last 2 decades, Bermuda saw the rise of many other recording artists, whose CDs are available in local stores. A five-man calypso band, **The Bermuda Strollers,** with their lively rhythms, can be heard on their album *The Best of* (Edmar 20G6), and also in a collection of musical odes to the island's natural beauty, *South Shore Bermuda* (Edmar 1156). Another balladeer and comic of great talent is **Gene Steede.** His popular album is called *South Shore Bermuda* (Edmar 2003). A challenger is **Jay Fox,** known for his songs of love, joy, and sorrow, all heard in the album *Island Paradise* (Jay Fox 1601).

Bermuda ballads, songs of love, and calypsos are also performed by **Stan Seymour,** a popular soloist who has been compared to Harry Belafonte. Look for *Our Man in Bermuda* (Edmar 1070).

The lively calypsos of Trinidad and the pulsating rhythms of Jamaica have also influenced musical tastes in Bermuda. **Youth Creation,** a dreadlock-sporting local reggae group, adopts the Rastafarian style in *Ja's on Our Side* (Edmar 2002).

For those who find that nothing quite stirs the blood as well as good old-fashioned oompah, there are the live as well as recorded performances of the **Bermuda Regiment,** whose bagpipes, trumpets, and drum tattoos evoke the finest British military traditions—and must strike a nostalgic chord or two in many a British or Bermudian listener. The regiment's album *Drummers Call Bermuda* (Edmar 1152) is a perennial favorite.

The late **Lance Hayward** was a Bermuda-born musician who established his musical reputation far from home. His most appreciative audiences were found in the smoke-filled jazz houses of New York's Greenwich Village. With a musical style that has been compared to the soft jazz of George Shearing, his most popular album is *Killing Me Softly* (Island 90683).

A Bermuda-born trio, **Steel Groove,** became known for performing only instrumentals in the Trinidadian style. Their trademark adaptations used the calypso-derived steel pan combined with a keyboard, an electric guitar, and often a bass guitar. Their most popular album became *Calypso Hits.* An even earlier Calypso group, **Esso Steel Band,** also became widely known island-wide with the release of their albums, *The Esso Steel Band* (Sunshine 1003) and *It's a Beautiful World.*

EATING & DRINKING

For years, Bermuda wasn't known for its cuisine; the food was too often bland and lacking in flavor. However, the culinary scene has notably changed. Chefs seem better trained, and many top-notch (albeit expensive) restaurants dot the archipelago. Italian food is in vogue, as is Chinese. (On the other side of the coin, fast food, including KFC, has arrived, too.)

In recent years, some Bermudians have shown an increased interest in their heritage. They've revived many traditional dishes and published the recipes in books devoted to Bermudian cooking (not a bad idea for a souvenir).

As the population grows, less and less farmland is available on the island, so Bermuda imports most of its food from the United States (which means you might want to focus on dishes made with the local ingredients noted below as much as possible; there's no telling how long that imported meat has been in storage). But lots of people still tend their own gardens; at one home, we were amazed at the variety of vegetables grown on a small plot of land, including sorrel, oyster plants, and Jerusalem artichokes.

What's Cooking?

SEAFOOD   Any local fisherman will be happy to tell you that more species of shore and ocean fish—including grunt, angelfish, yellowtail, gray snapper, and the ubiquitous rockfish—are found off Bermuda's coastline than any other place.

Rockfish, which is similar to Bahamian grouper, appears on nearly every menu. From the ocean, it weighs anywhere from 15 to 135 pounds (or even more). Steamed, broiled, baked, fried, or grilled, rockfish is a challenge to any chef. There's even a dish known as "rockfish maw," which we understand only the most old-fashioned cooks (there is still a handful on St. David's Island) know how to prepare. It's the maw, or stomach, of a rockfish, stuffed with a dressing of forcemeat (seasoned chopped fish) and simmered slowly on the stove. If you view dining as an adventure, you may want to try it.

The most popular dish on the island is **Bermuda fish chowder,** made with a variety of white fish (often rockfish). Waiters usually pass around a bottle of sherry peppers and some black rum, which you add to your soup; these lend a distinctive Bermudian flavor.

Shark isn't as popular on Bermuda as it used to be, but many traditional dishes, including hash, are made from shark. Some people use shark-liver oil to forecast the

Dress Up for Your Evening Out

As most of the world dresses more and more casually, Bermuda's dress codes have loosened up a bit—but this is still a more formal destination than many other islands. Most restaurants prefer that men wear a jacket and tie after 6pm; women usually wear casual, chic clothing in the evening. It's always wise to ask about required dress when you're reserving a table. And during the day, no matter what the establishment, be sure to wear a cover-up—don't arrive for lunch sporting a bikini.

See the "Etiquette" section under "Fast Facts: Bermuda" in chapter 10 for more information.

weather; it's said to be more reliable than the nightly TV report. The oil is left in the sun in a small bottle. If it lies still, fair weather is ahead; if droplets form on the sides of the bottle, expect foul weather.

The great game fish in Bermuda is **wahoo,** a sweet fish that tastes like albacore. If it's on the menu, go for a wahoo steak. Properly prepared, it's superb.

The **Bermuda lobster** (or "guinea chick," as it's known locally) has been called a first cousin of the Maine lobster. It's in season from September to March. Its high price tag has led to overfishing, forcing the government to issue periodic bans on its harvesting. In those instances, lobster is imported.

You can occasionally get good **conch stew** at a local restaurant. **Sea scallops,** though still available, have become increasingly rare. **Mussels** are cherished in Bermuda; one of the most popular traditional dishes is Bermuda-style mussel pie, with a filling of papaya, onions, potatoes, bacon, curry powder, lemon juice, thyme, and, of course, steamed mussels.

FRUITS & VEGETABLES In restaurants and homes, **Portuguese red-bean soup**—the culinary contribution of the Portuguese farmers who were brought to the island to till the land—precedes many a meal.

The **Bermuda onion** figures in many recipes, including onion pie. Bermuda-onion soup, an island favorite, is usually flavored with Outerbridge's Original Sherry Peppers.

Bermudians grow more **potatoes** than any other vegetable; the principal varieties are Pontiac red and Kennebec white. The traditional Sunday breakfast of codfish and bananas cooked with potatoes is still served in some homes.

"Peas and plenty" is a Bermudian tradition. Black-eyed peas are cooked with onions, salt pork, and sometimes rice. Dumplings or boiled sweet potatoes may also be added to the mix at the last minute. Another peas-and-rice dish, **Hoppin' John,** is eaten as a main dish or as a side dish with meat or poultry.

Both Bermudians and Bahamians share the tradition of **Johnny Bread,** or **Johnnycake,** a simple pan-cooked cornmeal bread. Fishermen would make it at sea over a fire in a box filled with sand to keep the flames from spreading to the boat.

The starchy **cassava** root, once an important food on Bermuda, is now used chiefly as an ingredient in the traditional Christmas cassava pie. Another dish with a festive holiday connection is **sweet-potato pudding,** traditionally eaten on Guy Fawkes Day (Nov 5).

Bermuda grows many **fresh fruits,** including strawberries, Surinam cherries, guavas, avocados, and, of course, bananas. Guavas are made into jelly, which in turn often goes into making the famous Bermuda syllabub, traditionally accompanied by Johnnycake.

What to Wash It All Down With

For some 300 years, **rum** has been the drink of Bermuda. Especially popular are Bacardi (formerly a Cuban company, their headquarters are now in Bermuda) and Demerara rum (also known as black rum). The rum swizzle (with rum, citrus juices, and club soda) is the most famous cocktail in Bermuda.

For decades, the true Bermudian has preferred a drink called **"Dark and Stormy."** Prepared with black rum and ginger beer (pronounced *burr*), it has been called the national drink of the island.

Local Dining Customs

One of Bermuda's most delightful traditions is the English ritual of **afternoon tea,** which many local homes and hotels maintain.

In hotels, the typical afternoon tea is served daily from 3 to 5pm. Adding a contemporary touch, it's often served around a pool, with guests partaking in their bathing suits—a tolerated lapse from the usual formal social and dress code.

At some places, more formal tea is served at a table laid with silver, crisp white linens, and fine china, often imported from Britain. The usual accompaniments include finger sandwiches made with thinly sliced cucumber or watercress, and scones served with strawberry jam.

An intriguing drink is **loquat liqueur.** It can be made with loquats (a small plumlike local fruit), rock candy, and gin, or more elaborately with brandy instead of gin and the addition of such spices as cinnamon, nutmeg, cloves, and allspice.

You'll find all the usual name-brand alcoholic beverages in Bermuda, but prices on mixed drinks can run high, depending on the brand.

Like the British, Bermudians often enjoy a sociable **pub lunch.** There are several pubs in the City of Hamilton, St. George, and elsewhere on the island. For the visitor, a pub lunch—say, fish and chips or shepherd's pie, a pint or two of ale, and an animated discussion about politics, sports, or the most recent royal visit—is an experience to be cherished as truly Bermudian.

WHEN TO GO

The Weather

A semitropical island, Bermuda enjoys a mild climate; the term "Bermuda high" has come to mean sunny days and clear skies. The Gulf Stream, which flows between the island and North America, keeps the climate temperate. There's no rainy season, and no typical month of excess rain. Showers may be heavy at times, but the skies clear quickly.

Being farther north in the Atlantic than The Bahamas, Bermuda is much cooler in winter. Springlike temperatures prevail from mid-December to late March, with the average temperature ranging from 60° to 70°F (16°–21°C). Unless it rains, winter is fine for golf and tennis but not for swimming; it can be cool, and you may even need a sweater or a jacket. Water temperatures in winter are somewhat like the air temperature, ranging from about 66°F (19°C) in January to 75°F (24°C) through March. Scuba divers and snorkelers will find Bermuda's waters appreciably cooler than Caribbean waters in winter. From mid-November to mid-December and from late March to April, be prepared for unseasonable spurts of spring or summer weather.

In summer, the temperature rarely rises above 85°F (29°C). There's nearly always a cool breeze in the evening, but some hotels have air-conditioning. And local water temperatures can be as high as 86°F (30°C) during the summer—warmer than many inshore and offshore Caribbean waters.

As a result, Bermuda's off season is the exact opposite of that in the Caribbean. It begins in December and lasts until about March 1. In general, hotels offer off-season rates, with discounts ranging from 20% to 60%. This is the time to go if you're traveling on a tight budget. During autumn and winter, many hotels also offer discounted package deals. Some hotels close for a couple of weeks or months at this period.

A look at the official chart of temperature and rainfall will give you a general idea of what to expect during your visit.

Bermuda's Average Daytime Temperatures & Rainfall

	JAN	FEB	MAR	APR	MAY	JUNE	JULY	AUG	SEPT	OCT	NOV	DEC
TEMP (°F)	65	64	64	65	70	75	79	80	79	75	69	65
TEMP (°C)	19	18	18	19	21	24	30	27	30	24	21	19
RAINFALL (IN.)	4	5	4.6	3	3.9	5.2	4	5.3	5.3	6	4.5	3

The Hurricane Season

This curse of the Caribbean, The Bahamas, and Bermuda lasts officially from June to November, but fewer tropical storms pound Bermuda than the U.S. mainland. Bermuda is also less frequently hit than islands in the Caribbean. Satellite forecasts are generally able to give adequate warning of any really dangerous weather.

If you're concerned, you can call the nearest branch of the National Weather Service (it's listed under the U.S. Department of Commerce in the phone book). Radio and TV weather reports from the National Hurricane Center in Coral Gables, Florida, will also keep you posted.

To find the current weather conditions in Bermuda, and a 5-day forecast, go to Bermuda Weather at **www.weather.bm**.

Holidays

Bermuda observes the following public holidays: New Year's Day (Jan 1), Good Friday, Easter, Bermuda Day (May 24), the Queen's Birthday (first or second Mon in June), Cup Match Days (cricket; Thurs and Fri preceding first Mon in Aug), Labour Day

GETTING SUCKED IN: THE OFFICIAL WORD ON THE bermuda triangle

In response to a flood of concern from travelers about the possibility of getting sucked into the so-called Bermuda Triangle and disappearing forever, the U.S. Board of Geographic Names has issued an official statement: "We do not recognize the Bermuda Triangle as an official name and do not maintain an official file on the area. The 'Bermuda or Devil's Triangle' is an imaginary area located off the southeastern Atlantic coast of the United States, which is noted for a high incidence of unexplained losses of ships, small boats, and aircraft. The apexes of the triangle are generally accepted to be Bermuda, Miami, and San Juan. In the past, extensive but futile Coast Guard searches prompted by search-and-rescue cases such as the disappearances of an entire squadron of TBM Avengers shortly after take-off from Fort Lauderdale, or the traceless sinking of *Marine Sulphur Queen* in the Florida Straits, have lent credence to the popular belief in the mystery and the supernatural qualities of the Bermuda Triangle."

(first Mon in Sept), Christmas Day (Dec 25), and Boxing Day (Dec 26). Public holidays that fall on a Saturday or Sunday are usually celebrated the following Monday.

Bermuda Calendar of Events

For an exhaustive list of events beyond those listed here, check **http://events.frommers.com**, where you'll find a searchable, up-to-the-minute roster of what's happening in cities all over the world.

JANUARY & FEBRUARY

Bermuda Festival. Throughout January and February, island-wide events abound. They include golf and tennis invitationals; an international marathon; a dog show; open house and garden tours; and the Bermuda Festival, a 6-week international festival of the performing arts, held in the City of Hamilton. It features drama, dance, jazz, classical, and popular music, as well as other entertainment by the best international artists. Some tickets for the festival are reserved until 48 hours before curtain time for visitors. For details and a schedule for the 2013 festival, contact **Bermuda Festival,** P.O. Box HM 297, Hamilton HM AX, Bermuda (www.bermudafestival.org; © **441/295-1291**).

The Bermuda International Race Weekend, with international and local runners, takes place the third weekend in January. For further information and entry forms, contact the **International Race Weekend Committee,** Bermuda Track and Field Association, P.O. Box DV 397, Devonshire DV BX, Bermuda (www.bermudaraceweekend.com; © **441/296-0951**).

MARCH

Bermuda International Film Festival. Film buffs and filmmakers (mainly independent ones) descend on Bermuda for the annual festival that combines screenings of independent works with movies from personal workshops in Bermuda and also with important films from abroad. Participants get to meet and speak with industry leaders. After each film there is a Q&A session. During the festival, three daily screenings are held. For more information, log on to www.biff.bm or contact Duncan Hall at © **441/293-7769.** Mid-March.

Home & Garden Tours. Each spring, the Garden Club of Bermuda lays out the welcome mat at a number of private homes and gardens. A different set of houses, all conveniently located in the same parish, is open every Wednesday during this event. The program usually includes a total of 20 homes, many of them dating from the 17th and 18th centuries. The Bermuda Department of Tourism Office (see "Visitor Information" under "Fast Facts" in chapter 10) provides a complete listing of homes and viewing schedules. You can also contact the organizers of many of the house and garden events, the Garden Club of Bermuda, P.O. Box HM 1141, Hamilton HMEX Bermuda (www.gardenclubbermuda.org; © **441/232-1273**). The tours usually run from the end of March to mid-May.

APRIL

Peppercorn Ceremony. His Excellency the governor collects the annual rent of one peppercorn for use of the island's Old State House in St. George. Mid- to late April. For information and the exact date, call The Peppercorn Ceremony Corporation in St. Georges at © **441/297-1532.**

Agriculture Exhibit. Held over 3 days in late April at the Botanical Gardens in Paget, this event is a celebration of Bermuda's agrarian and horticultural bounty. In addition to prize-winning produce, the Agriculture Exhibit provides a showcase for local arts and crafts. For more information, contact the **Department of Environmental Protection,** P.O. Box HM 834, Hamilton HM CX, Bermuda (© **441/236-4201**), or the Bermuda Department of Tourism (see "Visitor Information" under "Fast Facts" in chapter 10).

International Race Week. Every year, during late April and early May, this yachting event pits equivalent vessels from seven classes of sailing craft against one another. Yachting enthusiasts around the world follow the knockout elimination-style event with avid interest. The **Marion-to-Bermuda Race** and **Newport–Bermuda Race** (see below) take place in June.

Unfortunately for spectators, the finish lines for the island's sailing races usually lie several miles offshore. Afterward, boats are often moored in Hamilton Harbour; any vantage point on the harbor is good for watching the boats come in. Even better: Head for any of the City of Hamilton's harborfront pubs, where racing crowds celebrate their wins (or justify their losses) over pints of ale.

For information on all sailing events held off the coast of Bermuda, contact the **Sailing Secretary,** Royal Bermuda Yacht Club, 15 Point Pleasant Road, Hamilton, HM 11, Bermuda (www.rbyc.bm; © **441/295-2214**), or (for races originating off the U.S. coast) the **New York Yacht Club,** 37 W. 44th St., New York, NY 10036 (www.nyyc.org; © **212/382-1000**).

MAY

Beating Retreat Ceremony. The Bermuda Regiment and massed pipes and drums (a military band and a drum corps) create an event that combines a marching band concert and a parade. The ceremony's roots are in the 17th century, when British soldiers were stationed on the island and a roll of the drums called them back to their garrisons at nightfall. It's presented once or twice per month, rotating among the City of Hamilton, St. George, and the Royal Naval Dockyard. The ceremony usually takes place from May to October. The Bermuda Department of Tourism Office (see "Visitor Information" under "Fast Facts" in chapter 10) supplies exact times and schedules.

Bermuda Heritage Day and Month. Bermuda Heritage Month culminates on **Bermuda Day,** May 24, a public holiday that's Bermuda's equivalent of Independence Day. Bermuda Day is punctuated with parades

through downtown Hamilton, dinghy and cycling races, and the Bermuda Half-Day Marathon (open only to island residents). For the rest of the month, a program of cultural and sporting events is presented (the schedule will be available at the tourist office). Any hotel in town can fill you in on the events planned for the year's biggest political celebration, or contact the Bermuda Department of Tourism Office (see "Visitor Information" under "Fast Facts" in chapter 10).

JUNE

Queen's Birthday. The queen's birthday is celebrated with a parade down Front Street in the City of Hamilton. First or second Monday in June; contact the Bermuda Department of Tourism Office at www.gotobermuda.com or © **800/BERMUDA** [237-6832] for exact schedules.

Marion-to-Bermuda Race. This 1,038km (645-mile) sailboat race from Marion, Massachusetts, to Bermuda is held in mid-June. See the entry for "International Race Week," under April, above, for details on international sailing events. For more information, visit www.marionbermuda.com, or call © **441/295-2214.**

Newport–Bermuda Race. The world's most famous wind-driven contest is held each June. The record to date, which starts in Newport, Rhode Island, is a 56-hour transit. See "International Race Week," above, for advice on viewing this race.

JULY & AUGUST

Cup Match and Somers Days. Also known as the Cup Match Cricket Festival, this annual event celebrates the year's bounty with Bermuda's most illustrious cricket match. It's often compared to American Thanksgiving. Cricketers from the East End (St. George's Cricket Club) play off against those from the West End (Somerset Cricket Club), with lots of attendant British-derived protocol and hoopla. Tickets cost about $20; they're available at the gate on match day. The event is held on Thursday and Friday before the first Monday in August. For more information, click on www.bermudacupmatch.com or www.bermudacricketboard.com or call © **441/292-8958.**

SEPTEMBER

Labour Day. This public holiday, held on the first Monday in September, features a host of activities; it's also the ideal time for a picnic. The high point is a parade from Union Square in the City of Hamilton's Bernard Park.

Marine Science Day. Lectures, hands-on demonstrations, and displays for adults and children mark this day devoted to the study of the sea. It is hosted by the **BBSR** (Bermuda Biological Station for Research, Inc.). Visit www.bios.edu or call ✆ **441/297-1880** for more information. End of September.

OCTOBER

Match Racing. For Match Racing, pairs of identical sailing vessels, staffed by a rotating roster of teams from throughout the world, compete in elimination-style contests throughout the month. For details on international sailing events, see the entry for "International Race Week," under April, above.

NOVEMBER

Bermuda Heart & Soul. Travelers 50 years of age or older can enjoy specially designed cultural activities between the months of November and March during this Golden Rendezvous month. Many hotels offer reduced rates to mature travelers, and discount coupons are also available at the Visitors Information Centre in Hamilton. For more information, call the **Bermuda Heart and Soul** "Program in the Dockyard" at ✆ **441/234-3208.**

Guy Fawkes Day. A small annual celebration with a minifair marks this day. The celebration starts with the traditional burning of 17th-century British traitor Guy Fawkes's effigy at the Keepyard of the Bermuda Maritime Museum, Royal Naval Dockyard, at 4:30pm. November 5.

The Opening of Parliament. A traditional ceremony, with a military guard of honor,

celebrates the opening of Parliament by His Excellency the governor, as the Queen's personal representative. In anticipation of the entry of the members of Parliament (MPs) at 11am, crowds begin gathering outside the Cabinet Building around 9:30 or 10am. Spectators traditionally include lots of schoolchildren being trained in civic protocol, as well as nostalgia buffs out for a whiff of British-style pomp. For more information, call ✆ **800/223-6106.** November 6.

Invitation Tennis Weeks. More than 100 visiting players vie with Bermudians during 2 weeks of matches. Unlike Wimbledon—this event's role model—nearly everyone buys tickets at the gate. For information, contact the **Bermuda Lawn Tennis Association,** P.O. Box HM 341, Hamilton HM BX, Bermuda (www.blta.bm; ✆ **441/296-0834**). Early November.

Remembrance Day. Bermudian police, British and U.S. military units, Bermudians, and veterans' organizations participate in a small parade in remembrance of all who have given their lives in battle. November 11.

World Rugby Classic. Former international rugby players, who have recently retired from the international stage, compete with Bermudians at the Bermuda National Sports Club (www.worldrugby.bm; ✆ **441/295-6574**). Mid-November.

DECEMBER

Bermuda Goodwill Tournament. Pro-amateur foursomes from international golf clubs play more than 72 holes on four of Bermuda's eight courses. Anyone who wants to compete must pass the sponsors' stringent requirements and may appear only by invitation. Spectators are welcome to watch from the sidelines for free. For more information, contact the **Bermuda Goodwill Golf Tournament,** P.O. Box HM 2896, Hamilton HM LX, Bermuda (www.bermudagoodwill.org; ✆ **441/295-4640**). Early December.

BERMUDA'S NATURAL WORLD

Lying 920km (570 miles) east-southeast of Cape Hatteras, North Carolina, Bermuda is actually a group of some 300 islands, islets, and coral rocks clustered in a fishhook-shaped chain about 35km (22 miles) long and 3km (2 miles) wide at its broadest point. The archipelago, formally known as "The Bermudas," forms a land-mass of about 54 sq. km (21 sq. miles).

Only 20 or so of the islands are inhabited. The largest one, called the "mainland," is Great Bermuda; about 23km (14 miles) long, it's linked to nearby major islands by a series of bridges and causeways. Bermuda's capital, the City of Hamilton, is on Great Bermuda.

The other main inhabited islands include Somerset, Watford, Boaz, and Ireland in the west, and St. George's and St. David's in the east. This chain of major islands encloses the archipelago's major bodies of water, which include Castle Harbour, St. George's Harbour, Harrington Sound, and Great Sound. Most of the other smaller islands, or islets, lie within these bodies of water.

Bermuda is far north of the Tropic of Cancer, which cuts through the Bahamian archipelago. Bermuda's archipelago is based on the upper parts of an extinct volcano, which may date from 100 million years ago. Through the millennia, wind and water brought limestone deposits and formed these islands far from any continental land-mass. Today, the closest continental landmass is the coast of the Carolinas. Bermuda is about 1,250km (775 miles) southeast of New York City, some 1,660km (1,030 miles) northeast of Miami, and nearly 5,555km (3,445 miles) from London. It has a balmy climate year-round, with sunshine prevailing almost every day. The chief source of Bermuda's mild weather is the Gulf Stream, a broad belt of warm water formed by equatorial currents. The stream's northern reaches separate the Bermuda islands from North America and, with the prevailing northeast winds, temper the wintry blasts that sweep across the Atlantic from west and north. The islands of Bermuda are divided, for administrative purposes, into parishes. (See chapter 3.)

More Than Onions: The Island's Flora

Bermuda's temperate climate, abundant sunshine, fertile soil, and adequate moisture account for the exceptionally verdant gardens that you'll find on the archipelago. Some of the best gardens, such as the Botanical Gardens in Paget Parish, are open to the public. Bermudian gardeners pride themselves on their mixtures of temperate-zone and subtropical plants, both of which thrive on the island, despite the salty air.

Bermuda is blessed with copious and varied flora. Examples include the indige-nous **sea grape,** which flourishes along the island's sandy coasts (it prefers sand and saltwater to more arable soil), and the **cassava plant,** whose roots resemble the tubers of sweet potatoes. When ground into flour and soaked to remove a mild poi-son, the cassava root is the main ingredient for Bermuda's traditional Christmas pies. Also growing wild and abundant are **prickly pears, aromatic fennel, yucca,** and the **Spanish bayonet,** a spiked-leaf plant that bears a single white flower in season.

Bermuda's only native palm, the **palmetto,** proved particularly useful to the early settlers. Its leaves were used to thatch roofs, and when crushed and fermented, the palm fronds produced a strong alcoholic drink called bibby, whose effects the early Puritans condemned. Palmetto leaves were also fashioned into women's hats during a brief period in the 1600s, when they represented the height of fashion in London.

The **banana,** one of Bermuda's most dependable sources of fresh fruit, was intro-duced to the island in the early 1600s. It is believed that Bermudian bananas were the first to be brought back to London from the New World. They created an immediate sensation, leading to the cultivation of bananas in many other British colonies.

The plant that contributed most to Bermuda's renown was the **Bermuda onion** (*Allium cepa*). Imported from England in 1616, it was grown from seeds brought from the Spanish and Portuguese islands of Tenerife and Madeira. The Bermuda onion became so famous along the East Coast of the United States that Bermudians themselves became known as "Onions." During the 1930s, Bermuda's flourishing export trade in onions declined due to high tariffs, increased competition from similar species grown in Texas and elsewhere, and the limited arable land on the island.

Today, you'll see oleander, hibiscus, royal poinciana, poinsettia, bougainvillea, and dozens of other flowering shrubs and vines decorating Bermuda's gently rolling land. Of the island's dozen or so species of morning glory, three are indigenous; they tend to grow rampant and overwhelm everything else in a garden.

Close Encounters with the Local Fauna

AMPHIBIANS

Because of the almost total lack of natural freshwater ponds and lakes, Bermuda's amphibians have adapted to seawater or slightly brackish water. Amphibians include **tree frogs** (*Eleutherodactylus johnstonei* and *Eleutherodactylus gossei*), whose nighttime chirping newcomers sometimes mistake for the song of birds. Small and camouflaged by the leafy matter of the forest floor, the frogs appear between April and November.

More visible are Bermuda's **giant toads,** or road toads (*Bufo marinus*), which sometimes reach the size of an adult human's palm. Imported from Guyana in the 1870s in hopes of controlling the island's cockroach population, giant toads search out the nighttime warmth of the asphalt roads—and are often crushed by cars in the process. They are especially prevalent after a soaking rain. The road toads are not venomous and, contrary to legend, do not cause warts.

Island reptiles include colonies of harmless **lizards,** often seen sunning themselves on rocks until approaching humans or predators scare them away. The best-known species is the Bermuda rock lizard (*Eumeces longirostris*), also known as a skink. It's said to have been the only nonmarine, nonflying vertebrate on Bermuda before the arrival of European colonists. Imported reptiles include the Somerset lizard (*Anolis roquet*), whose black eye patches give it the look of a bashful bandit, and the Jamaican anole (*Anolis grahami*), a kind of chameleon.

BIRD LIFE

Partly because of its ample food sources, Bermuda has a large bird population; many species nest on the island during their annual migrations. Most of the birds arrive

---

Impressions

A major problem for Bermudians remained the question of whether to obtain independence. The Bermuda people have always been under the Union Jack, unlike many other British colonies, and while the British Empire has only a little of its former glory, it still gives a degree of safety for those who shelter under its wing.

—W. S. Zuill, *The Story of Bermuda and Her People*

during the cooler winter months, usually between Christmas and Easter. Birders have recorded almost 40 different species of eastern warblers, which peacefully coexist with martins, doves, egrets, South American terns, herons, fork-tailed flycatchers, and some species from as far away as the Arctic Circle.

Two of the most visible imported species are the **cardinal,** introduced during the 1700s, and the **kiskadee.** Imported from Trinidad in 1957 to control lizards and flies, the kiskadee has instead wreaked havoc on the island's commercial fruit crops.

The once-prevalent eastern bluebird has been greatly reduced in number since its preferred habitat, cedar trees, was depleted by blight. Another bird native to Bermuda is the gray-and-white **petrel,** known locally as a cahow, which burrows for most of the year in the sands of the isolated eastern islands. During the rest of the year, the cahow feeds at sea, floating for hours in the warm waters of the Gulf Stream. One of the most elusive birds in the world—it was once thought to be extinct—the petrel is now protected by the Bermudian government.

Also native to Bermuda is the **cliff-dwelling tropic bird,** which you can identify by the elongated plumage of its white tail. The bird resembles a swallow and is the island's harbinger of spring, appearing annually in March.

Although the gardens and golf courses of many of the island's hotels attract dozens of birds, some of the finest bird-watching sites are maintained by the Bermuda Audubon Society (**www.audubon.bm**) or the National Trust. Isolated sites known for sheltering thousands of native and migrating birds include Paget Marsh, just south of the City of Hamilton; the Idwal Hughes Nature Reserve in Hamilton Parish; and Spittal Pond in Smith's Parish.

SEA LIFE

In the deep waters off the shores of Bermuda are some of the finest game fish in the world: blackfin tuna, marlin, swordfish, wahoo, dolphin, sailfish, and barracuda. Also prevalent are bonefish and pompano, both of which prefer sun-flooded shallow waters closer to shore. Any beachcomber is likely to come across hundreds of oval-shaped chitons (*Chiton tuberculatus*), a mollusk that adheres tenaciously to rocks in tidal flats; locally, it is known as "suck-rock."

Beware of the **Portuguese man-of-war** (*Physalia physalis*), a floating colony of jellyfish whose stinging tentacles sometimes reach 15m (50 ft.) in length. Give this dangerous and venomous marine creature a wide berth: Severe stings may require hospitalization. Avoid the creature when it washes up on Bermuda beaches, usually between March and July—the man-of-war can sting even when it appears to be dead.

The most prevalent marine animal in Bermuda is responsible for the formation of the island's greatest tourist attraction—its miles of pale pink sand. Much of the sand consists of broken shells, pieces of coral, and the calcium carbonate remains of other marine invertebrates. The pinkest pieces are shards of crushed shell from a single-celled animal called foraminifer. Its vivid pink skeleton is pierced with holes, through which the animal extends its rootlike feet

> ## Impressions
>
> *Bermuda . . . it's a nutty, nutty place.*
> —Paul Shaffer, *Late Night
> with David Letterman*

(*pseudopodia*), which cling to the underside of the island's reefs during the animal's brief life, before its skeleton is washed ashore.

RESPONSIBLE TRAVEL

The ecotourist will find Bermuda a rich stamping ground with its bird-watching and nature trails. Regrettably, because of lack of business, most so-called "green tours" are no longer offered. You can, however, map out your own tour.

Some of these chief attractions include the following:

o **The Arboretum,** Middle Road in Devonshire Parish, is 7.7 pristine hectares (19 acres) close to the City of Hamilton, with a large expanse of open space and a small woodland.

o **Bermuda Railway Trail,** West End. Totaling 34km (21 miles), this trail provides a scenic route from East to West. It is used by walkers and birders alike.

GENERAL RESOURCES FOR green travel

The following websites provide valuable wide-ranging information on sustainable travel.

o **Responsible Travel** (www. responsibletravel.com) is a great source of sustainable travel ideas; the site is run by a spokesperson for ethical tourism in the travel industry. **Sustainable Travel International** (www.sustainable travelinternational.org) promotes ethical tourism practices and manages an extensive directory of sustainable properties and tour operators around the world.

o In the U.K., **Tourism Concern** (www.tourismconcern.org.uk) works to reduce social and environmental problems connected to tourism. The **Association of Independent Tour Operators** (**AITO;** www.aito.co.uk) is a group of specialist operators leading the field in making vacations sustainable.

o **Carbonfund** (www.carbonfund. org), **TerraPass** (www.terrapass. com), and **Carbon Neutral** (http://coolclimate.berkeley.edu)

provide info on "carbon offsetting," or offsetting the greenhouse gas emitted during flights.

o **Greenhotels** (http://greenhotels. com) recommends green-rated member hotels around the world that fulfill the company's stringent environmental requirements. **Environmentally Friendly Hotels** (www.environmentallyfriendly hotels.com) offers more green accommodations ratings.

o For information on animal-friendly issues throughout the world, visit **Tread Lightly** (www. treadlightly.org). For information about the ethics of swimming with dolphins, visit the **Whale and Dolphin Conservation Society** (www.wdcs.org).

o **Volunteer International** (www. volunteerinternational.com) has a list of questions to help you determine the intentions and the nature of a volunteer program. For general info on volunteer travel, visit **www.goabroad.com** and **www.idealist.org**.

- **Blue Hole Park,** Hamilton Parish. An abundance of wildlife exists in nearly 5 hectares (12 acres), with a natural small pond and caves close by.
- **Hog Bay Park,** Sandys Parish. On 15 hectares (38 acres), this park has well-maintained trails, vegetable gardens, and wooded hillsides with native and endemic vegetation.
- **Spittal Pond Nature Reserve,** Smith's Parish. At South Road, 14 hectares (34 acres) of nature form the largest and most accessible nature reserve on the island. There are excellent trails plus bird-watching at several observation points, where you can see a large variety of wildlife.

SUGGESTED ITINERARIES

For visitors on the run, who are forced by their schedules to see Bermuda in anywhere from 1 to 3 days, we've devised a trio of self-guided tours, written as three 1-day itineraries. With these ready-made itineraries, you can have a complete, unforgettable trip, even though time is short.

You can cover much of Bermuda, especially the harbor City of Hamilton and the historic town of St. George, on foot. A week's visit will let you break up your sightseeing trips with time on the beach, boating, or engaging in some of the island's other outdoor activities, such as golf or scuba diving. Hitting the beach is the first priority for most visitors—but you don't need us to tell you how to schedule your time in the sun.

THE PARISHES OF BERMUDA

For administrative purposes, the islands of Bermuda are divided into **parishes,** all named for shareholders of the Bermuda Company, which was formed by English investors in the early 1600s to develop Bermuda as a profit-making enterprise. From west to east, the parishes are listed below.

Sandys Parish

In the far western part of the archipelago, Sandys (pronounced *Sands*) Parish encompasses the islands of **Ireland, Boaz,** and **Somerset.** This parish (named for Sir Edwin Sandys) is centered in Somerset Village, on Somerset Island. Sandys Parish is often called Somerset.

Some visitors to Bermuda head directly for Sandys Parish and spend their entire time here; they feel that the far western tip, with its rolling hills, lush countryside, and tranquil bays, is something special and

---

 Planning Pointer

It's enlightening to take a ferry ride around the inner harbor before or after your City of Hamilton walking tour. You can get an overview of the city before concentrating on specific landmarks or monuments, or gain a new perspective on what you've just seen.

Bermuda's Parishes

ATLANTIC OCEAN

National Museum of Bermuda
Ireland Island North
Royal Naval Dockyard (King's Wharf)
Ireland Island South
Two Rock Passage
Mangrove Bay
Somerset Village
Watford Bridge
Ely's Harbour
SANDYS
Bay Rd.
North Shore Rd.
Fort Scaur
Great Sound
PEMBROKE
Ocean View Golf Course
Hamilton
Long Island
Hawkins Island
Waterville (House)
Somerset Bridge
Ferry
Hamilton Harbour
Botanical Gardens
Ports Island
Middle Rd.
Hinson Island
PAGET
Port Royal Golf Course
Little Sound
Darrell Island
Harbour Rd.
Belmont Hotel Golf & Country Club
Riddells Bay Golf & Country Club
Middle Rd.
WARWICK
South Rd.
SOUTHAMPTON
Gibbs Hill Lighthouse
Princess Golf Club

unique. (This area has always stood apart from the rest of Bermuda: During the U.S. Civil War, when most Bermudians sympathized with the Confederates, Sandys Parish supported the Union.) Sandys Parish has areas of great natural beauty, including **Somerset Long Bay,** the biggest and best public beach in the West End (which the Bermuda Audubon Society is developing into a nature preserve), and **Mangrove Bay,** a protected beach in the heart of **Somerset Village.** Take a walk around the old village; it's filled with typically Bermudian houses and shops. On Somerset Road is the **Scaur Lodge Property,** whose waterfront hillside is open daily at no charge.

The parish boasts some of the most elegant places to stay in Bermuda, but if you want to be near the shops, restaurants, and pubs of the City of Hamilton, you may want to stay in a more central location and visit Sandys Parish on a day trip. You can

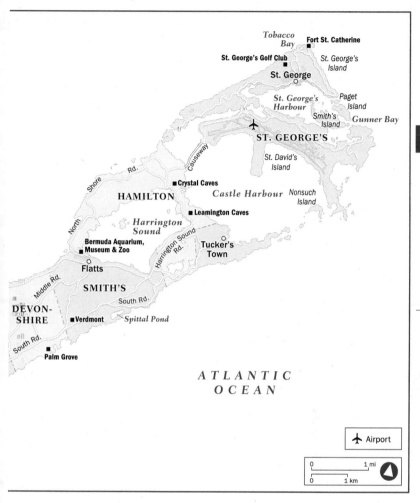

commute to the City of Hamilton by ferry, but it's a bit time-consuming. Those who prefer tranquility and unspoiled nature to shopping or lingering over an extra pint in a pub will be happy here. Another advantage of staying here is that Sandys has several embarkation points for various types of sea excursions.

Southampton Parish

Southampton Parish (named for the third earl of Southampton) is a narrow strip of land opening at its northern edge onto Little Sound and on its southern shore onto the Atlantic Ocean. It stretches from Riddells Bay to Tucker's Island, and is split by Middle Road.

If dining at waterfront restaurants and staying at big resort hotels is part of your Bermuda dream, then Southampton is your parish; it's the site of such famed resorts as the Fairmont Southampton and the Sonesta Beach Resort. Southampton is also the best place to stay if you plan to spend a great deal of time on the island's fabled pink, sandy beaches. Among Southampton's jewels is **Horseshoe Bay,** one of Bermuda's most attractive public beaches, with changing rooms, a snack bar, and space for parking.

Southampton lacks the intimacy and romance of Sandys, but it has a lot of razzle-dazzle going for it. It's the top choice for a golfing vacation. If you like to sightsee, you can easily occupy 2 days just exploring the parish's many attractions. It also has more nightlife than Sandys—although not as much as the City of Hamilton.

Warwick Parish

Named in honor of the second earl of Warwick, this parish lies in the heart of Great Bermuda Island. Like Southampton, it is known for its long stretches of rosy sand. Along the south shore is **Warwick Long Bay,** one of Bermuda's best public beaches. Warwick also offers parklands bordering the sea, winding country roads, two golf courses, and a number of natural attractions. This area is the best on the island for horseback riding, which is the ideal way to see pastoral Bermuda up close.

Warwick is a great choice for visitors seeking cottage or apartment rentals (where you can do some of your own cooking to cut down on the outrageous expense of food). The parish is not strong on restaurants; one of its disadvantages is that you have to travel a bit if you like to dine out. Nightlife is also spotty—just about the only action you can find after dark is in hotel lounges. This parish is for tranquility seekers, but because of its more central location, it doesn't offer quite the seclusion that Sandys does.

Paget Parish

Paget Parish lies directly south of the capital City of Hamilton, separated from it by Hamilton Harbour. Named after the fourth Lord Paget, it has many residences and historic homes and it's also the site of the 15-hectare (37-acre) **Botanical Gardens.** But the south-shore beaches—the best in the chain of islands—are what draw visitors here in droves. Paget Parish is also the site of **Chelston,** on Grape Bay Drive, the official residence of the U.S. consul general. Situated on 5.8 hectares (14 acres) of landscaped grounds, it's open only during the Garden Club's Home and Garden Tours in the spring (see "Bermuda Calendar of Events," in chapter 2, for details).

This is one of the best parishes to stay in; it has many excellent accommodations, including Elbow Beach Hotel. It's close enough to the City of Hamilton for an easy commute, but far enough away to escape the hordes. Because public transportation is all-important (you can't rent a car), Paget is a good place to situate yourself; it has some of the best and most convenient ferry connections and bus schedules. There are docks at Salt Kettle, Hodson's, and Lower Ferry; you can even "commute" by ferry to Warwick Parish or Sandys Parish, to the west. Paget's relatively flat terrain, rural lanes, and streets lined with old mansions make this an ideal place for biking. And hikers will find many small trails bordering the sea.

If you don't like big resort hotels, you can rent a cottage or one of several little guesthouses here. Unlike Warwick, Paget has a number of dining choices, too. Elbow Beach offers the most, but other fine options include Fourways Inn and Paraquet Restaurant. Most of the parish's nightlife centers on Elbow Beach.

Finding an Address

The island chain of Bermuda doesn't follow a rigid system of street addresses. Most hotels, even in official government listings, don't bother to include an address, although they do include post office boxes and postal codes. Bermudians just assume that everybody knows where everything is, which is fine if you've lived on Bermuda all your life. But if you're a first-time visitor, get a good map before setting out—and don't be shy about asking directions. In general, people are very helpful.

Most of the establishments you'll be seeking are on some street plan. However, some places use numbers in their street addresses, and others—perhaps their neighbors—don't. The actual building number is not always important, because a building such as a resort hotel is likely to be set back so far from the main road that you couldn't see its number anyway. Look for signs with the name of the hotel rather than the street number. Cross streets will also aid you in finding an address.

There are no major disadvantages to staying in Paget. You will find overcrowded beaches during spring break, however, and congestion in the City of Hamilton in the summer, when many cruise ships arrive.

Pembroke Parish

This parish (named after the third earl of Pembroke) houses one quarter of Bermuda's population. It is home to the **City of Hamilton,** Bermuda's capital and its only full-fledged city. The parish opens at its northern rim onto the vast Atlantic Ocean and on its southern side onto Hamilton Harbour; its western border is on Great Sound. The City of Hamilton is the first destination that most cruise-ship passengers will see.

This parish is not ideal for those seeking a tranquil vacation. Pembroke Parish, already packed with the island's greatest population density, also attracts the most visitors. The little city is especially crowded when cruise ships are in the harbor and travelers pour into the stores and restaurants. Yet for those who like to pub-crawl English style, shop until they drop, and have access to the largest concentration of dining choices, Pembroke—the City of Hamilton, in particular—is without equal on Bermuda.

Whether or not you stay in Pembroke, try to fit a shopping (or window-shopping) stroll along Front Street into your itinerary. The area also boasts a number of sightseeing attractions, most of which are easily accessible on foot (a plus because you don't have to depend on taxis, bikes, or scooters—which can get to be a bit of a bore after a while). Nightlife is the finest on the island. Don't expect splashy Las Vegas–type revues, however; instead, think restaurants, pubs, and small clubs.

Devonshire Parish

Lying east of Paget and Pembroke parishes, near the geographic center of the archipelago, Devonshire Parish (named for the first earl of Devonshire) is green and hilly. It has some housekeeping (self-catering) apartments, a cottage colony, and one of Bermuda's oldest churches, the **Old Devonshire Parish Church,** which dates from 1716. Three of Bermuda's major roads traverse the parish: the aptly named South Road (also unofficially referred to as South Shore Rd.), Middle Road, and North

Shore Road. As you wander its narrow lanes, you can, with some imagination, picture yourself in the parish's namesake county of Devon, England.

Golfers flock to Devonshire to play at the **Ocean View Golf Course.** Along North Shore Road, near the border of Pembroke Parish, is **Devonshire Dock,** long a seafarer's haven. In fact, during the War of 1812, British soldiers came to Devonshire Dock to be entertained by local women. Today, fishermen still bring in grouper and rockfish, so you can shop for dinner if you're staying at a nearby cottage with a kitchen.

Devonshire has a number of unspoiled nature areas. The **arboretum** on Montpelier Road is one of the most tranquil oases on Bermuda. This open space, created by the Department of Agriculture, Fisheries, and Parks, is home to a wide range of Bermudian plant and tree life, especially conifers, palms, and other subtropical trees. Along South Road, west of the junction with Collector's Hill, is the **Edmund Gibbons Nature Reserve.** This portion of marshland, owned by the National Trust, provides living space for a number of birds and rare species of Bermuda flora.

Devonshire is one of the sleepy residential parishes, known for its hilly interior, beautiful landscape, and fabulous estates bordering the sea. There's little sightseeing here; all those stunning private estates aren't open to the public, so unless you get a personal invitation, you're out of luck. But the parish is right in Bermuda's geographic center, so it's an ideal place to base yourself if you'd like to explore both the West End and the East End. There are two major drawbacks, though: With a few notable exceptions, the parish has very few places to stay and almost no dining choices.

Smith's Parish

Named for Sir Thomas Smith, this parish faces the open sea to the north and south. To the east is Harrington Sound; to the west, bucolic Devonshire Parish.

The parish encompasses **Flatts Village,** one of the island's most charming parish towns (take bus no. 10 or 11 from the City of Hamilton). It was a smugglers' port for about 200 years and served as the center of power for a coterie of successful "planter politicians" and landowners. Flatts Village's government was second in importance to that of St. George, which was once Bermuda's capital. People gathered at the rickety Flatts Bridge to "enjoy" such public entertainment as hangings; if the offense was serious enough, victims were drawn and quartered here. From Flatts Village, you have panoramic views of both the inlet and Harrington Sound. At the top of McGall's Hill is St. Mark's Church, based on the same designs used for the Old Devonshire Parish Church.

Most visitors view Smith's Parish as a day trip or a half-day trip, although the parish does have places to stay, such as the Pink Beach Club and Cottages. Dining choices are extremely limited, however, unless you stick to the hotels. Again, if you're seeking lots of nighttime diversion, you'll have to go to another parish. Because the **Spittal Pond Nature Reserve** is here, many nature lovers prefer Smith's to the more populated parishes. Basically, Smith's Parish is for the visitor who wants serenity and tranquility but not at the celestial prices charged at the "cottages" of Sandys.

Hamilton Parish

Not to be confused with the City of Hamilton (which is in Pembroke Parish), Hamilton Parish lies directly north of Harrington Sound, opening onto the Atlantic. It's bordered on the east by St. George and on the southwest by Smith's Parish. Named for the second marquis of Hamilton, the parish surrounds Harrington Sound, a

Finding Your Way

The Bermuda Department of Tourism publishes a free **Bermuda Handy Reference Map.** The tiny pocket map, distributed by the tourist office and available at most hotels, includes an overview and orientation map of Bermuda, highlighting its major attractions, golf courses, public beaches, and hotels. (It does not, however, pinpoint individual restaurants unless they are attached to hotels.) On the other side is a detailed street plan of the City of Hamilton, indicating all its major landmarks and service facilities, such as the ferry terminal and the post office. There's also a detailed map of the Royal Naval Dockyard, the West End, and the East End, plus tips on transportation—ferries, taxis, buses—and other helpful hints, such as a depiction of various traffic signs. For exact locations of Visitors Information Centre branches where you can pick up a copy of the *Bermuda Handy Reference Map,* see "Visitor Information" in the "Fast Facts" section of chapter 10.

The Parishes of Bermuda

saltwater lake stretching some 10km (6¼ miles). On its eastern periphery, the parish opens onto Castle Harbour.

The big attractions here are the **Bermuda Aquarium** and the **Crystal Caves.** Scuba diving and other watersports are also very popular in the area.

Around **Harrington Sound,** the sights differ greatly from those of nearby St. George (see below). You'll find such activities as fishing, swimming, sunfish sailing, and kayaking at Harrington Sound, but it doesn't offer the historical exploration that St. George does. Some experts believe that Harrington Sound was a prehistoric cave that fell in. Harrington Sound's known gateway to the ocean is an inlet at Flatts Village (see "Smith's Parish," above). However, evidence suggests that there are underwater passages as well—several deep-sea fish have been caught in the sound.

For the best panoramic view of the north shore, head for **Crawl Hill,** the highest place in Hamilton Parish, just before you come to Bailey's Bay. "Crawl" is a corruption of the word *kraal,* which is where turtles were kept before slaughter. **Shelly Bay,** named for one of the passengers of the British ship *Sea Venture* that foundered on Bermuda's reefs in 1609, is the longest beach along the north shore.

At Bailey's Bay, **Tom Moore's Jungle** consists of wild woods. The poet Tom Moore is said to have spent many hours writing verse here under a calabash tree (which is still standing). The jungle is now held in private trust, so you must obtain permission from a security guard to enter it. It's much easier to pay your respects to the Romantic poet by going to **Tom Moore's Tavern** (p. 138).

Although the parish has some major resorts, such as Grotto Bay Beach Hotel, most visitors come here for sightseeing only. We have to agree: Hamilton is a good place to go exploring for a day or half-day, but you're better off staying elsewhere. If you stay here, you'll spend a great deal of your vacation time commuting into the City of Hamilton or St. George. Bus no. 1 or 3 from the City of Hamilton gets you here in about an hour.

St. George's Parish

At Bermuda's extreme eastern end, this historic parish encompasses several islands. The parish borders Castle Harbour on its western and southern edges; St. George's

ISLAND-HOPPING ON your own

Most first-time visitors think of Bermuda as one island, but in fact it's a small archipelago. Many of the islands that make up the chain are uninhabited. If you're a bit of a skipper, you can explore them on your own. With a little guidance and the proper maps, you can discover small islands, out-of-the-way coral reefs, and hidden coves that seem straight out of the old Brooke Shields B-movie *The Blue Lagoon*.

For this boating adventure, rent a Boston Whaler with an outboard engine. The name of these small but sturdy boats reveals their origins: New Englanders once used similar boats in their pursuit of Moby Dick. It's important to exercise caution, remembering that the English found Bermuda in 1612 only after the *Sea Venture*, en route to the Jamestown Colony, was wrecked off the Bermuda coast.

In the East End, you can explore Castle Harbour, which is almost completely surrounded by islands, forming a protected lake. If you stop to do some fishing, snapper will be your likely catch.

(Visitors who rent condos or apartments often take their quarry back to their kitchenette to prepare it for dinner.) To avoid the often-powerful swells, drop anchor on the west side of Castle Harbour, near Castle Harbour Golf Club and Tucker's Town. Then head across Tucker's Town Bay to Castle Island and Castle Island Nature Reserve. In 1612, Governor Moore ordered the construction of a fort on Castle Island, the ruins of which you can see today.

In the West End, begin your exploration by going under Somerset Bridge into well-protected Ely's Harbour. To the north, you can visit Cathedral Rocks before making a half-circle to Somerset Village; from here, you can explore the uninhabited islands off Mangrove Bay.

You can rent a 4m (13-ft.) Boston Whaler—and pick up some local guidance—at **Blue Hole Water Sports,** Grotto Bay Beach Hotel, Hamilton Parish (www.blueholewater.bm; ℭ **441/293-2915**). Prices begin at $90 for 2 hours, $135 for 4 hours, and $195 for 8 hours. Rates do not include gas.

Harbour divides it into two major parts, **St. George's Island** and **St. David's Island.** A causeway links St. David's Island to the rest of Bermuda, and St. George's is also linked by a road. Many parish residents are longtime sailors and fishers. St. George's Parish also includes **Tucker's Town** (founded in 1616 by Gov. Daniel Tucker), on the opposite shore of Castle Harbour.

Settled in 1612, the **town of St. George** was once the capital of Bermuda; the City of Hamilton succeeded it in 1815. The town was settled 3 years after Sir George Somers and his shipwrecked party of English sailors came ashore in 1609. (After Admiral Somers died in Bermuda, in 1610, his heart was buried in the St. George area, while the rest of his body was taken home to England for burial.) Founded by Richard Moore, of the newly created Bermuda Company, and a band of 60 colonists, St. George was the second English settlement in the New World, after Jamestown, Virginia. Its coat of arms depicts St. George (England's patron saint) and a dragon.

Almost 4 centuries of history come alive here. Generations of sailors have set forth from its sheltered harbor. St. George even played a role in the American Revolution: Bermuda depended on the American colonies for food, and when war came, supplies grew dangerously low. Although Bermuda was a British colony, the loyalties of its people were divided because many Bermudians had relatives living on the American mainland. A delegation headed by Col. Henry Tucker went to Philadelphia to petition the Continental Congress to trade food and supplies for salt. George Washington had a different idea. He needed gunpowder, and a number of kegs of it were stored at St. George. Without the approval of the British Bermudian governor, the parties struck a deal. The gunpowder was trundled aboard American warships waiting in the harbor of Tobacco Bay under cover of darkness. In return, the grateful colonies supplied Bermuda with food.

Although St. George still evokes a feeling of the past, it's actively inhabited. When cruise ships are in port, it's likely to be overrun with visitors. Many people prefer to visit St. George at night, when they can walk around and enjoy it in relative peace and quiet. You won't be able to enter any of the sightseeing attractions, but they're of minor importance. After dark, a mood of enchantment settles over the place: It's like a storybook village.

Would you want to live here for a week? Probably not. Once you've seen the glories of the town of St. George—which you can do in a day—you're isolated at the easternmost end of Bermuda for the rest of your stay. Several chains, including Club Med, have tried and failed to make a go of it here. Accommodations are limited, although there are a number of restaurants (many of which, frankly, are mediocre). For history buffs, no place in Bermuda tops St. George's. But as a parish to base yourself in, you might do better in the more centrally located and activity-filled Pembroke or Southampton parishes. As for nightlife in St. George, you can always go to a pub on King's Square.

ICONIC BERMUDA IN 1 DAY

If you have only 1 day for sightseeing, we suggest you spend it in the historic former capital of **St. George,** a maze of narrow streets with quaint names: Featherbed Alley, Duke of York Street, Petticoat Lane, Old Maid's Lane, and Duke of Kent Street. You can spend a day exploring British-style pubs, seafood restaurants, shops (several major City of Hamilton stores have branches here), old forts, museums, and churches.

And what would a day in Bermuda be without time spent on the beach? **Elbow Beach** and **Warwick Long Bay** are among the most appealing spots. The no. 7 bus will take you there from St. George.

At the eastern end of Bermuda, St. George was the second English town established in the New World (after Jamestown, Virginia). For the history buff, it holds more interest than the City of Hamilton.

We begin the tour at:

1 King's Square

Also known as Market Square and King's Parade, the square is the very center of St. George. Only about 200 years old, it's not as historic as St. George itself. This was formerly a marshy part of the harbor—at least when the shipwrecked passengers and crew of the *Sea Venture* first saw it. At the water's edge stands a branch of the Visitors Information Centre, where you can pick up additional information on the area. On the square you'll notice a replica of a pillory and stocks. The devices were used to punish criminals—and, in many cases, the innocent. You could be severely punished here for such "crimes" as casting a spell over your neighbor's turkeys.

From the square, head south across the small bridge to:

2 Ordnance Island

The British army once stored gunpowder and cannons on this island, which extends into St. George's Harbour. Today, the island houses the *Deliverance,* a replica of the vessel that carried the shipwrecked *Sea Venture* passengers on to Virginia. Alongside the vessel is a ducking stool, a contraption used in 17th-century witch trials.

Retrace your steps across the bridge to King's Square. On the waterside stands the:

3 White Horse Tavern

This restaurant juts out into St. George's Harbour. Consider the tavern as a possible spot for lunch later (p. 142). For now, we focus on its history: It was once the home of John Davenport, who came to Bermuda in 1815 to open a dry goods store. Davenport was a bit of a miser; upon his death, some £75,000 in gold and silver was discovered stashed in his cellar.

Across the square stands the:

4 Town Hall

Located near the Visitors Information Centre, this is the meeting place of the corporation governing St. George. It has antique cedar furnishings and a collection of photographs of previous lord mayors. *Bermuda Journey,* a multimedia audiovisual presentation, is shown here several times a day.

From King's Square, head east along King Street, cutting north (left) on Bridge Street. You'll come to the:

5 Bridge House

Constructed in the 1690s, this was once the home of several governors of Bermuda. Located at 1 Bridge St., it's furnished with 18th- and 19th-century antiques and houses an art gallery and souvenir shop.

Return to King Street and continue east to the:

6 Old State House

The Old State House opens onto Princess Street, at the top of King Street. This is the oldest stone building in Bermuda, dating from 1620, and was once the home of the Bermuda Parliament. It's the site of the Peppercorn Ceremony, in which the Old State House pays the government a "rent" of one peppercorn annually. See chapter 5 for details on this grand ceremony.

Continue your stroll down Princess Street until you come to Duke of York Street and the entrance to:

7 Somers Garden

The heart of Sir George Somers, the admiral of the *Sea Venture,* is buried here. The gardens, opened in 1920 by the Prince of Wales, contain palms and other tropical plants.

Walk through Somers Gardens and up the steps to the North Gate onto Blockade Alley. Climb the hill to the structure known as "the folly of St. George," the:

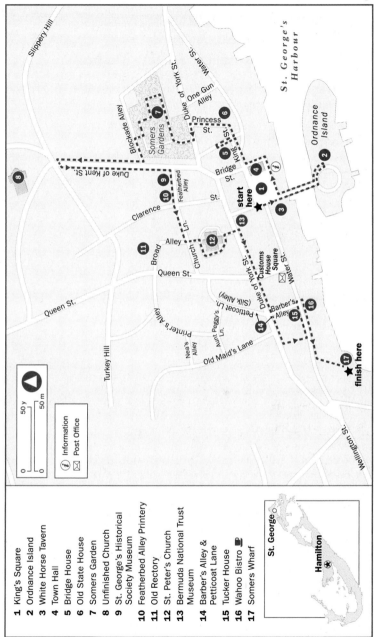

1 King's Square
2 Ordnance Island
3 White Horse Tavern
4 Town Hall
5 Bridge House
6 Old State House
7 Somers Garden
8 Unfinished Church
9 St. George's Historical Society Museum
10 Featherbed Alley Printery
11 Old Rectory
12 St. Peter's Church
13 Bermuda National Trust Museum
14 Barber's Alley & Petticoat Lane
15 Tucker House
16 Wahoo Bistro
17 Somers Wharf

8 Unfinished Church

This cathedral was intended to replace St. Peter's Church (see stop 12 on this tour). Work began on the church in 1874, but ended when the church was beset by financial difficulties and a schism in the Anglican congregation.

After viewing the cathedral, turn left onto Duke of Kent Street, which leads down to the:

9 St. George's Historical Society Museum

Located at Featherbed Alley and Duke of Kent Street, the museum building is an example of the rather plain 18th-century Bermudian architecture. It contains a collection of Bermudian historical artifacts and cedar furniture.

Around the corner on Featherbed Alley is the:

10 Featherbed Alley Printery

Here you can see a working replica of the type of printing press invented by Johannes Gutenberg in Germany in the 1450s.

Go up Featherbed Alley and straight onto Church Street. At the junction with Broad Lane, look to your right to see the:

11 Old Rectory

The Old Rectory is at the head of Broad Alley, behind St. Peter's Church. Now a private home administered by the National Trust, it was built in 1705 by a reformed pirate. You can go inside only on Wednesdays from noon to 5pm.

After seeing the Old Rectory, go through the church's backyard, opposite Broad Alley, to reach:

12 St. Peter's Church

The church's main entrance is on Duke of York Street. St. Peter's is the oldest Anglican place of worship in the Western Hemisphere. In the churchyard, you'll see many headstones, some 300 years old. The assassinated governor, Sir Richard Sharples, was buried here. The present church was built in 1713, with a tower added in 1814.

Across the street is the:

13 Bermuda National Trust Museum

When it was the Globe Hotel, this was the headquarters of Maj. Norman Walker, the Confederate representative in Bermuda. It was once a hotbed of blockade running (artillery smuggling during the Civil War).

Go west along Duke of York Street to:

14 Barber's Alley & Petticoat Lane

Barber's Alley honors Joseph Hayne Rainey. A former slave from South Carolina, Rainey fled to Bermuda with his French wife at the outbreak of the Civil War. He became a barber in St. George and eventually returned to South Carolina, where in 1870 he was elected to the U.S. House of Representatives—the first African American to serve in Congress.

Nearby is Petticoat Lane, also known as Silk Alley. The name dates from the 1834 emancipation, when two former slave women who'd always wanted silk petticoats like their former mistresses finally purchased some—and paraded up and down the lane to show off their new finery.

RATTLE & SHAKE: THE bermuda railway trail

One of the most unusual sightseeing adventures in Bermuda is following the Bermuda Railway Trail (or parts thereof), which stretches for 34km (21 miles) along the old railroad way, across three of the interconnected islands that make up Bermuda. Construction of this rail line may have been one of the most costly ever on a per-kilometer basis. Opened in 1931, the Bermuda Railway ceased operations in 1948. Once the island's main mode of transportation, the train eventually gave way to the automobile.

Before setting out on this trek, arm yourself with a copy of the *Bermuda Railway Trail Guide,* which is available at the Bermuda Department of Tourism in the City of Hamilton and the Visitors

Information Centres in Hamilton and St. George. You're now ready to hit the trail of the old train system that was affectionately called "Rattle and Shake." You can explore the trail on horseback, bicycle, or foot.

Although the line covered 34km (21 miles), from St. George in the east to Somerset in the west, a 5km (3-mile) stretch has been lost to roads in and around the capital City of Hamilton. For the most part, however, the trail winds along an automobile-free route.

In the West End, the trail begins near the Watford Bridge, but there are many convenient access points. In the East End, it's easiest to pick up the trail on North Shore Road.

Continue west until you reach:

15 Tucker House

Opening onto Water Street, this was the former home of a prominent Bermudian family, whose members included an island governor, a treasurer of the United States, and a captain in the Confederate Navy. The building houses an excellent collection of antiques, including silver, portraits, and cedar furniture. One room is devoted to memorabilia of Joseph Hayne Rainey.

16 Wahoo Bistro

Near Tucker House, this family friendly cafe at 36 Water St. (*©* **441/297-1307**), has an outdoor terrace overlooking the harbor. It features everything from an ice-cream parlor to a pizza oven, and even full meals, in its tutti-frutti-colored dining room.

End your tour across the street at:

17 Somers Wharf

This multimillion-dollar waterfront restoration project contains shops, restaurants, and taverns.

ICONIC BERMUDA IN 2 DAYS

Spend **Day 1** as indicated above. Devote **Day 2** to sightseeing and shopping in the City of Hamilton. If you're staying in Paget or Warwick, a ferry from either parish will take you right into the city. For many visitors, the City of Hamilton's shops are its most compelling attraction. Try to time your visit to avoid the arrival of cruise ships; on those days, the stores and restaurants in the city can get really crowded. You can obtain a schedule of cruise-ship arrivals and departures from the tourist office.

If you took our advice and went to the beach yesterday, try a different one today. After all, Bermuda isn't just about sightseeing and shopping—it's about those marvelous pink sands, too.

Begin your tour along the harborfront at the:

1 Visitors Information Centre/Ferry Terminal
Pick up some free maps and brochures of the island here.

From the bureau, you'll emerge onto Front Street, the City of Hamilton's main street and principal shopping area. Before 1946, there were no cars here. Today, the busy traffic includes small automobiles (driven only by Bermuda residents), buses, mopeds, and bicycles. You'll also see horse-drawn carriages, which are the most romantic (and, alas, the most expensive) way to see the City of Hamilton.

At the docks behind the Ferry Terminal, you can find the ferries to Warwick and Paget parishes; for details on their attractions, see chapter 5. You can also take a ferry across Great Sound to the West End and Somerset.

Walk south from the Ferry Terminal toward the water, taking a short side street between the Visitors Information Centre and the large Bank of Bermuda. You'll come to:

2 Albouy's Point
This is a small, grassy park with benches and trees, which opens onto a panoramic vista of the boat- and ship-filled harbor. Nearby is the Royal Bermuda Yacht Club, which has been an elite rendezvous for the Bermudian and American yachting set—including the rich and famous—since the 1930s. To use the word "royal" in its name, the club obtained special permission from Prince Albert, Queen Victoria's consort. The club sponsors the widely televised Newport-Bermuda Race.

After taking in the view, walk directly north, toward Front Street. Continue east along Front Street to the intersection with Queen Street. This is the site of the:

3 "Birdcage"
This is the most photographed sight in Bermuda. Here you can sometimes find a police officer directing traffic. If the "bobby" is a man, he's likely to be wearing regulation Bermuda shorts. The traffic box was named after its designer, Michael "Dickey" Bird. It stands at Heyl's Corner, which was named for an American southerner, J. B. Heyl, who operated a nearby apothecary in the 1800s.

Continue north along Queen Street until you reach:

4 Par-la-Ville Park
This was once a private garden attached to the town house of William B. Perot, Bermuda's first postmaster. Perot, who designed the gardens in the 19th century, collected rare and exotic plants from all over the globe, including an Indian rubber tree, which was seeded in 1847. Mark Twain wrote that he found the tree "disappointing" in that it didn't bear rubber overshoes and hot-water bottles.

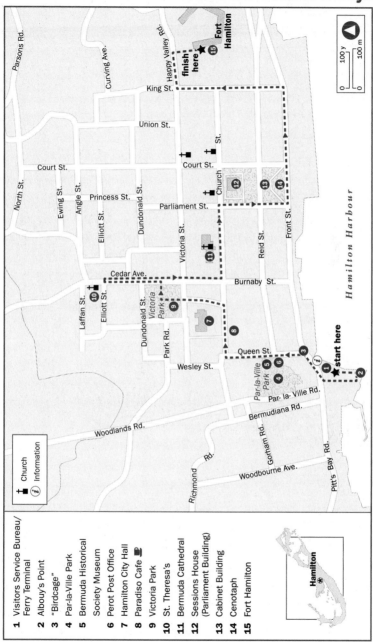

Church
(i) Information

1 Visitors Service Bureau/
   Ferry Terminal
2 Albouy's Point
3 "Birdcage"
4 Par-la-Ville Park
5 Bermuda Historical
   Society Museum
6 Perot Post Office
7 Hamilton City Hall
8 Paradiso Cafe 🍴
9 Victoria Park
10 St. Theresa's
11 Bermuda Cathedral
12 Sessions House
   (Parliament Building)
13 Cabinet Building
14 Cenotaph
15 Fort Hamilton

Hamilton

Also opening onto Queen Street at the entrance to the park is the:

5 Bermuda Historical Society Museum

This museum, at 13 Queen St., is also the Bermuda Library. It's filled with curiosities, including cedar furniture, collections of antique silver and china, hog money (the original monetary unit minted in Bermuda), Confederate money, a 1775 letter from George Washington, and other artifacts. The library has many rare books, including a 1624 edition of John Smith's *General Historie of Virginia, New England and the Somers Isles,* which you can ask to view. If you'd like to rest and catch up on your reading, you'll also find a selection of current local and British newspapers and periodicals here.

Across the street is the:

6 Perot Post Office

William Perot ran this post office from 1818 to 1862. It's said that he'd collect the mail from the clipper ships, then put it under his top hat in order to maintain his dignity. As he proceeded through town, he'd greet his friends and acquaintances by tipping his hat, thereby delivering their mail at the same time. He started printing stamps in 1848. A Perot stamp is extremely valuable today— only 11 are known to exist, and Queen Elizabeth II owns several. The last time a Perot stamp came on the market, in 1986, it fetched $135,000.

Continue to the top of Queen Street, then turn right onto Church Street to reach:

7 Hamilton City Hall

Located at 17 Church St., the city hall dates from 1960 and is crowned by a white tower. The bronze weather vane on top is a replica of the *Sea Venture.* Portraits of the queen and paintings of former island leaders adorn the main lobby. The Bermuda Society of Arts holds frequent exhibitions in this hall. The Benbow family's collection of rare stamps is also on display.

8 Paradiso Café 🍴

The Paradiso Cafe (p. 134), on the ground floor of the Washington Mall, a shopping and office complex on Reid Street, which is parallel to Church Street to the south (📞 441/295-3263), serves the most irresistible pastries in town. You can also order ice cream, tartlets, quiches, croissant sandwiches, espresso, and cappuccino.

In back of Hamilton City Hall, opening onto Victoria Street, lies:

9 Victoria Park

Office workers frequent this cool, refreshing oasis on their lunch breaks. It features a sunken garden, ornamental shrubbery, and a Victorian bandstand. The 1.6-hectare (4-acre) park was laid out in honor of Queen Victoria's Golden Jubilee in 1887. Outdoor concerts are held here in summer. Contact the tourist office for dates.

Cedar Avenue is the eastern boundary of Victoria Park. If you follow it north for 2 blocks, you'll reach:

10 St. Theresa's

This Roman Catholic cathedral is open daily from 8am to 7pm and for Sunday services. Its architecture was inspired by the Spanish Mission style. Dating from

1927, it's one of a half-dozen Roman Catholic churches in Bermuda; its treasure is a gold-and-silver chalice—a gift from Pope Paul VI when he visited the island in 1968.

After seeing the cathedral, retrace your steps south along Cedar Avenue until you reach Victoria Street. Cedar Avenue now becomes Burnaby Street; continue south to Church Street and turn left. A short walk along this street (on your left) will bring you to the:

11 Bermuda Cathedral

Also known as the Cathedral of the Most Holy Trinity, this is the seat of the Anglican Church of Bermuda, and it towers over the city skyline. Its style is neo-Gothic, characterized by stained-glass windows and soaring arches. The lectern and pulpit duplicate those of St. Giles in Edinburgh, Scotland.

Leave the cathedral and continue east along Church Street to the:

12 Sessions House (Parliament Building)

Located on Parliament Street, between Reid and Church streets, the Sessions House is open to the public Friday at 10am. The speaker wears a full wig and a flowing black robe. The Parliament of Bermuda is the third oldest in the world, after Iceland's and England's.

Continue south along Parliament Street to Front Street, and turn left toward the:

13 Cabinet Building

The official opening of Parliament takes place here in late October or early November. Wearing a plumed hat and full regalia, the governor makes his "Throne Speech." If you visit on a Wednesday, you can see the Bermuda Senate in action. The building is open Monday through Friday from 9am to 5pm.

In front of the Cabinet Building is the:

14 Cenotaph

The Cenotaph is a memorial to Bermuda's dead from both World Wars. In 1920, the Prince of Wales laid the cornerstone. (In 1936, as King Edward VIII, he abdicated to marry an American divorcée, Wallis Simpson, and during World War II, as the Duke of Windsor, he served as governor of The Bahamas.) The landmark is a replica of the Cenotaph in London.

Continue east along Front Street until you reach King Street, then turn left and head north until you come to Happy Valley Road. Go right on this road until you see the entrance (on your right) to:

15 Fort Hamilton

This imposing old fortress lies on the eastern outskirts of town. The Duke of Wellington ordered its construction beginning in 1868 to protect Hamilton Harbour. Filled with underground passageways and complete with a moat and 18-ton guns, the fort was outdated before it was even completed, and it never fired a shot. It does, however, offer panoramic views of the city and the harbor, and it's worth a trip just for the view. In summer, try to be here at noon, when the kilted Bermuda Isles Pipe Band performs a skirling ceremony on the green, accompanied by dancers and drummers.

ICONIC BERMUDA IN 3 DAYS

Spend **Days 1 and 2** as outlined above. On **Day 3,** take the ferry from the City of Hamilton across Great Sound to Somerset. You'll disembark at the western end of Somerset Island in Sandys Parish, which consists of Somerset Island (the largest and southernmost island), and Watford, Boaz, and Ireland islands. When Bermudians cross into Somerset on Somerset Bridge, they say they are "up the country."

Craggy coastlines, beaches, nature reserves, fishermen's coves, old fortifications, winding lanes, and sleepy villages characterize this area. All of Sandys' major attractions lie along the main road from Somerset Bridge to the Royal Naval Dockyard, which is at the end of Ireland Island.

Although we describe this as a walking tour, you may want to rent a bicycle or moped to help you cover the longer stretches.

To begin the tour, take the ferry from the City of Hamilton to:

1 Somerset Bridge

This bridge links Somerset Island with the rest of Bermuda. It was among the first three bridges constructed on Bermuda in the 1600s, and it's said to be the smallest drawbridge in the world; its opening is just wide enough to accommodate a sailboat mast. Near the bridge you can see the old Somerset Post Office and an 18th-century cottage known as Crossways.

Next, walk up Somerset Road about 70m (230 ft.) to the entrance to the:

2 Railway Trail

Open only to pedestrians and bikers, the trail follows the path of old "Rattle and Shake," the Bermuda Railway line that once ran the length of the island. This section of the trail—between Somerset Bridge and Sound View Road—is one of the most attractive segments (good to know if you don't want to walk the whole trail—although some hearty visitors do just that). Parts of the trail open onto the coast, affording panoramic vistas of the Great Sound. See "Rattle & Shake: The Bermuda Railway Trail," earlier, for more information.

3 Take a Break 🍴

The trail goes across the parkland of Fort Scaur (see below), with its large moat. If you're here around noontime, you might want to consider this as a picnic spot (get your picnic fixings in the City of Hamilton). If you can spend all day in Somerset (which we highly recommend), you might also want to take time out for a swim before returning to your walking or cycling.

Follow the signposts to:

4 Fort Scaur

In the 1870s, the British feared an attack from the United States, so they built this fort on the highest hill in Somerset to protect Her Majesty's Royal Naval Dockyard. It sits on 9 hectares (22 acres) of land and opens onto Somerset Road; the huge dry moat cuts right across Somerset Island. You can wander around this fort, which proved to be unnecessary because the American invasion never materialized. If you stand on the ramparts, you'll be rewarded with a marvelous view of Great Sound. Through a telescope, you can see such distant sights as St. David's Lighthouse and Fort St. Catherine in the East End of

1 Somerset Bridge
2 Railway Trail
3 Fort Scaur
4 Sound View Road
5 Cavello Bay
6 Royal Naval Dockyard (King's Wharf)
7 Bermuda Arts Centre
8 Lagoon Park
9 Somerset Village
10 Somerset Country Squire Pub & Restaurant
11 Somerset Long Bay Park

Bermuda. If you follow the eastern moat all the way down to the Great Sound shore, you'll find ideal places for swimming and fishing.

After exploring the surrounding Scaur Hill Fort Park, resume your walk along the railway track and continue north for more than 1.5km (1 mile), then turn right onto:

5 Sound View Road

Take a stroll along this sleepy residential street, which has some of the finest cottages in Bermuda.

Continue around a wide arc, passing Tranquillity Hill and Gwelly and Saltsea lanes. When you come to Scott's Hill Road, take a right and go about 80m (260 ft.) to East Shore Road. At the first junction, take Cavello Lane, which branches off to the right; it will take you to:

6 Cavello Bay

The sheltered cove is a stopping point for the City of Hamilton ferry.

Wait for the next ferry and take it (with your cycle or moped) to Watford Bridge or directly to the:

7 Royal Naval Dockyard

There's so much to see here, you could spend an entire afternoon exploring the area. The dockyard is a sprawling complex encompassing 2½ hectares (6¼ acres) of Ireland Island. The major attraction is the **Bermuda Maritime Museum** (p. 89), opened by Queen Elizabeth II in 1975. There's an exhibit of Bermuda's old boats, documenting the island's rich maritime history. You can cross a moat to explore the keep and the 9m-high (30-ft.) defensive ramparts.

Across the street from the Bermuda Maritime Museum is the Old Cooperage Building, site of the Neptune Cinema. Adjacent to the cinema is the Craft Market, which sells interesting items. Next door is the:

8 Bermuda Arts Centre

Princess Margaret dedicated the center in 1984. Showcasing the visual arts and crafts of the island, this not-for-profit organization has a volunteer staff.

From the dockyard, it's 19km (12 miles) to Somerset Village, but many people who have walked or cycled the distance consider it one of the highlights of their Bermuda trip. Most opt to walk for only an hour or two before they tire and decide to take a bus. You'll find some of the best beaches here, so if you get tired along the way, take time out for a refreshing dip in the ocean.

Leave through the dockyard's south entrance and walk down Pender Road about 1km (⅔ mile). Cross Cockburn's Cut Bridge and go straight along Cockrange Road, which will take you to:

9 Lagoon Park

Enter the park as you cross over the Cut Bridge onto Ireland Island South. Walking trails crisscross the park, which has a lagoon populated with ducks and other wild fowl. There are places for picnicking in the park, which is free and open to the public.

Spend **Days 1 through 3** as outlined above. Make **Day 4** a beach day. Head for **Horseshoe Bay Beach,** in Southampton Parish, in the morning. Spend most of your time there, exploring hidden coves in all directions. Have lunch right on the beach at a concession stand. In the afternoon, visit **Gibbs Hill Lighthouse.** After a rest at your hotel, sample some Bermudian nightlife.

On **Day 5,** conclude your stay with an excursion to **Flatts Village,** which lies in the eastern sector of Smith's Parish.

Explore the **Bermuda Aquarium, Natural History Museum & Zoo,** and consider an undersea walk (see the box "A Look Under Bermuda's Waters," on p. 70).

Spend the rest of the day at the fabled **Elbow Beach.** After relaxing over afternoon tea at one of the hotels, arrange to see an evening show—if it's scheduled, make it gombey dancing, which has its roots in Africa and which remains a strong cultural symbol in Bermuda (p. 92).

To continue, cross Grey's Bridge to Boaz Island, and walk or cycle along Malabar Road. On your right, you'll see the calm waters of Mangrove Bay. You'll eventually arrive at:

10 Somerset Village

Somerset is one of the most charming villages on Bermuda. Only one road goes through the village. Most of the stores are branches of larger stores in the City of Hamilton.

11 Somerset Country Squire Pub & Restaurant ☕

Somerset Country Squire Pub & Restaurant (✆ 441/234-0105; p. 115) is an English-style pub that serves sandwiches, burgers, and such pub grub as steak-and-kidney pie and bangers and mash (sausages and mashed potatoes). The kitchen is also noted for its desserts.

Follow Cambridge Road west to:

12 Somerset Long Bay Park

Families like this park because of its good beach and shallow waters, which open onto Long Bay. You can picnic here. The Bermuda Audubon Society operates the nature reserve, and the pond attracts migrating birds, including the Louisiana heron, the snowy egret, and the purple gallinule, in both spring and autumn.

FUN ON & OFF THE BEACH

Although people visit Bermuda mainly to relax on its spectacular pink sand beaches, the island also offers a wealth of activities, both onshore and off. In fact, Bermuda's sports facilities are better than those on most Caribbean and Bahamian islands.

The most popular outdoor pursuits in Bermuda are tennis and golf, but sailing ranks high, too. If you hesitate to pick up a racket or golf club because you've neglected your game, fear not: Your Bermudian partner, on the court or on the links, would deem it quite improper to remark that your play was anything but superb. If a word of friendly criticism is ever offered, be assured that it will be as gentle as the island's ocean breezes.

Bermuda's waters are the clearest in the western Atlantic. Reefs, shipwrecks (many in such shallow water that they're even accessible to snorkelers), a variety of marine life and coral formations, and underwater grottoes make Bermuda ideal for scuba diving and snorkeling. For locations of many of these activities, see the maps throughout this chapter.

BEACHES

Bermuda is one of the world's leading beach resorts. It boasts miles of pink shoreline, broken only now and then by cliffs that form sheltered coves. Many stretches have shallow, sandy bottoms for some distance out, making them safe for children and nonswimmers. Some beaches (usually the larger ones) have lifeguards; others do not. The Parks Division of the Department for Agriculture and Fisheries supervises public facilities. Hotels and private clubs often have their own beaches and facilities. Even if you're not registered at a hotel or resort, you can often use their beach and facilities if you become a customer by having lunch there.

You'll find dozens of spots for sunbathing, swimming, and beachcombing; here's a list of the island's most famous sands, arranged clockwise beginning with the south-shore beaches closest to the City of Hamilton.

Elbow Beach ★★★

One of the most consistently popular beaches in Bermuda, Paget Parish's Elbow Beach incorporates almost 1.5km (1 mile) of (occasionally interrupted) pale pink sand. Private homes and resort hotels dot the edges. Because protective coral reefs surround it, Elbow Beach is one of the safest beaches on the island—and it's the family favorite.

Bermuda's government provides lifeguards as a public service. The **Elbow Beach Hotel** (www.mandarinoriental.com/bermuda; ✆ **441/236-3535**) offers a variety of facilities and amenities free to hotel guests, but they're off-limits to others. Amenities and facilities include sun chairs, cabanas, changing rooms, showers, restrooms, and beach towels distributed three times a day by beach attendants who are trained in water safety and lifeguard techniques. The on-site Dive Shop also rents paddle boats and sea kayaks for $30 per hour for a single, $40 per hour for a double, and snorkeling equipment ($15 per hour) to anyone on the beach. Take bus no. 2 or 7 from the City of Hamilton. For more information, see www.divebermuda.com.

Astwood Cove ★

This Warwick Parish public beach has no problem with overcrowding during most of the year; it's in a remote location, at the bottom of a steep, winding road that intersects with South Road. Many single travelers and couples head here to escape the families that tend to overrun beaches, such as Elbow Beach, in the high season. We prefer this beach for many reasons, one of them being that its cliffs are home to nesting Bermuda longtails, also known as white-tailed tropic birds. Astwood Beach has public restrooms but not many other facilities. An added advantage is nearby Astwood Park, a favorite picnic and hiking area. If you prefer your beaches small and secluded, head here. Take bus no. 2 or 7 from Southampton.

Warwick Long Bay ★★

Like Astwood Cove, this is one of the best places for people who want to escape the family crowds and find solitude. Unlike the sheltered coves of nearby Chaplin and Horseshoe bays (see below), this popular beach features the longest uninterrupted stretch of pink sand on the island. This expanse is conducive to social interaction, but also offers plenty of space to stretch out solo—it all depends on what you prefer. Against a backdrop of scrubland and low grasses, the beach lies on the southern side of South Shore Park, in Warwick Parish. Despite the frequent winds, the waves are surprisingly small thanks to an offshore reef. Jutting above the water less than 60m (200 ft.) from the shore is a jagged coral island that, because of its contoured shape, appears to be floating above the water's foam. There are restrooms at the beach's western end, plus lots of parking, but no other facilities. There are no lifeguards because the undertow is not very strong. Take bus no. 7.

Jobson's Cove ★

This Warwick Parish beach has the feel of a secret hideaway, thanks to pink sands, gentle waves, and calm waters. It's only 9m (30 ft.) wide where the horseshoe-shaped bay opens to the ocean. Adjacent to the much larger and more popular Warwick Long Bay, it's excellent for snorkeling—the water is about 2m (6½ ft.) deep for a long way out into the bay. There are no buildings along the water, adding to the feeling of seclusion and peace. There are no facilities here, but it's close enough to Warwick Long Bay to walk over and use their restrooms if necessary. Take bus no. 7.

Stonehole Bay

Near Jobson's Cove in Warwick Parish, Stonehole Bay is more open and less sheltered than Jobson's, with a sandy shoreline that's studded with big rocks. It's almost never crowded, and wading is safe even though strong waves sometimes make the

Bermuda's Best Public Beaches & Snorkel Sites

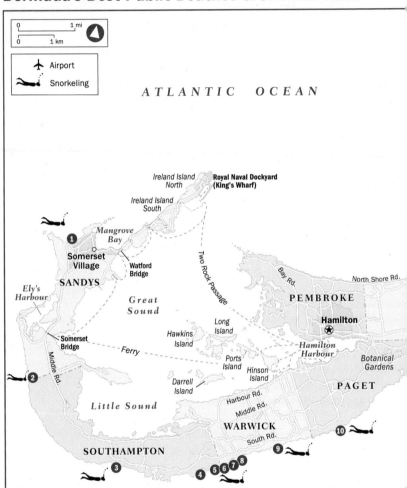

waters cloudy (so they're less than ideal for snorkeling). There are no facilities at Stonehole Bay. Take bus no. 7.

Chaplin Bay

Straddling the boundary between Warwick and Southampton parishes, this small but secluded beach disappears almost completely during storms and exceptionally high tides. Geologists come here to admire the open-air coral barrier that partially separates one half of the beach from the other. Chaplin Bay, like its more famous neighbor, Horseshoe Bay (see below), lies at the southern extremity of South Shore Park. From Chaplin, you can walk over to use the facilities and equipment at Horseshoe,

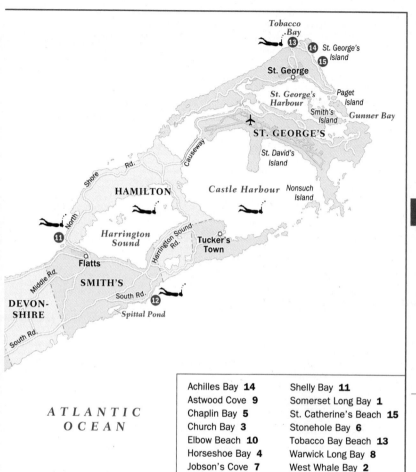

ATLANTIC
OCEAN

Achilles Bay **14**	Shelly Bay **11**
Astwood Cove **9**	Somerset Long Bay **1**
Chaplin Bay **5**	St. Catherine's Beach **15**
Church Bay **3**	Stonehole Bay **6**
Elbow Beach **10**	Tobacco Bay Beach **13**
Horseshoe Bay **4**	Warwick Long Bay **8**
Jobson's Cove **7**	West Whale Bay **2**
John Smith's Bay **12**	

but you'll enjoy more solitude here than at the more active Horseshoe Bay. Take bus no. 7.

Horseshoe Bay Beach ★★

With its long, curved strip of pink sand, Horseshoe Bay, on South Road in Southampton Parish, is one of Bermuda's most famous beaches. That means it's likely to be crowded, especially if cruise ships are in port. Although families flock here, Horseshoe Bay isn't the safest beach on Bermuda. Don't be fooled by the seemingly smooth surface; there can be dangerous undercurrents. If you're using the beach after a storm, be especially careful that you don't encounter a Portuguese man-of-war—they often wash up here in greater numbers than elsewhere on Bermuda.

A lifeguard is on duty here from May to September. ***Insider's tip:*** When you tire of the crowds at Horseshoe Bay, take one of the little trails that wind through the park nearby; they'll lead you to secluded cove beaches that afford more privacy. Our favorites are Port Royal Cove to the west, and Peel Rock Cove and Wafer Rocks Beach to the east. You might also sneak over to Chaplin Bay to the east (see above). Take bus no. 7.

Church Bay

This beach off West Side Road lies along Bermuda's southwestern edge, at the point in Southampton Parish where the island hooks off to the northeast. The waves pound much of the shore mercilessly, but rows of offshore reefs shelter Church Bay. Marine life abounds in the relatively calm waters, much to the delight of snorkelers. If you're just planning to lounge in the sun, this is a great place: The beach offers unusually deep pink sands. There are toilets at the top of the hill near the parking area, and a concession stand (May 1–Oct 31 Mon–Sat 10am–5pm) sells soda and chips, and rents out masks and fins for snorkeling. Take bus no. 7 or 8.

Somerset Long Bay

When offshore storms stir up the waters northwest of Bermuda, the water here is unsafe for swimming. Because its bottom isn't always sandy or of a consistent depth, many people find Somerset Long Bay better suited to beachcombing or long walks than to swimming. Nevertheless, many single travelers favor this beach when they're looking for seclusion. The undeveloped parkland of Sandys Parish shelters it from the rest of the island, and the beach's crescent shape and length—about .5km (⅓ mile)—make it unusual by Bermudian standards. It has restrooms and changing facilities. We think this is one of the best places on Bermuda to watch the sunset. A plus is the beach's proximity to the **Bermuda Audubon Society Nature Reserve** (www.audubon.bm), where you can go for long walks and enjoy moments of solitude—except on weekends, when family picnics abound. Take bus no. 7 or 8.

Shelly Bay

This beach of abundant pink sand is suitable for both families and those seeking solitude. Because it's not well-known, it's unlikely to be crowded, and its calm, shallow basin makes it safe for swimming. Off North Shore Road in Hamilton Parish, Shelly Bay lies in a cove whose encircling peninsula partially shelters it from mid-Atlantic waves. There are trees to sit under when the beach gets too hot, and the beach house rents snorkeling equipment, lounge chairs, beach towels, and other items; there are also public restrooms. Buses from the City of Hamilton heading east along the north shore, primarily no. 11, stop here.

Tobacco Bay, Achilles Bay & St. Catherine's Beach

St. George's Island's beaches include Achilles Bay, Tobacco Bay, and St. Catherine's Beach (formerly known as the Club Med beach), all of which are sandy, with water so clear you can see to the bottom of the ocean floor.

Lovely Tobacco Bay is an East End family favorite. It's the most popular beach on St. George's Island, especially among those who come for the day to visit the historic town of St. George. With its broad sands, Tobacco Bay resembles a south-shore beach. Its pale pink sand lies within a sheltering coral-sided cove just a short walk west of Fort St. Catherine and St. Catherine's Beach. The major disadvantage here is that the beach is likely to be overrun with cruise-ship passengers; when they're in port, you may want to seek more secluded beaches such as St. Catherine's. You can sunbathe here and even go for a swim, but don't venture out too far; the currents are dangerously strong, and a lot of seaweed washes up on the shore.

On site are toilets, changing rooms, showers, and a snack bar, open erratically during high season. At beachfront kiosks, you can rent flotation devices and snorkeling gear for $10 per hour or $25 per day from May to September. Stands also sell sodas and sandwiches (tuna, grilled cheese, hamburgers, hot dogs, and the like). Take bus no. 10 or 11.

John Smith's Bay

This is the only public beach in Smith's Parish. It's more popular with residents of Bermuda's eastern end than with visitors, who often don't know about it. It's ideal for those seeking solitude. Long, flat, wide, and rich with pale pink sand, this beach has a lifeguard daily from 10am to 6pm May 24 to mid-September. Some shallow areas are perfect for snorkeling; however, the bay occasionally experiences rip currents. There are toilet and changing facilities. Take bus no. 1.

SNORKELING

Bermuda is known for the gin-clear purity of its waters and for its vast array of coral reefs. If you're ready to explore, all you need are a snorkel, mask, and fins—if you can swim, you can snorkel. A handful of companies can help you (we recommend our favorite, below); otherwise, you can hit the water on your own.

The best places to go snorkeling are public beaches (see above). Many hotels that are right on the beach will lend or rent you fins, masks, and snorkels, and will advise you of the best sites in your area. You almost never have to travel far.

Die-hard snorkelers—some of whom visit Bermuda every year—prefer **Church Bay** above all other snorkeling spots on Bermuda. It lies on the south shore, west of the Fairmont Southampton Golf Club and Gibbs Hill Lighthouse. The little cove, which seems to be waiting for a movie camera, is carved out of coral cliffs. It's well protected and filled with snug little nooks. Another advantage is that the reefs are fairly close to land. But remember, the seas can be rough (as is true anywhere in Bermuda); use caution.

A LOOK UNDER BERMUDA'S waters

The Ocean Discovery Centre at the Bermuda Underwater Exploration Institute, East Broadway (www.buei.org; ☎ 441/292-7219), hopes to give visitors an underwater adventure. The highlight of a visit is a simulated dive 3,600m (12,000 ft.) to the bottom of the Atlantic. Author Peter Benchley's videotaped commentary adds to the fun of exploring Bermuda's reefs. You'll learn about newly discovered ocean animals that live in the murky depths. Displays include large murals of sea creatures, artifacts rescued from long-sunken vessels off the coast, and even a scale model of a ship that wrecked centuries ago. On-site facilities include gift shops, a theater showing films, and La Coquille, a French bistro that specializes, of course, in seafood. Admission is $13 for adults, $6 for children 6 to 17, free for children 5 and under; hours are Monday through Friday from 9am to 5pm, Saturday and Sunday from 10am to 5pm. Bus: 1, 3, 7, or 8.

At the eastern end of the south shore, **John Smith's Bay,** east of Spittal Pond Nature Reserve and Watch Hill Park, is another top spot, especially if your hotel is nearby. Even more convenient, especially for snorkelers staying at St. George or at a hotel near the airport, is **Tobacco Bay,** north of St. George's Golf Club. Another small but reliable snorkeling spot is **West Whale Bay;** it lies along the south shore at the west end of Southampton, west of the Port Royal Golf Course.

Although snorkeling is a year-round pursuit, it's best from May to October. Snorkelers usually wear wet suits in winter, when the water temperature dips into the 60sF (15–20°C). The waters of the Atlantic, which can be tempestuous at any time of the year, can be especially rough in winter.

Some of the best snorkeling sites are accessible only by boat. If you want to head out on your own, and you have a knowledge of Bermuda's waters, we suggest renting a small boat (see "Sailing," under "More Fun in the Water," later in this chapter), some of which have glass bottoms. If you rent a boat, the rental company will advise you on where to go and not to go. Countless wrecked boats lie on the many reefs that surround Bermuda. If you're not familiar with Bermuda's waters, you should stay in the sounds, harbors, and bays, especially in Castle Harbour and Harrington Sound. If you want to visit the reefs, it's better and easier to contact one of the diving outfitters recommended below than to captain your own boat. The use of snorkeling equipment is included in the prices listed.

Jessie James Cruises This outfitter operates some of the best snorkeling trips on the islands, and novices are welcome (they're accompanied by a crew member in shallow water). Some of the shipwrecks you'll visit include the *Constellation* and the *Montana.* The most stunning snorkel trip is a 3-hour experience taking you to a spectacular coral reef and sea garden. Operating from April to October, trips cost $65 for adults and children 11 or older, and $45 for ages 8 to 10.

Glen Court, Warwick. www.jessiejames.bm. ☎ 441/335-1072. Bus: 7.

SCUBA DIVING

Bermuda is a world-class dive site, known for its evocative and often eerie shipwrecks, teeming with marine life. All scuba diving outfitters go to all sites. If you're diving, talk to the dive master about what you'd like to see, including any or all of the various wrecks that are accessible off the coast and not viewed as dangerous. For the locations of many of these sites, see the map on p. 66.

The Diving Sites

CONSTELLATION When Peter Benchley was writing *The Deep* (later made into a film), he came here to study the wreck of the *Constellation* for inspiration. Lying in 9m (30 ft.) of water, this wreck is 13km (8 miles) northwest of the Royal Naval Dockyard. Built in 1918, the *Constellation* was a four-masted, wooden-hulled schooner. During World War II, it was the last wooden cargo vessel to leave New York harbor. It wrecked off the coast of Bermuda on July 31, 1943, and all the crew survived. Today, the hull, broken apart, can be seen on a coral and sand bottom. You can see the 36,300kg (80,000 lb.) of cement it was carrying, and morphine ampoules are still found at this site. Large populations of parrotfish, trumpet fish, barracuda, grouper, speckled eels, and octopus inhabit the wreck today.

CRISTOBAL COLON Bermuda's largest shipwreck is the *Cristóbal Colón,* a Spanish luxury liner that went down on October 25, 1936, between North Rock and North Breaker. A transatlantic liner, it weighed in excess of 10,000 tons. The ship was traveling to Mexico to load arms for the Spanish Civil War when it crashed into a coral reef at a speed of 15 knots. During World War II, the U.S. Air Force used the ship as target practice before it eventually settled beneath the waves. Its wreckage is scattered over a wide area on both sides of the reef. It is recommended that you take two dives to see this wreck. Most of the wreck is in 9 to 17m (30–56 ft.) of water, but the depth range actually varies from 4.5m (15 ft.) at the ship's bow to 24m (79 ft.) at its stern. Some artillery shells from World War II remain unexploded, so don't have a blast, please.

HERMES This 1984 American freighter rests in some 24m (79 ft.) of water about 1.5km (1 mile) off Warwick Long Bay on the south shore. The 825-ton, 50m (164-ft.) freighter is popular with divers because its U.S. Coast Guard buoy tender is almost intact. The crew abandoned this vessel (they hadn't been paid in 6 months), and the Bermuda government claimed it for $1, letting the dive association deliberately sink it to make a colorful wreck. The visibility at the wreck is generally the finest in Bermuda, and you can see its galley, cargo hold, propeller, and engines.

L'HERMINIE This 1838 French frigate lies in 6 to 9m (20–30 ft.) of water off the west side of Bermuda, with 25 of its cannons still visible. A large wooden keel remains, but the wreck has rotted badly. However, the marine life here is among the most spectacular of any shipwreck off Bermuda's coast: brittle starfish, spiny lobster, crabs, grouper, banded coral shrimp, queen angels, and tons of sponges.

MARIE CELESTE This is one of the most historic wrecks in the Atlantic, a 207-ton paddle-wheel steamer from the Confederacy. The steamer was a blockade runner during the Civil War. In exchange for guns, this vessel would return to Bermuda with cotton and cash. Evading capture throughout most of the war, it was wrecked off the coast of Bermuda on September 25, 1864. The ship sank in 17m (56 ft.) of water, where its ruins lie like a skeleton today. This is not a great dive site for observing marine life, but the wreck is evocative and offers many caves and tunnels to explore.

NORTH CAROLINA This iron-hulled English bark lies in 7.5 to 12m (25–39 ft.) of water off Bermuda's western coast. While en route to England, it went down on New Year's Day in 1879 when it struck the reefs. The bow and stern remain fairly intact. There is often poor visibility here, making the wreck appear almost like a ghost ship. Hogfish, often reaching huge sizes, inhabit the site, along with schools of porgies and snapper.

RITA ZOVETTA   This Italian cargo steamer was built in 1919 in Glasgow and went aground off St. David's Island in 1924. The ship lies in 6 to 21m (21–69 ft.) of water just off St. David's Head. The wreck measures 120m long (395 ft.), and its stern is relatively intact. Divers go through the shaft housings to see the large boilers. Stunning schools of rainbow-hued fish inhabit the site.

SOUTH WEST BREAKER   Some 2.5km (1½ miles) off Church Bay, this was the location chosen for the famous Jacqueline Bisset scene in Peter Benchley's movie *The Deep*. The breaker was supposed to be a hideout for a man-eating squid. In reality, the breaker was created from fossilized prehistoric worms (believe it or not). It has an average depth of 8.5m (28 ft.), and on most days a visibility of 30m (98 ft.). New divers prefer this site because it's not considered dangerous and it has a large variety of hard and soft coral. It's also a good place for snorkelers. A large tunnel split through the center of the breaker provides a protective cover for green moray eels and spiny lobsters. Schools of barracuda are also encountered here.

TARPON HOLE   This series of large breakers lies directly off the western extremity of Elbow Beach. The site is named Tarpon Hole because of the large schools of tarpon that often cluster here, some in excess of 2m (6½ ft.) long. It is a sea world of lush fans and soft corals, made all the more intriguing with its tunnels, caves, and overhangs.

TAUTON   This Norwegian coastal steamer ran afoul on Bermuda's treacherous reefs on November 24, 1920. The 68m (228-ft.) steel-hulled vessel sank in 3 to 12m (10–39 ft.) of water off the northern end of Bermuda. Its boilers and steam engines are still visible. This is a favorite dive for beginners, as the wreck lies in shallow water. Because of its breathtaking varieties of fish, it's a favorite site for photographers.

Diving Schools & Outfitters

Diving in Bermuda is great for novices, who can learn the fundamentals and go diving in 6 to 7.5m (20–25 ft.) of water on the same day as their first lesson. In general, Bermuda's reefs are still healthy, despite talk about dwindling fish and dying coral formations. On occasion, in addition to the rainbow-hued schools of fish, you may even find yourself swimming with a barracuda.

Although scuba fanatics dive all year, the best diving months are May through October. The sea is the most tranquil at that time, and the water temperature is moderate—it averages 62°F (17°C) in the spring and fall, 83°F (28°C) in the summer.

Weather permitting, scuba schools function daily. Fully licensed scuba instructors oversee all dives. Most dives are conducted from a 12m (39-ft.) boat, and outfitters cover a wide range of dive sites. Night dives and certifications are also available.

All dive shops display a map of wreck sites that you can visit; there are nearly 40 in all, the oldest of which dates from the 17th century. Although locals believe there may be some 300 wrecks, the mapped sites are the best known and in the best condition. Dive depths at these sites run 7.5 to 26m (25–85 ft.). Inexperienced divers may want to stick to the wreck sites off the western coast, which tend to be in shallower waters—about 9.5m (31 ft.) or less. These shallow wreck sites are popular with snorkelers as well.

A yacht OF YOUR VERY OWN . . . SORT OF

M.Y. Bermuda IV, No. 3 Stowe Hill in Paget Parish (www.bermudaiv.com; *©* **441/232-7000**), is Bermuda's only live-aboard scuba-diving charter yacht. Both divers and underwater photographers book charters aboard this luxury vessel in one of three double en-suite staterooms. A highly trained chef prepares gourmet meals, and the charter includes up to five dives per day, as overseen by a professional diving instructor. The cost is $3,200 per person (six- to eight-person minimum), including accommodations for 5 nights and all meals and diving costs. Even if you don't live aboard, it's possible to book the yacht for $600 per hour, or else you can call and try to arrange a dinner aboard the yacht, costing $150 per person for a gourmet five-course meal, including cocktails, wine, and beer.

Many hotels have their own watersports equipment. If yours doesn't, the outfitters below rent equipment.

Note: Spearfishing is not allowed within 1.5km (1 mile) of any shore, and spear guns are not permitted in Bermuda.

Bermuda Scuba This is one of the island's leading dive operators. It offers a popular "Discover Scuba" resort course that costs $165 for 3 hours and begins daily at 1:15pm. Course participants get to complete a shallow-water scuba dive by the end of the day. All dives are from a 12m (39-ft.) boat. A two-tank dive, including a view of a shipwreck and the exploration of a reef in 7.5 to 9m (25–30 ft.) of water, costs $135 (equipment not included). It costs $165 with equipment. This is a PADI, five-star center.

At the Fairmont Southampton, 101 South Rd., Southampton Parish. www.bermudascuba.com. *©* **441/238-2332.** Daily 8:30am–4:30pm. Bus: 8.

Blue Water Divers & Watersports Ltd. Bermuda's oldest and largest full-service scuba-diving operation offers introductory lessons for between $135 and $185, and daily one- and two-tank dive trips for $85 and $125, respectively. Snorkeling trips cost $50. Full certification courses are available through PADI, NAUI, and SSI. Equipment costs extra, and reservations are required. The outfitter offers underwater scooters called DPVs or "diver propulsion vehicles." This exciting vehicle takes adventurers through underwater caves and canyons. Who knows? You may even discover a shipwreck from long ago.

Robinson's Marina, Sandy's Parish. www.divebermuda.com. *©* **441/234-1034.** Daily 9am–5pm. Bus: 7 or 8.

Triangle Diving This outfitter appeals to the serious scuba diver and to the helmet diver alike. It sets out every day to explore the shipwrecks off the East End along with stunning coral reefs. PADI certification courses are also a feature. The reefs it explores daily at North Rock are among the most beautiful on the island. Two-tank dives cost $120 for the dives, plus $40 for the equipment.

Grotto Beach Hotel, 11 Blue Hill, Bailey's Bay, Hamilton Parish. www.trianglediving.com. *©* **441/293-7319.** Bus: 1, 3, 10, or 11.

4

FUN ON & OFF THE BEACH

Scuba Diving

MORE FUN IN THE WATER

Fishing

Bermuda is one of the world's finest destinations for anglers, especially in light-tackle fishing. Blue marlin catches have increased dramatically in recent years, and Bermuda can add billfishing (for marlin, swordfish, and sailfish) to its already enviable reputation. In January 2012 a 960-pound bluefin tuna was caught in local waters, a catch that reinforced belief in the waters around Bermuda as a fertile site for sports fishermen. Fishing is a year-round sport, but it's best from May to November. No license is required.

You can obtain more information about game fishing from the **International Game Fish Association's** website, **www.igfa.org**.

DEEP-SEA FISHING

Wahoo, amberjack, blue marlin, white marlin, dolphin, tuna, and many other varieties of fish call Bermuda's warm waters home. A number of island outfitters offer the equipment to help you fish for them. One of the best known and respected of the lot includes:

Fish Bermuda   This outfitter offers one of the largest charter boats in Bermuda, with a fully air-conditioned cabin. Owner Allen DeSilva operates a 56-foot custom fishing vessel called *Mako*. It is outfitted with tackle that's updated every year. A standard three-quarter-day trip costs $1,600, rising to $2,000 for a full-day trip. Fishing is best, and waters at their most "cooperative," between May and October.

Mill's Creek, 11 Abri Lane, Pembroke. http://fishbermuda.com. © **441/295-0835.** Bus: 7 or 8.

REEF FISHING

Three major reef banks lie off Bermuda, and they're likely to yield such catches as greater amberjack, almaco jack, great barracuda, little tunny, Bermuda chub, gray snapper, yellowtail snapper, and assorted bottom fish. The closest reef, the Inner System, begins about 1km (⅔ mile) offshore and stretches for nearly 8km (5 miles). The Challenger Bank is about 23km (14 miles) offshore, and the Argus Bank is about 50km (31 miles) distant. The farther out you go, the more likely you are to turn up larger fish.

Several companies offer half- or full-day charters. Arrangements can be made through the activities desks of the big resort hotels as well as various charter companies.

Anglers Aweigh: How to Make Your Big Catch a Winning One

The **Bermuda Game Fishing Tournament** is open to any angler who takes the time and trouble to fill out the tournament application when he or she catches a really big fish. No special license is required, but your catch must be weighed and three witnesses must sign an affidavit attesting to its weight. Special prizes are awarded each year for top catches of 17 species of game fish. For more information on registering the ones that didn't get away, contact the **Bermuda Department of Tourism,** Global House, 43 Church St., Hamilton HM 12, Bermuda (www.bermudatourism.com; © **441/292-0023**). Open daily 9am to 5pm.

More Fun in the Water | FUN ON & OFF THE BEACH

SHORE FISHING

Shore fishing turns up such catches as bonefish, palometa (pompano), gray snapper, and great barracuda. Locals and most visitors prefer shore fishing at Spring Benny's Bay or West Whale Bay; Great Sound and St. George's Harbour are other promising grounds. The activities director at your hotel can help make fishing arrangements for you.

Sailing

Bermuda is one of the world's sailing capitals. Sail-yourself boats are available to rent for 2, 4 (half-day), and 8 (full-day) hours. A number of places charter yachts with licensed skippers.

Blue Hole Water Sports   This outfitter rents sail-yourself Windsurfers or Sunfish for $30 to $35 per hour. A wide range of other equipment is on hand, including single ($20) and double ($30) kayaks.

Grotto Bay Beach Hotel, 11 Blue Hole Hill, Hamilton Parish. www.blueholewater.bm. © **441/293-2915.** Apr–Oct daily 8:30am–5:30pm. Bus: 1, 3, 10, or 11.

Pompano Beach Club Watersports Centre   This is one of the island's best outfitters, mainly because of its variety of modern boats. Windsurfers, which hold one novice or experienced passenger, rent for $30 per hour. One or two people can rent a Sunfish sailboat for $35 per hour. Single-person kayaks go for $20 for 1 hour; double kayaks, $30 for 1 hour. Two-person Sun Cats, which travel 9.5kmph (6 mph) and look like motorized lawn chairs, go for $50 per hour.

36 Pompano Beach Rd., Southampton Parish. www.pompanobeachclub.com. © **441/234-0222.** May–Oct daily 10am–6pm. Bus: 7 or 8.

Sail Bermuda   Charter sailing and snorkeling are the features of this outfitter, in business since 1997. Clients are allowed great leeway in designing their own tours (within reason, of course). Several watersports options are also available, including parasailing, jet skiing, and scuba diving. Charters for up to six persons range from $500 for a 3-hour jaunt to $900 for a 6-hour boat trip; for more than six, it's $25 per person plus $150 per additional cruising hour.

Caleb Zuill, 71 Harbour Rd., Paget Parish. www.sailbermuda.com. © **441/737-2993.**

Somerset Bridge Watersports   Somerset Bridge is the best outlet for renting Boston Whalers for island-hopping on your own. A 4m (13-ft.) Whaler (25 or 30 hp) carries four and costs $75 for 2 hours, $120 for 4 hours, and $200 for 8 hours, plus a gas fee of $25. Somerset provides lots of extras, such as canopies, special maps, a ladder, a viewing box, and a fish and coral ID card. "Jet Ski Adventures" cost $105 for 1 hour and 10 minutes for one person, $125 for a double. The jet ski reaches speeds of up to 81kmph (50 mph).

Robinson's Marina, Somerset Bridge, Ely's Harbour, Sandys Parish. www.watersportssomerset bridge.com. © **441/234-3145.** Daily 8am–sunset. Bus: 7 or 8.

Water-Skiing

You can water-ski in the protected waters of Hamilton Harbour, Great Sound, Castle Harbour, Mangrove Bay, Spanish Point, Ferry Reach, Ely's Harbour, Riddells Bay, and Harrington Sound. May through September, when the waters are usually calm, is the best time for water-skiing. Bermuda law requires that a licensed skipper take waterskiers out. Only a few boat operators handle this sport, and charges fluctuate with

HANGING OUT WITH THE dolphins

The well-publicized **Dolphin Quest Experience,** at the National Museum of Bermuda (aka the Bermuda Maritime Museum) in the Royal Naval Dockyard (www.dolphinquest.org; © **441/234-4464**), offers in-the-water encounters with Atlantic bottlenose dolphins. Seven dolphins are kept in a holding pen that's 1 to 3.5m (3¼–11 ft.) deep and separated from the open sea with underwater netting. Typically, up to 10 swimmers, as many as 100 of them per day during the midsummer peak, each wearing bathing suits in summer and wet suits in winter (Nov–May), cavort in the water with the dolphins. The price for the most intensive encounters—in the water, up-front, and personal—costs $250 for a 30-minute encounter and $310 for its otherwise equivalent 45-minute counterpart. Other packages are available, with prices varying from $60 to $160 per person according to the time spent either in the water or standing (or lying) on a dock for

pettings, feedings, and interchanges with the dolphins. Call or check the organization's website for details. In winter, it's easy to get a slot, but in summer, there's a much heavier demand.

Is all this cruel to the dolphins? The staff is rigorous about protecting and caring for them; the overall atmosphere is playful and lighthearted; and the dolphins have a fairly large area to swim in. But we can't help worrying that continued contact with hordes of people and separation from their natural habitat must have a traumatizing effect on these beautiful animals. For more (mostly troubling) information, check out the Whale and Dolphin Conservation Society's website at **www.wdcs.org**. For more information about responsible travel in general, check out these websites: Tread Lightly (www.treadlightly.org) and the International Ecotourism Society (www.ecotourism.org).

fuel costs. Rates include the boat, skis, safety belts, and usually an instructor. Hotels and guesthouses can assist with arrangements.

Bermuda Waterski Centre Up to five people can water-ski at the same time from a specially designed Ski Nautique. Lessons are also available. The charge for a party of any size (not per person) is $75 for a 15-minute session, $100 for a 30-minute session, and $170 for a 60-minute session. The driver is included in the price.

Robinson's Marina, Somerset Bridge, Sandys Parish. © **441/234-3354.** May to mid-Sept daily 8am–7:30pm. Bus: 6 or 7.

WHERE TO PLAY WORLD-CLASS GOLF

Since the island's first course was laid out in 1922, golf has been one of Bermuda's most popular sports. You can play year-round, but spring, fall, and early winter offer the best seaside conditions. You must arrange tee times at any of the island's eight courses in advance through your guesthouse or hotel. Women's and men's clubs (right- and left-handed) are available at each course, and most leading stores in Bermuda sell golf balls. Generally speaking, children under 18 are usually not welcome on golf courses; definitely check in advance if you have any underage duffers in your party.

The Golfer's Dress Code

Remember to dress appropriately for your golf game. Most courses have strict dress codes that require shirts with collars, Bermuda-length shorts or slacks, and soft-spiked golf shoes or tennis shoes. No bathing suits, cutoffs, short shorts, or jeans.

The Rosewood **Tucker's Point Club** is one of the most scenic courses on the island (though it is a private club), while the **Port Royal** course, designed by Robert Trent Jones, Sr., is a challenge. Two famous courses—the **Mid Ocean Club** at Tucker's Town and the **Riddells Bay Golf and Country Club**—are private, although Riddells Bay has relaxed its policies considerably in recent years, and will welcome qualified visitors to the island with access to their greens if they reserve several days or weeks in advance. One of the most photographed courses on Bermuda is the **Fairmont Southampton Golf Club,** where a landscape of rolling hills and flowering shrubs adds to the players' enjoyment.

The golf courses listed below that are part of hotel complexes permit nonguests to use their facilities. All of these golf courses have pros and offer lessons.

Top players participate in tournaments throughout the year. For information, contact the **Bermuda Golf Association,** The Victoria Place Building, 31 Victoria St., Hamilton HM BX, Bermuda (www.bermudagolf.org; ✆ **441/295-9972**).

Belmont Hills Golf & Country Club   This course, one of the most respected in Bermuda, was originally designed by Scotsman Emmett Devereux in 1923. In 2002, California-based designer Algie M. Pulley, Jr., radically reconfigured its layout as a means of adding a series of golf "features" that brought the standards and allure of this course up to the demands of modern-day golf pros. Since its reopening, amid justifiable brouhaha surrounding the most extensive golf course rebuilding in the history of Bermuda, there has been endless discussion about the peculiar features of this relatively short (6,017 yd.) but challenging course. Despite the fact that some of the undulations in its terrain were flattened during the 2002 overhaul, an interconnected network of caves beneath the turf sometimes cause the ball to roll unpredictably. Another odd feature involves exceptionally narrow fairways. But despite these quirky disadvantages, golf pros recommend the Belmont for beginners as well as seasoned pros. Although the first hole is said to be "confidence building," holes 2, 6, and 12 are all relatively difficult (each with a par of 5). Likewise, the 17th and 18th holes, arguably the most difficult on the course, reward golfers with some of the best ocean views. It's estimated that with a 9 or 10 handicap, golfers will shoot in the 70s at Belmont—but there aren't any guarantees. With the exception of the above-mentioned 17th and 18th holes, most of the course is inland, so unlike most of the other golf courses in Bermuda, this one provides few views of the Atlantic.

Greens fees (which do not include golf carts) are $120 daily. A full set of clubs rents for about $45 to $60 depending on the brand you select. Carts rent for $35.

Btw. Harbour and Middle rds., Warwick Parish. www.newsteadbelmonthills.com. ✆ **441/236-6060.** Daily 7am–5pm. Holes: 18. Par: 70. Length: 5,501m (6,017 yd.). Ferry from the City of Hamilton. Bus: 8.

Fairmont Southampton Golf Club   On the grounds of one of the most luxurious hotels on Bermuda, this course, one of the shortest on the island, occupies not only the loftiest but also one of the most scenic settings on the island. Elevated tees, strategically placed bunkers, and plenty of water hazards make it a challenge, and golfers have been known to use every club in their bag when the wind blows in from the Atlantic. Against the backdrop of the Gibbs Hill Lighthouse, the 16th hole sits in a cup ringed by flowering bushes. The vertical drop on the 1st and 2nd holes is almost 60m (200 ft.). Even experienced golfers like to "break in" on this course before taking on some of Bermuda's more challenging ones. Its 18 holes are usually completed in 2½ to 3 hours (as opposed to around 5 hr. at most of the others) Greens fees for 18 holes of play cost $86 and include the use of a golf cart. This well-irrigated course is often green when some other courses suffer a summer brownout.

This venue offers reduced rates ("Sunset Rates") if you begin your round of golf between 2:30pm and 3:30pm. During that period, adults can "walk" (that is, without benefit of a golf cart) the course's 18 holes for $45 or navigate with use of a cart for $67. There are no caddies, and club rental is $25.

101 South Rd., Southampton Parish. www.fairmont.com/southampton. ✆ **441/238-8000.** Daily 7am–sunset. Holes: 18. Par: 3. Length: 2,454m (2,684 yd.). Bus: 7 or 8.

4

Ocean View Golf Course   In the 1950s, this was a club for black Bermudians. Later, as other clubs started to admit black players, the course was neglected and fell into disrepair. Ocean View's reputation for spotty maintenance lives on despite a $2-million renovation and a takeover by the Bermudian government that improved the course early in the millennium. In the center of Bermuda, in Devonshire Parish, it offers panoramic views of the ocean from many of its elevated tees. Many golfers consider the terrain unpredictable; that, combined with rambling hills and winds from the Great Sound, makes the course more challenging than it appears. A few holes have as many as six tees. The green on the 162m (177-yd.), par-3 5th hole has been cut into the coral hillside. Because the hole is draped with semitropical vines, golfers sometimes have the eerie feeling that they're hitting the ball into a cave.

On weekdays, this course tends to be the least crowded on Bermuda. Greens fees are $77 for 18 holes and $50 for 9 holes, a price which includes use of a golf cart. In its way, this is the least pretentious golf course in Bermuda. Golf shoes (soft spikes) or tennis shoes will work.

2 Barkers Hill Rd., Devonshire Parish. www.oceanview.bm. ✆ **441/295-9092.** Daily 7:30am–6:30pm. Holes: 9 (18 tee positions). Par: 35. Length: 2,688m (2,940 yd.). Bus: 2, 10, or 11.

Port Royal Golf Course ★★   Originally designed by Robert Trent Jones, Sr., in 1970, this stellar golf course was restored and reopened in June 2009 after a multi-million-dollar overhaul and a takeover by the Bermudian government. Golfers cite its 7th and 8th holes as being particularly difficult, subject as they are to steep dogleg turns and occasional high winds, and the 15th and 16th holes as "gorgeous but treacherous," thanks to their location on windy cliff tops ringing the periphery of Whale Bay. Greens fees for 18 holes of play cost $180 per person, with use of a golf cart included.

5 Middle Rd., Southampton Parish. www.portroyalgolf.bm. ✆ **441/234-0974.** Daily 7:30am–6pm. Holes: 18. Par: 71. Length: 5,999m (6,561 yd.). Bus: 7 or 8.

Riddells Bay Golf Course ★★   Although technically, this stalwart and relent-lessly upscale bastion of golf on Bermuda is a private, members-only club, it relaxes its policies when confronted with off-island newcomers who want to experience a layout of greens and fairways that are the oldest (established in 1922) on Bermuda.

Communicate your wishes to the well-intentioned staff as long in advance of your arrival as possible, and if you're at all experienced in the game, you'll probably be assigned a tee-off time. Greens fees cost $155 per person, including the use of a golf cart.

26 Riddle's Bay Rd., Warwick Parish WK 04 Bermuda. www.riddellsbay.com. *(C)* **441/238-3225.** Daily 7:30am–5:30pm. Holes: 18. Par: 70. Length 5,269m (5,854 yd.). Bus: 7.

OTHER OUTDOOR PURSUITS
Biking

With a year-round average temperature of 70°F (21°C), Bermuda offers ideal weather for bicycling. Plus, biking is a great way to have fun and stay in shape, and it allows you to take a hands-on approach to your sightseeing. But be forewarned: Most roads aren't suitable for beginners. Think carefully and ask around when you're deciding where you or your children can ride safely and comfortably.

In general, roadways are well paved and maintained. The island's speed limit is 32kmph (20 mph) for all vehicles, but the roads are narrow and winding, and car traffic, especially during the day, tends to be heavy. *Always* exercise caution when riding a bike or scooter. Most drivers are considerate of cyclists, but a car may approach without warning because the government discourages unnecessary horn honking. Fellow cyclists might even overtake you—bicycle racing is one of the most popular local sports.

Much of the island's terrain consists of flat stretches, although the hills provide what the locals call "challenges." Some climbs are steep, especially on roads that run north and south. South Road, through Southampton and Warwick parishes, often leaves bikers huffing and puffing.

RENTING A BIKE
Push bikes or pedal bikes, the terms Bermudians use to distinguish bicycles from mopeds, are a popular form of transportation. You can rent a bicycle by the hour, by the day, or for your entire stay. For information about bicycle and scooter rentals, see "Getting Around," in chapter 10. All recommended scooter and cycle shops rent bicycles. Many hotels have bicycles for guests' use, with or without a fee. Rentals generally cost $35 for 1 day, $60 for 2 days. Ten- and 12-speed bikes are usually available. It's always a smart idea to call as far in advance as possible, because demand is great, especially from April to October.

WHERE TO BIKE ON BERMUDA
Only the hardiest cyclists set out to traverse the complete 34km (21-mile) length of Bermuda in 1 day. For most people, it's far better to focus on smaller sections at different times. So, decide what interests you parish by parish, and proceed from there. To save time, you can take your bike aboard various ferries (they're free), and then begin cycling.

A safe choice for beginning riders is the **Bermuda Railway Trail** (see below). Some of the most interesting cycling trails are in **Devonshire** and **Smith's parishes.** The hills throughout these areas guarantee that you'll get your exercise for the day, and the beautiful landscapes make your effort worthwhile. **Spittal Pond,** a wildlife sanctuary with bike paths running along seaside cliffs, is one of the most rewarding destinations. Stop by a cycle shop for a trail map and some advice. Nearly all bike shop owners know Bermuda intimately and will mark up a map for you or give you any special guidance you need.

If you're a real demon on a bike, you can go farther west for the challenge of pumping up to **Gibbs Hill Lighthouse,** the oldest cast-iron lighthouse in the world. From here, you'll have one of the most panoramic views in Bermuda.

If you'd like to combine a picnic with your bicycle outing, head for **Sandys Parish.** First cross Somerset Bridge, the smallest drawbridge in the world, then pedal along Somerset Road to Fort Scaur Park. There you can relax and admire the view of Ely's Harbour while enjoying your picnic.

THE BERMUDA RAILWAY TRAIL   An interesting bicycle option is the **Bermuda Railway Trail** (see the box "Rattle & Shake: The Bermuda Railway Trail," on p. 55), which is restricted to bicyclists and pedestrians. The Railway Trail consists of seven non-contiguous sections, each with its own character. You can decide how much of the trail you'd like to cover in 1 day, and which sections to focus on. Pick up a copy of the *Bermuda Railway Trail Guide,* available at the Bermuda Department of Tourism in the City of Hamilton, or the Visitors Information Centres in the City of Hamilton and St. George, to help you plan your route.

Horseback Riding

Spicelands Riding Centre   This stable, the best recommended in Bermuda, offers 30-minute riding lessons for $60 each, and hour-long trail rides for between $60 and $160 per person, depending on the degree to which its participants want to restrict their group to their friends, family, and members of their entourage. Book your lesson or trail ride at least 1 day ahead, calling between 6am and 7pm.

Middle Rd., Warwick Parish. www.spicelandsriding.com. ☏ **441/238-8212.** Bus: 8.

Tennis

Nearly all the big hotels (and many of the smaller ones) have courts, most of which can be lit for night play. Pack your tennis clothing and sneakers, because a tennis outfit (though it no longer needs to be white) may be required.

Each of the facilities listed below has a tennis pro on duty, and lessons can be arranged. All rent racquets and sell balls.

Elbow Beach Hotel   The Elbow Beach Hotel has five Laykold courts (one for lessons only). Lessons cost $75 for 1 hour. The 1-hour court fee is $12. Racquets can be rented for $7 per hour, and balls are $8 per can of three.

60 South Rd., Paget Parish. ☏ **441/236-3535.** Call for bookings daily mid-Oct to mid-Apr 8am–5:30pm; mid-Apr to mid-Oct 8am–7pm (3 courts are floodlit for night play 7–9pm). Bus: 1, 2, or 7.

The Fairmont Southampton   This resort has Bermuda's largest tennis court layout, with six Plexipave courts, three of which are lit for night play. The price for guests and nonguests is $15 per hour. Evening rates are $6 extra. Racquets rent for $8 per hour, balls cost $7 per can. Lessons are $80 for 1 hour.

101 South Rd., Southampton Parish. ☏ **441/238-8000.** Daily 8am–7pm (until 6pm in winter). Bus: 7 or 8.

Government Tennis Stadium (W. E. R. Joell Tennis Stadium)   There are three clay and five Plexicushion courts here. Charges to play are $10 per hour for adults, $5 per hour for juniors (12 and under). Playing at night on one of the three lit

Other Outdoor Pursuits

FUN ON & OFF THE BEACH

EXPLORING BERMUDA'S natural wonderlands

The National Trust in Bermuda has wisely protected the island's nature reserves. If you play by the rules—that is, don't disturb animal life or take plant life as a souvenir—you can explore many of these natural wonderlands. If you enjoy nature trails, they're one of the most rewarding reasons to visit Bermuda.

The best and largest sanctuary is **Spittal Pond Nature Reserve** in Smith's Parish. Birders visit the reserve—especially from September to April—to see herons, ducks, flamingos, terns, and many migratory fowl (which can't be seen after March). This 24-hectare (59-acre) untamed seaside park is always open to the public with no admission charge. **The Department of Parks (© 441/236-4201)** offers free guided tours. Tours are

offered primarily from November to May; call for schedules and additional information.

The island abounds with other places of natural wonder. Craggy formations shaped over the centuries out of limestone and coral dot the beaches along the southern coast, with towering cliffs forming a backdrop. Some of Bermuda's natural beauty spots were badly damaged by recent hurricanes, but 344 hectares (850 acres) of trails, parks, and preserves are up and running again. You can join one of the many interpretative tours offered by local ecoheritage groups. To learn what's available at the time of your visit, contact the **Bermuda Audubon Society** in Hamilton (www. audubon.bm).

courts costs $8 extra. Tennis attire is mandatory. Racquets rent for $7 per hour; balls cost $6 per can.

Cedar Ave., Pembroke Parish. © **441/292-0105.** Mon–Fri 8am–10pm; Sat–Sun 8am–7pm. Bus: 1, 2, 10, or 11.

Grotto Bay Beach Club   This resort across from the airport has some of the best tennis courts on the island. The 8.5-hectare (21-acre) property offers four Plexipave courts, two of which are well-lit for night games. During the day, guests play for $10, nonguests $12; at night, guests pay $15, nonguests $17. The hotel also rents rackets for $4 and sells tennis balls for $6 a can at the on-site pro shop.

11 Blue Hole Hill, Hamilton Parish. © **441/293-8333.** Daily, 24 hrs. Bus: 1, 3, 10, or 11.

SPECTATOR SPORTS

In this tradition-bound British colony, the most popular spectator sports are cricket, soccer, field hockey, and the not terribly genteel game of rugby. As you might expect, boating, yachting, and sailing are also popular. The Bermuda Department of Tourism can provide dates and venues for upcoming events; see "Visitor Information" under "Fast Facts" in chapter 10. Also see the "Bermuda Calendar of Events" in chapter 2.

Cricket

Far more Bermudians than you might suspect have memorized this terribly British sport's arcane rules. If you arrive in midsummer (the game's high season), you'll probably see several regional teams practicing on cricket fields throughout the island. Each match includes enough pageantry to remind participants of the game's imperial antecedents and enough conviviality (picnics, socializing, and chitchat among the spectators) to give you a real feel for Bermuda.

The **Cup Match Cricket Festival** is Bermuda's most passionately watched cricket event, with hundreds of viewers turning out to cheer on family members and friends. Conducted during late July or early August, it pairs Bermuda-based teams against one another. The event usually occurs at the headquarters of two of the island's approximately 30 cricket teams, either the **St. George's Cricket Club,** Willington Slip Road (✆ **441/297-0374**), or the **Somerset Cricket Club,** Cricket Lane, Broome Street off Somerset Road (✆ **441/234-0327**). Buy your tickets at the gate on the day of each event, and expect to pay between $18 and $20 per ticket for entrance to this long-standing Bermuda tradition.

Golf Tournaments

Bermuda offers some of the finest golfing terrain in the world, partly due to the climate, which supports lush driving ranges and putting greens. In addition, the ever-present golfers play at surprisingly high levels. Golf tournaments are held throughout the year, culminating in the annual, much-publicized **Bermuda Open** at the Port Royal Golf Course in early October. Amateurs and professionals are welcome to vie for one of the most sought-after golfing prizes in the world. For information or an application, contact the secretary of the **Bermuda Golf Association** (www.bermuda golf.org; ✆ **441/295-9972**).

Horse Racing & Equestrian Competitions

Contact the **National Equestrian Centre** (formerly known as the Vesey Street Racetrack), Vesey Street, Devonshire Parish (✆ **441/291-7223**), for information about upcoming events. From September to May, harness races take place about twice a month.

A major equestrian event is in October: the FEI/Samsung Dressage Competition and Show-Jumping. Details are available from the **Bermuda Equestrian Federation,** P.O. Box DV 583, Devonshire DV BX, Bermuda (www.bef.bm; ✆ **441/234-0485**).

Soccer

Bermudians view soccer as an important part of elementary education and actively encourage children and teenagers to participate. In early April, teams from countries around the Atlantic and Caribbean compete in three age divisions for the Diadora Youth Soccer Cup. Games are held on various fields throughout the island. More accessible to spectators at other times are the many high-school games held regularly throughout the year. Contact the tourist office for a schedule.

Yachting

Bermuda capitalizes on its geographical position in the mid-Atlantic to lure the yachting crowd. The racing season runs from March to November, with most races scheduled on weekends in the relatively calm waters of Bermuda's Great Sound. The best land vantage points include Spanish Point, the islands northeast of Somerset, and Hamilton Harbour. Shifting sightlines can make it confusing to watch races from land. Better views are available from the decks of privately owned boats that anchor near the edge of the racecourse, so it's good to befriend a private boat owner. Although the carefully choreographed regattas might be confusing to newcomers, the sight of a fleet of racing craft with spinnakers and pennants aloft is always exciting.

Bermuda is the final destination in two of the most important annual yacht races: the **Annapolis-Bermuda Race** (www.bermudaoceanrace.com) and the even more prestigious **Newport-Bermuda Race** (www.bermudarace.com), both held in late June during alternate years. Both provide enough visual distraction and maritime pageantry to keep you enthralled. Participating yachts range from 9 to 30m (30–98 ft.) in length, and their skippers are said to be among the most dedicated in the world.

Around Halloween, the autumn winds propel dozens of less exotic racing craft through the waters of the Great Sound. They compete in a series of one-on-one playoffs for the **King Edward VII Gold Cup International Match Racing Tournament.**

The island's yachting events are by no means limited to international competitions. Bermuda's sheltered bays and windswept open seas provide year-round enticement for anyone who has ever wanted to experience the thrill of a snapping jib and taut mainsail. See "Sailing," under "More Fun in the Water," earlier in this chapter, for details on yacht charters.

4

FUN ON & OFF THE BEACH

Spectator Sports

SEEING THE SIGHTS

Even though a large number of people live on this small island, you should never feel crowded. There are no billboards or neon signs, and, except for the rush hour in and around Hamilton, relatively few cars to spoil the rolling countryside. Most houses seem to fit quite naturally into the landscape.

5

Because of Bermuda's small size, it's easy to get to know the island parish by parish. There's much to see, whether you travel by bike, ferry, bus, or taxi. You'll need plenty of time, however, because the pace is slow. Cars and other motorized vehicles, such as mopeds, must observe the maximum speed of 24kmph (15 mph) in the City of Hamilton and St. George, and 32kmph (20 mph) in the countryside. The speed limits are rigidly enforced, and there are severe penalties for violations.

If you're visiting for the first time, you may want to follow the traditional tourist route. The Aquarium, Devil's Hole, and cruise-boat outings are all popular for first-time visitors. For travelers on a second, third, or fourth visit to Bermuda, a different experience unfolds. Once you've done all the "must-sees," you'll want to walk around and make discoveries on your own. The best parishes for walking are Somerset and St. George's, and the City of Hamilton.

But don't fill your days with too much structured sightseeing. You'll also want time to lounge on the beach, play in the water, or hit the links; and to enjoy moments such as sitting by the harbor in the late afternoon,

 The Fun of Getting Lost

Many guidebooks contend that you can't get lost in Bermuda. Don't believe them! As you travel along the narrow, winding roads, originally designed for the horse and carriage, you may go astray— several times—especially if you're looking for an obscure guesthouse on some long-forgotten lane. But don't worry, you won't stay lost for long. Bermuda is so narrow— only about 3km (1¾ miles) wide at its broadest point—that if you keep going east or west, you'll eventually come to a main road. The principal arteries are North Shore Road, Middle Road, and South Road (also unofficially referred to as South Shore Rd.), so you'll usually have at least some sense of what part of the island you're in.

Strolling Bermuda's Pink Sands The pink sand beaches are reason enough to come to Bermuda. Find your favorite cove (perhaps Whale Bay, Astwood Cove, or Jobson's Cove) and stroll aimlessly at dawn, at twilight, or whenever your fancy dictates. See the map "Bermuda's Best Public Beaches & Snorkel Sites" on p. 66.

Touring the Commissioner's House at the Royal Naval Dockyard Around 1850, it was the most visible symbol in the mid-Atlantic of the imperial power of the British Navy. After the turn of the millennium, it was majestically restored from a dilapidated ruin into a glowing memorial to another age and time.

Visiting the Bermuda Masterworks Collection in the Botanical Gardens A source of enormous civic pride, it contains the largest assortment of Bermudian and Bermuda-inspired artwork in the world—proof positive that lots of other artistically sensitive people have loved the island as much as we do.

Viewing Bermuda from Gibbs Hill Lighthouse Climb the 185 steps of the oldest cast-iron lighthouse (p. 92) in the world for one of the greatest views of the Atlantic Ocean. Springtime visitors may be lucky enough to see migrating whales beyond the shore reefs.

enjoying the views as the yachts glide by. Absorbing Bermuda's beauty at your own pace and stopping to chat with the occasional islander will give you a real taste of Bermuda.

In this chapter, we go on a do-it-yourself tour, parish by parish. Also consider taking one or more of the walking tours that we describe in chapter 3.

SANDYS PARISH

Sandys Parish is one of the island's real beauty spots. If you're looking for a place to just wander about and get lost on a summer day, this lovely parish is well worth your time. Fort Scaur and the Royal Naval Dockyard on Ireland Island are the major attractions. If you're pressed for time, skip the Gilbert Nature Reserve and St. James' Anglican Church.

To explore this tip of the fishhook that is Bermuda, it's best to take a ferry (the fare is $4). The trip from the City of Hamilton to The Dockyards takes 20 to 40 minutes, depending on the number of stops en route, and you can take your bike onboard free (there's an additional $4 charge for scooters and mopeds). Ferries originating in the City of Hamilton sometimes also stop at Cavello Bay, Somerset Bridge, and Boaz Island, before arriving at the Royal Naval Dockyard. The **Visitors Information Centre** is at the Royal Naval Dockyard (*C* **441/799-4842**), across from the ferry terminal. From May to October, hours are daily, 9am to 5pm. From November to April, hours are Thursday and Friday 9:30am to 4:30pm, Saturday and Sunday 10am to 4:30pm. For more information on the ferry service, visit www.seaexpress.bm or call *C* **441/295-4506.**

Gilbert Nature Reserve NATURE RESERVE In the center of the island lies the Gilbert Nature Reserve, 2 hectares (5 acres) of unspoiled woodland. It bears the

Attractions Around the Island

0   1 mi
0   1 km

✈ Airport

ATLANTIC   OCEAN

2 1

Ireland Island North
3
Royal Naval Dockyard (King's Wharf)

Ireland Island South

Mangrove Bay
Somerset Village

4

SANDYS

Watford Bridge

14

Bay Rd.

15 16 North Shore Rd.

PEMBROKE

Ely's Harbour

6 5
7

8

9

Great Sound

Two Rock Passage

Long Island

Hawkins Island

Hamilton
★ 17
18
19

22

Hamilton Harbour

21

20

PAGET

Ferry

Ports Island

Hinson Island

Darrell Island

Little Sound

Harbour Rd.

Middle Rd.

13

WARWICK

South Rd.

10

SOUTHAMPTON

11

12

Middle Rd.

Admiralty House Park **14**

Bermuda Aquarium, Museum & Zoo **28**

Bermuda Arts Centre **2**

Bermuda Biological Station for Research **30**

Bermuda Craft Market **2**

Bermuda Historical Society Museum **17**

Bermuda National Gallery **17**

Bermuda National Museum (Bermuda Maritime Museum) **1**

The Bermuda National Trust Museum **32**

Bermuda Underwater Exploration Institute **18**

"Birdcage" **17**

Birdsey Studio **21**

Black Watch Well **15**

Botanical Gardens **22**

Bridge House Gallery **29**

Carter House (St. David's Island Historical Site) **31**

Cathedral of the Most Holy Trinity **17**

Christ Church **13**

Crystal Caves **29**

Deliverance **33**

Paget Marsh **20**

Palm Grove **25**

Perot Post Office **17**

Royal Naval Dockyard **3**

Scaur Hill Fort Park/
Fort Scaur **7**

St. George's Historical
Society Museum **32**

St. James' Anglican Church **6**

St. Peter's Church **32**

Sessions House **17**

Seymour's Pond
Nature Reserve **10**

Somerset Bridge **8**

Somers Garden **32**

Spittal Pond
Nature Reserve **27**

Town Hall (St. George's) **32**

Tucker House Museum **32**

Unfinished Church **32**

Verdmont **26**

Warwick Long Bay **12**

Warwick Pond **13**

Waterville **19**

Firefly and Freer Cox
Memorial **23**

Fort Hamilton **17**

Fort St. Catherine **34**

Gates Fort **35**

Gibbs Hill Lighthouse **11**

Gilbert Nature Reserve **4**

Government House **16**

Hamilton City Hall
& Arts Centre **17**

Heydon Trust **5**

Hog Bay Park **9**

Idwal Hughes
Nature Reserve **29**

The Masterworks Museum
of Bermuda Art **22**

Old Devonshire Parish
Church **24**

Old Rectory **32**

Old State House **32**

The World's Smallest Drawbridge

After leaving Fort Scaur, you can continue over the much-photographed 17th-century **Somerset Bridge,** the world's smallest drawbridge. During the very rare moments when it's open for marine traffic, the space between the spans is a mere 56cm (22 in.) at road level—just large enough for the mast of a sailboat to pass through.

name of the family that owned the property from the early 18th century until 1973, when the Bermuda National Trust acquired it (in conjunction with the Bermuda Audubon Society). The reserve is one of the best places on the island for bird-watching, and it is riddled with paths that connect to the Railway Trail that crosses Bermuda. In the northeastern corner of the reserve are the finest examples of mature Bermuda cedars on the island.

Springfield, 29 Somerset Rd. www.bnt.bm. ✆ **441/236-6483.** Free admission. Daily dawn–dusk. Organized tours available. Bus: 7 or 8 from the City of Hamilton.

Scaur Hill Fort Park ★ HISTORIC SITE   On the highest hill in Sandy's Parish, Fort Scaur was part of a ring of fortifications constructed in the 19th century, during a period of troubled relations between Britain and the United States. Intended as a last-ditch defense for the Royal Naval Dockyard, the fort was skillfully constructed, taking advantage of the land contours to camouflage its presence from detection at sea. The fort has subterranean passages and a dry moat that stretches across the land from Ely's Harbour to Great Sound.

Open to visitors since 1957, Fort Scaur has become one of Somerset's most popular tourist attractions. The fort has panoramic views of Ely's Harbour and Great Sound; using the free telescope, you'll see such faraway points as St. David's Lighthouse and Fort St. Catherine. The fort sits on 9 hectares (22 acres) of parkland filled with interesting trails, picnic areas, a rocky shoreline for fishing, and a public dock. Picnic tables, benches, and restrooms are available.

Ely's Harbour, Somerset Rd. No phone. Free admission. Daily sunrise–sunset. Bus: 7 or 8 from the City of Hamilton.

St. James' Anglican Church CHURCH   This is one of the most beautiful churches on Bermuda. It was constructed on the site of a structure that was destroyed by a hurricane in 1780. The present church was built 9 years later. A unique feature is the altar, which faces west instead of the customary east. The north and south aisles were added in 1836, the entrance gate in 1872, and the spire and chancel in 1880. The church was struck by lightning in 1939 and restored shortly thereafter.

90 Somerset Rd. ✆ **441/234-0834.** Free admission. Daily 8am–5pm. Bus: 7 or 8 from the City of Hamilton.

Ireland Island & the Royal Naval Dockyard

The American War of Independence created a crisis for Britain's military planners: Ports along the U.S. Atlantic seaboard were closed to British warships for repairs and replenishments. And during the Napoleonic Wars with France, the need for a British-controlled stronghold in the mid-Atlantic became something approaching an obsession with Britain's military leaders. Beginning in 1809, foundations for a massive

Sandys Parish

SEEING THE SIGHTS

A park OF YOUR OWN

Just when you thought that everything in "Paradise" (as locals call Bermuda) had been discovered, you happen upon 15-hectare (37-acre) **Hog Bay Park**. In spite of its unattractive name, this is one of the beauty spots of Bermuda, and one of its least visited attractions. To reach the park from the City of Hamilton, take a ferry across Great Sound, getting off at the Somerset Bridge ferry stop. Cross the Somerset drawbridge and follow the trail of the old Bermuda Railway.

Cross Middle Road into the park. Once at the park you'll pass ruins of kilns once used for making lime to paint the famous whitewashed roofs of island homes. As you meander, you'll come across old abandoned cottages, finally reaching Sugar Loaf Hill with its Look Out Point. From here, you'll be rewarded with one of the greatest panoramic views on Bermuda. As Barbra Streisand might put it: "On a clear day, you can see forever."

naval fortress evolved, based mostly on enforced labor from slaves (and later freed slaves), prisoners, and prisoners-of-war.

Today, the Royal Naval Dockyard is one of the premier attractions of Bermuda. Within the sprawling compound are a scattering of shops and restaurants, and the attractions listed below.

Bermuda Arts Centre COMMERCIAL ART GALLERY   Works by local artists are the focus in this gallery, with exhibits changing about every 4 to 6 weeks. An eclectic range of original art and prints is for sale. Local artists in residence include a cedar sculptor and a jewelry maker. You'll see four artists laboring in their respective mediums: wood-sculpting, jewelry making, oil painting, and weaving. There's a small gift shop on-site, displaying and selling the wares of these and other artists.

Maritime Lane. www.artbermuda.bm. © **441/234-2809.** Free admission. Daily 10am–5pm. Bus 7 or 8 leaves the City of Hamilton for the Royal Naval Dockyard Mon–Sat every 15 min. 6:45am–11:45pm. The trip takes 1 hr. and costs $4 for adults, $2 for children 5–16, free for children 4 and under. **Note:** Drivers accept this exact bus fare in coins only.

Bermuda Craft Market MARKET   This is the prime place to watch local artists at work and to buy their wares, some of which make ideal souvenirs. Established in 1987, within the shadowy, thick-walled premises of what was originally conceived as a warehouse and boat repair yard, this market offers items made from Bermuda cedar, candles, clothing, dolls, fabrics, hand-painted goods, jewelry, metal and gem sculpture, needlework, quilts, shell art, glass panels, and woven-cane goods, among other things.

In the Cooperage Bldg., 4 Freeport Rd. © **441/234-3208.** Free admission. Mon–Sat 11am–5pm; Sun 11am–5pm. Bus 7 or 8 leaves the City of Hamilton for the Royal Naval Dockyard Mon–Sat every 15 min. 6:45am–11:45pm. The trip takes 1 hr. and costs $4 for adults, $2 for children 5–16, free for children 4 and under. **Note:** Drivers accept this exact bus fare in coins only.

Bermuda National Museum (Bermuda Maritime Museum) ★★ ☺ MUSEUM Housed in a 19th-century fortress built by convict labor, this museum exhibits artifacts, models, and maps pertaining to Bermuda's nautical heritage. The fortress's massive buildings of fitted stone, with their vaulted ceilings of English brick, would be worth visiting even if they weren't crammed with artifacts and exhibits. So are the

9m (30-ft.) defensive ramparts; the underground tunnels, gun ports, and magazines; and the water gate and pond designed for boats entering from the sea. Exhibits in six large halls illustrate the island's long, intimate connection with the sea—from Spanish exploration to 20th-century ocean liners, from racing dinghies to practical fishing boats, from shipbuilding and privateering to naval exploits.

The compound's most impressive component is the **Commissioner's House,** dating from around 1834. The world's first cast-iron building was once the British colonial government's equivalent of the White House in Washington, D.C. Although its life as a historic monument began after its restoration in 2000, many of its exhibits weren't fully operational until about 7 years later. Today, glistening with a richly restored sense of Imperial Britain at the height of the Victorian age, it contains exhibits associated with slavery and the slave trade, antique maps, a collection of 19th- and 20th-century maritime paintings, watercolors with maritime themes painted in Bermuda, exhibits linking Bermuda's trade and emigration patterns to the Azores and the West Indies, and testimonials to the cooperative efforts of the British and U.S. Navies.

Don't omit a visit to the half-dozen stone and masonry buildings surrounding the Commissioner's House. The best of these is the 1837 **Shifting House,** which opened for viewing by the public in 1979. The artifacts inside include gold bars, pottery, jewelry, silver coins, and other items recovered from 16th- and 17th-century shipwrecks. The collection includes some earthenware and pewter that belonged to the English settlers on their way to Jamestown aboard the *Sea Venture,* which was wrecked in 1609. Most visitors come here to gaze at the Tucker Treasure. A well-known local diver, Teddy Tucker, made a significant find in 1955 when he discovered the wreck of the *San Antonio,* a Spanish vessel that had gone down off the coast of Bermuda in a violent storm in 1621. One of the great treasures of this find, the Pectoral Cross, was stolen in 1975 just before Queen Elizabeth II officially opened the museum. The priceless original cross was replaced by a replica, and the original cross has not been recovered—its mysterious disappearance is still the subject of much discussion.

As you enter the Parade Ground at the entrance to the museum, you'll notice a 3m-high (9¾-ft.) figure of King Neptune. This replica in Indiana limestone is modeled on a figure that was recovered from HMS *Irresistible,* when the ship was broken up in 1891. The **Queen's Exhibition Hall** houses general maritime exhibits, including displays on navigation, whaling, and cable and wireless communications. A "Bermuda in Five Hours" exhibit focuses on Pan American's early "flying boats." The building itself was constructed in 1850 for the purpose of storing 4,860 barrels of gunpowder. Some of the most intriguing objects on display within this building were salvaged from 16th- and 17th-century wrecks discovered in Bermuda's offshore waters.

The **Forster Cooper Building** (1852) illustrates the history of Bermuda and its Atlantic trade routes. The **Boatloft** houses part of the museum's boat collections, including the century-old fitted dinghy *Victory,* the 5m (16-ft.) *Spirit of Bermuda,* and the *Rambler,* the only surviving Bermuda pilot gig (a commanding officer's light boat kept on a large ship). On the upper floor, the original dockyard clock, which is still working, chimes every quarter-hour. Admission to the Shifting House, Queen's Exhibition Hall, Forster Cooper Building, Boatloft, and Commissioner's House are included in the entrance price to the Bermuda Maritime Museum.

Royal Naval Dockyard. www.bmm.bm. © **441/234-1418.** Admission $10 adults, $8 seniors, free for children 12 and under. Daily 9:30am–5pm (last ticket sold at 4pm). Closed Dec 25. Bus 7 or 8

STEPPING BACK INTO THE ice age

Bermuda has one of the highest concentrations of limestone caves in the world. Most began forming during the Pleistocene Ice Age. As early as 1623, the adventurer Capt. John Smith wrote that he had encountered "vary strange, darke, cumbersome caves."

In Bermuda, nature's patient, relentless underground sculpting has left behind a dream world for even the casual spelunker. Deep in the majestic silence of the earth's interior, you can roam in caverns full of great stalactites and stalagmites of Gothic grandeur, delicacy, and beauty. This awesome underground has been the inspiration for creative achievements as diverse as Shakespeare's *The Tempest* and Henson Associates' *Fraggle Rock*.

You can visit **Crystal Caves** on guided tours; the cave complex is along Harrington Sound Road in Hamilton Parish (p. 100).

leaves the City of Hamilton for the Royal Naval Dockyard Mon–Sat every 15 min. 6:45am–11:45pm. The trip takes 1 hr. and costs $4 for adults, $2 for children 5–16, free for children 4 and under. **Note:** Drivers accept this exact bus fare in coins only.

The Royal Naval Dockyard ★★★ HISTORIC SITE   The Dockyard, with its Bermuda Maritime Museum, is the number-one tourist attraction on Bermuda. Even if you plan to spend all your precious time on Bermuda's pink sandy beaches, try to schedule at least a half day to check it out.

The Royal Naval Dockyard has been transformed into a park, with Victorian street lighting and a Terrace Pavilion and bandstand for concerts. When the Bermudian government bought this dockyard, which had been on British Admiralty land, in 1953, it marked the end of British naval might in the western Atlantic. A multimillion-dollar cruise-ship dock has been built and a tourist village has emerged; today, vendors push carts filled with food, dry goods, and local crafts. There's a full-service marina with floating docks, a clubhouse, and showers. The area also houses the Bermuda Maritime Museum, the Neptune Cinema (a 118-seat cinema showing feature films two times a night, with matinees Fri–Sun; ✆ **441/292-7296**), the Craft Market, and the Bermuda Arts Centre, which are described above. The entire dockyard is closed Good Friday and Christmas Day. For more information about the Dockyard and its Maritime Museum, call ✆ **441/234-1333** or visit www.bmm.bm.

Ferries from the City of Hamilton stop at Ireland Island, at the western end of Bermuda, at intervals of btw. 20–90 minutes Mon–Fri 6:15am–6:30pm, and Sat–Sun 9am–5pm, with additional evening routes added during midsummer, based on demand and on special events offered within the Dockyards. Fare $4 each way. Depending on the day of the week, you might still be able to catch a ferry from Hamilton to the Dockyard at 8pm and then return to Hamilton as late as 11:30pm. Call ✆ **441/295-4506** for information on these later schedules. Bus 7 or 8 leaves the City of Hamilton for the Royal Naval Dockyard Mon–Sat every 15 min. 6:45am–11:45pm. The trip takes 1 hr. and costs $4 for adults, $2 for children 5–16, free for children 4 and under. **Note:** Drivers accept this exact bus fare in coins only.

SOUTHAMPTON PARISH

Most visitors stop by Southampton for the beaches if for no other reason. Even if you're not staying here, it's worth a journey to see the view from Gibbs Hill Lighthouse—there's no finer panorama in all of Bermuda.

Gibbs Hill Lighthouse ★ HISTORIC SITE   Southampton's main attraction is this completely restored lighthouse, built in 1846. It's the oldest cast-iron lighthouse in the world. Although there's a 185-step climb to the top, the panoramic view of Bermuda and its shoreline from the balcony make the exertion worthwhile. You can also view the same panorama that Queen Elizabeth II gazed on in 1953; just find the commemoration plaque by the entrance to the lighthouse. The lighthouse keeper will explain the workings of the machinery. If you visit in the spring, you may spot migrating whales beyond the south-shore reefs.

Gibbs Hill, Lighthouse Rd. (btw. South and Middle rds.). www.bermudalighthouse.com. ℂ **441/ 238-8069.** Admission $2.50; free for children 4 and under. Daily 9am–5pm. Closed Feb. Bus: 7 or 8 from the City of Hamilton.

WARWICK PARISH

This parish has few sightseeing attractions, but it is a place of natural beauty. Visitors come here mostly for the sandy beach, **Warwick Long Bay,** on South Road—it's one of the finest on Bermuda (see "Beaches," in chapter 4, for details). Nearby, you can visit **Christ Church,** across from the Belmont Hotel on Middle Road. Built in 1719, it's one of the oldest Scottish Presbyterian churches in the New World.

   Warwick is also the site of some of the best golf and horseback riding in Bermuda. See chapter 4 for specifics on these activities.

PAGET PARISH

On every visit to Bermuda, we schedule a long stopover at the Botanical Gardens with its associated art museum, the Masterworks Museum of Bermuda Art. They're worth the trip, even if you're staying in the East End. Once you're here, Waterville, one of the oldest houses in Bermuda, merits a look. You could cap your visit with a walk through unspoiled Paget Marsh, although you might skip it if you've already seen Spittal Pond (see "Smith's Parish," later in this chapter).

The Birdsey Studio COMMERCIAL ART GALLERY   Jo Birdsey Lindberg, daughter of the island's best-known artist, Alfred Birdsey (1912–96), sells original artwork, watercolors, and oils. An experienced painter, she continues a family tradition by producing and showing her work here, in a garden setting. Her impressionistic style appears in compositions ranging from landscapes of Bermuda to architectural and nautical themes. Also available are notecards reproduced from paintings by Alfred Birdsey. You must call ahead for an appointment.

5 Stowe Hill. ℂ **441/236-6658** or 441/236-5845 in the evening. Free admission. By appointment only. Bus: 8 from the City of Hamilton.

Botanical Gardens ★ PARK/GARDEN   This 14-hectare (35-acre) landscaped park, maintained by the Department of Natural Resources, is one of Bermuda's major attractions. Hundreds of clearly identified flowers, shrubs, and trees line the pathways. Attractions include collections of hibiscus and subtropical fruit, an aviary, banyan trees, and even a garden for the blind. A 90-minute tour leaves at 10:30am on Tuesday, Wednesday, and Friday, taking you through lushly planted acres. Guests meet at the Berry Hills entrance near the Botanical Gardens Visitor's Center. On the Tuesday and Friday tour, participants stop in at Camden, the official residence of Bermuda's premier, for a look around. The cafe sells sandwiches and salads (soup and chili in winter). Early in 2008, the Masterworks Museum of Bermuda Art (described below) opened within a much-restored, much rebuilt building in these gardens. And in the spring of 2008, the Botanical Gardens launched an ambitious 5-year plan to introduce four separate gardens of themed plants, including a Japanese Zen Garden, a 17th-century-style English Parterre Garden, a 12th-century-style Persian Garden, and a Tudor-style Children's Maze Garden.

Point Finger Rd. (at South Rd.). © **441/236-4201.** Free admission. Daily 9:30am–5:30pm. Tours Tues–Wed and Fri 10:30am. Bus: 1, 2, 7, or 8. By bike or moped, turn left off Middle Rd. onto Tee St.; at Berry Hill Rd., go right; about 1km (⅔ mile) farther on the left is the signposted turnoff to the gardens; take a right fork to the parking lot on the left.

The Masterworks Museum of Bermuda Art ★★ ART MUSEUM Ber-

muda's first purpose-built art museum was the subject of island-wide patriotic fervor when it opened early in 2008, and the crowds pouring in haven't abated since. It's housed within the much-altered, much-expanded premises of what functioned in 1900 as an arrowroot processing plant. As part of a skillful recycling of the once-decrepit building, it now boasts a state-of-the-art security system, sophisticated lighting, air-conditioning, preservation facilities, floors crafted from wide planks of exotic Brazilian hardwood, and a constantly shifting exposition of artworks crafted or painted by Bermudians, focusing on Bermuda, or merely inspired by Bermuda. Only about 5% of the total number of artworks within this museum's collection can be exhibited at any time. A visit to this collection will certainly impress upon you the artistic power of Bermuda as muse to a huge array of radically different artists. You'll see a lot of paintings by artists you might never have heard of before, as well as works by Winslow Homer and Georgia O'Keeffe, both of whom responded to Bermuda with artistic zeal. On your way into the museum, note the stately 18th-century mansion, Camden House, that's immediately adjacent: Closed to the public, it's the official residence of the premier of Bermuda, who rented the premises of what's now the museum to its curators for a fee of $1 a year. Prince Charles of Britain, incidentally, is this organization's most visible patron.

The Arrowroot Bldg. in the Botanical Gardens, 183 South Rd. www.bermudamasterworks.com. © **441/236-2950.** Admission free for members, $5 for nonmembers. Mon–Sat 10am–4pm; Sun 11:30am–4:30pm. Bus: 1, 2, 7, or 8.

Paget Marsh NATURE RESERVE This nature reserve comprises 10 hectares

(25 acres) of unspoiled native woods and marshland, with vegetation and bird life of ecological interest. Because it's a fully protected area with few trails, prospective visitors should call first and make special arrangements, and obtain a map from the Bermuda National Trust. A boardwalk allows you to view the marsh better. If you require a group tour, special speaker, or special program, then advance arrangements are necessary.

Middle Rd. © **441/236-6483.** Free admission. Mon–Fri dawn–dusk. Bus: 2, 7, or 8.

Waterville HISTORIC HOME Built before 1735, Waterville is one of the oldest

houses on Bermuda. It was home to seven generations of the prominent Trimingham family. From the house's cellar storage rooms in 1842, James Harvey Trimingham started the business that was to become Trimingham Brothers—one of Bermuda's finest Front Street department stores until it closed in 2005. Major renovations were undertaken in 1811, and the house has been restored in that period's style. The two main rooms hold period furnishings, mainly Trimingham family heirlooms specifically bequeathed for use in the house. Waterville is the headquarters of the Bermuda

National Trust, and houses its offices and reception rooms. It's just west of the Trimingham roundabout, near the City of Hamilton.

29 The Lane (Harbour Rd.), at Pomander Rd. www.bnt.bm. ✆ **441/236-6483.** Free admission. Mon–Fri 9am–5pm. Closed on holidays. Bus: 7 or 8 from the City of Hamilton.

PEMBROKE PARISH & THE CITY OF HAMILTON

For first-time visitors, the ideal way to see the City of Hamilton and its parish, Pembroke, is to sail in through Hamilton Harbour, past the offshore cays.

In 1852, the cornerstone was laid for the Hamilton Hotel, Bermuda's first hotel, completed in 1863 (a fire destroyed it in 1955). When the Hamilton Princess opened in 1887, it overshadowed the Hamilton Hotel and became the island's hotel of choice. The Hamilton Hotel's colorful history includes being taken over by Allied agents during World War II.

If Queen Victoria could visit Bermuda today, she would probably stay at **Government House,** on North Shore Road and Langton Hill. Because this is the residence of the governor of the island, it's not open to the public. This Victorian home has housed many notable guests, including Queen Elizabeth II and Prince Philip, Prince Charles, Sir Winston Churchill, and Pres. John F. Kennedy. In 1973, Gov. Sir Richard Sharples, his aide, Capt. Hugh Sayers, and the governor's dog were assassinated while they were walking on the grounds. A local named Erskine Burrows was hanged in 1977 after being found guilty of these murders as well as that of Police Commissioner George Duckett in 1972 and an armed robbery in 1973.

While touring Pembroke Parish, visitors often stop at **Black Watch Well,** at the junction of North Shore Road and Black Watch Pass. Excavated by a detachment of the Black Watch Regiment, the well was dug in 1894, when Bermudians were suffering through a long drought.

Another choice spot to visit is **Admiralty House Park,** off North Shore Road at Spanish Point Road. In 1816, a house was erected here to offer accommodations for the commanding British admiralty, which worked at the naval base at the dockyard. Over the years, the house was rebuilt several times. In the 1850s, it gained a series of subterranean tunnels, plus a number of galleries and caves carved into the cliffs above the sea. By 1951, the Royal Navy withdrew, and most of the house was torn down—except for a ballroom, which survives. Today, you can explore the parklike grounds. The sheltered beach at Clarence Cove is ideal for swimming.

The City of Hamilton ★★★

The capital of Bermuda was once known as the "show window of the British Empire." Both Mark Twain and Eugene O'Neill, who lived in lodgings that opened onto Hamilton Harbour, cited its beauty.

Named for former governor Henry Hamilton, the City of Hamilton was incorporated in 1793. Because of its central location and its large, protected harbor, it replaced St. George as the island's capital in 1815. The city encompasses only 73 hectares (180 acres) of land, so most visitors explore it on foot.

Long before it became known as "the showcase of the Atlantic," the City of Hamilton was a modest outlet for the export of Bermuda cedar and fresh vegetables. Today, it's the hub of the island's economy.

The City of Hamilton by Land and Sea

The City of Hamilton should be seen not only from land but also from the water. Try to make time for a boat tour of the harbor and its coral reefs. If you're visiting from another parish, the ferry will let you off at the west end of Front Street, which is ideal if you'd like to drop by the Visitors Information Centre (☎ **441/295-1480**), which is right near the Ferry Terminal, and pick up a map. The staff also provides information and helpful brochures; hours are Monday to Saturday 9am to 5pm.

More popular for its shops and restaurants than for its attractions, the City of Hamilton boasts the largest number of dining spots and bars on Bermuda, especially on and near Front Street. The restaurants have a wide range of prices, and there are many English-style watering holes if you'd prefer to go for a traditional pub-crawl. And religion isn't neglected—there are 12 churches within the city limits, the most interesting being the **Cathedral of the Most Holy Trinity** (p. 97).

If you'd like to go sightseeing, follow the plan laid out under "The Best of Bermuda in 2 Days," in chapter 3 for a comprehensive view of the City of Hamilton. The only sights that are worth in-depth visits are **Fort Hamilton,** the **Bermuda Historical Society Museum,** and the **Bermuda National Gallery.** You can safely skip the rest if you're pressed for time.

A stroll along **Front Street ★** will take you by some of the City of Hamilton's most elegant stores, but you'll also want to branch off into the little alleyways to check out the shops and boutiques. If you get tired of walking or shopping (or both), you can go down to the docks and take one of the boats or catamarans waiting to show you the treasures of Little Sound and Great Sound.

Ferries back to Paget, Warwick, and Sandys parishes leave daily between 6:50am and 11:20pm. On Saturday and Sunday, there are fewer departures. For schedules and fares, go to **www.seaexpress.bm**.

On certain days you may be able to see locals buying fresh fish—the part of the catch that isn't earmarked for restaurants—right from the fishers at the **Front Street docks.** Rockfish is the most abundant, and you'll also see snapper, grouper, and many other species.

Opposite the Visitors Information Centre stands the much-photographed **"Birdcage,"** where in years gone by, you'd see a Bermuda shorts–clad police officer directing traffic on a pedestal whose form was likened to a birdcage. Visitors often wondered if the traffic director was for real or placed there for tourist photographs. Such a sight is rare now.

Nearby is Albouy's Point, site of the Royal Bermuda Yacht Club, founded in 1844. The point, named after a 17th-century professor of "physick," is a public park overlooking Hamilton Harbour.

To reach the sights listed below, take bus no. 1, 2, 10, or 11.

Bermuda Historical Society Museum MUSEUM This museum has a collection of old cedar furniture, antique silver, early Bermudian coins called "hog money," and ceramics imported by early sea captains. You'll see the sea chest and navigating lodestone of Sir George Somers, whose flagship, the *Sea Venture,* became stranded on Bermuda's reefs in 1609, resulting in Bermuda's first European settlers. You'll also

AFRICAN DIASPORA heritage trail

Bermuda's African Diaspora Heritage Trail commemorates the role African slaves played in the formation of Bermuda. Free booklets, available from tourist offices, direct you along this self-guided tour of both tangible and intangible sites that highlight peak points in the cultural history of the island. A plaque marks each site.

Thirteen sites have been identified, including the site of the slave ship *Enterprise* incident, which, like the better-known *Amistad* affair, involved the rescue of slaves seeking refuge and freedom, and the historic Slave Graveyard at St. Peter's Church (ca. 1612), both located in St. George; the Crow Lane, site of the execution by burning of Sally Bassett, slave revolt leader; and sites associated with Mary Prince, the Bermudian slave who wrote the first account of slavery actually authored by a slave. Published in London in 1831, it played a key role in the struggle to abolish slavery. Another important site is Cobb's Hill Wesleyan Methodist Church, built by slaves by moonlight. The 13 sites highlighted in the brochure can be collectively visited through a combination of bus and fast ferry routes, and as such, require a full day to visit. Their densest concentration is in St. George's, where five of the sites lie within easy walking distance of one another. Some of the other sites are part of major attractions (for example, the Commissioner's House at the Royal Dockyard), which you might have otherwise visited independently. Even if you opt not to visit every single site (one, for example, commemorates a gibbet positioned long ago on offshore rocks, which are visible only from the shoreline of "mainland" Bermuda), you'll learn a lot about the sociology of Bermuda during its sometimes tormented formative years.

find portraits of Sir George and Lady Somers, and models of *Patience, Deliverance,* and the ill-fated *Sea Venture.*

The museum occupies part of the premises of the Bermuda National Library, in Par-la-Ville Park on Queen Street. It was designed by William Bennett Perot, the City of Hamilton's first postmaster (1818–62), who was a somewhat eccentric fellow; as he delivered mail around town, he is said to have placed letters in the crown of his top hat in order to preserve his dignity.

13 Queen St., Par-la-Ville Park. ℂ **441/295-2905.** Free admission. Mon–Thurs 8:30am–7pm; Fri 10am–5pm; Sat 9am–5pm; Sun 1–5pm.

Bermuda National Gallery ART MUSEUM   Located on the second floor of City Hall in the heart of the City of Hamilton, this is the home of the island nation's art collection, showing Bermudian and world art alike. The museum displays a diverse permanent collection as well as changing exhibitions. Both past and contemporary works from local and international painters not only tell the story of Bermuda's history, but also reflect its heritage. The gallery opened in 1992 with a core collection of European masters, including Gainsborough, Reynolds, and Murillo. The collection was bequeathed to Bermuda by the Hon. Hereward T. Watlington on the condition that the art be housed in a climate-controlled environment to protect it from humidity and damaging sunlight.

In addition to the Watlington Collection, the museum has an African collection (African figures, masks, and royal regalia), a Bermuda collection (which ranges from

17th-c. decorative arts to contemporary Bermudian work), and a wide range of Bermudian and international photographs, prints, and modern art.

City Hall, 17 Church St. www.bermudanationalgallery.com. ✆ **441/295-9428.** Free admission. Mon–Fri 10am–4pm; Sat 10am–2pm.

Bermuda Underwater Exploration Institute (BUEI) MUSEUM This blockbuster attraction is a glitzy, metallic, and electronic counterpart to the rich patina and genuine historicity of the Commissioner's House at the Royal Dockyard, with which it is sometimes compared. The force behind it is Teddy Tucker, the dynamic but endlessly controversial patriarch of Bermuda's underwater wreck explorations. At least some of the video presentations you'll see inside feature him as its spokesperson and centerpiece. There's something very akin to a museum of science and industry within this glistening, multimedia extravaganza. Various rooms are devoted to the underwater geology of Bermuda, one of the world's largest collections of seashells, bioluminescence and the creatures that produce it, and a showcase of the treasure that Tucker salvaged from underwater wrecks. Ironically, the exhibit that remains in our minds long after our visit involved a grove of Bermudian cedars that were covered by rising waters during the melting of glaciers after the last ice age, and which were ripped off the sea bed by one of Tucker's crew—proof positive of (relatively) recent drastic fluctuations in sea level.

40 Crow Lane, Pembroke Parish. www.buei.org. ✆ **441/292-7219.** Admission $13 adults, $10 seniors, $6 ages 6–16, children 5 and under free. Mon–Fri 9am–5pm; Sat–Sun 10am–5pm. Last ticket sold at 4pm.

Cathedral of the Most Holy Trinity (Bermuda Cathedral) CATHEDRAL This is the mother church of the Anglican diocese in Bermuda. It became a cathedral in 1894 and was formally consecrated in 1911. The building features a reredos (ornamental partition), stained-glass windows, and ornate carvings. If you have the stamina, climb the 157 steps to the top of the tower for a panoramic view of the City of Hamilton and the harbor.

Church St. www.anglican.bm. ✆ **441/292-4033.** Free admission to cathedral; admission to cathedral tower $3 adults, $2 children 6 and under and seniors 65 and over. Cathedral Mon–Fri 9:30am–4:30pm and for Sun services; tower Mon–Fri 10am–3pm.

Hamilton City Hall & Arts Centre CULTURAL INSTITUTION The City Hall, also home of the **Bermuda Society of Arts,** is an imposing white structure with a giant weather vane and wind clock to tell maritime-minded Bermudians which way the wind is blowing. Completed in 1960, the building is the seat of the City of Hamilton's municipal government. The theater on the first floor books stage, music, and dance productions throughout the year, and is the main site of the Bermuda Festival. The Bermuda National Gallery (see above) is also here.

Since 1956, the Bermuda Society of Arts has encouraged and provided a forum for contemporary artists, sculptors, and photographers. Its gallery, with ever-changing exhibitions, displays the work of local and visiting artists.

17 Church St. ✆ **441/292-1234** or 441/292-3824. Free admission to City Hall and Bermuda Society of Arts. City Hall Mon–Fri 9am–5pm, Sat 9am–noon; Bermuda Society of Arts Mon–Sat 10am–4pm.

Perot Post Office ARCHITECTURE/GOVERNMENT BUILDING Bermuda's first stamp was printed in this landmark building. Beloved by collectors from all over the world, the stamps—signed by William Bennett Perot, Bermuda's first postmaster—are priceless. It's said that Perot and his friend J. B. Heyl, who ran an apothecary, conceived of the first postage stamp to protect the post office from cheaters. People used to stop off at the post office and leave letters, but not enough pennies to send them. The postage stamps were printed in black or carmine.

Philatelists can purchase contemporary Bermuda stamps here. For its 375th anniversary, Bermuda issued a series of stamps honoring its discovery in 1609. One stamp portrays the admiral of the fleet, Sir George Somers, along with Sir Thomas Gates, the captain of the *Sea Venture*. Another depicts the settlement of Jamestown, Virginia, which was on the verge of extinction when Sir George and the survivors of the Bermuda shipwreck finally arrived with supplies late in 1610. A third shows the *Sea Venture* stranded on the coral reefs of Bermuda. Yet another shows the entire fleet, originally bound for Jamestown, leaving Plymouth, England, on June 2, 1609.

Queen St., at the entrance to Par-la-Ville Park. ℂ **441/292-9052** or 441/295-5151. Free admission. Mon–Fri 9am–5pm.

Sessions House ARCHITECTURE/GOVERNMENT BUILDING   This Italian Renaissance–style structure was originally built in 1819. Its clock tower, added in 1887, commemorates the Golden Jubilee of Queen Victoria. The House of Assembly meets on the second floor from November to May, and visitors are permitted in the gallery. Call ahead to find out when meetings are scheduled. On the lower level, the chief justice presides over the Supreme Court.

21 Parliament St. ℂ **441/292-7408.** Free admission. Daily 9am–12:30pm and 2–6pm. Tours, if demand warrants, Mon–Thurs at 10:30am and 2:30pm.

DEVONSHIRE PARISH

If you're passing through Devonshire, consider a stop at the following attractions.

Old Devonshire Parish Church CHURCH   The Old Devonshire Parish Church is believed to have been built on this site in 1624, although the present foundation dates from 1716. An explosion virtually destroyed the church at Easter in 1970, but it was reconstructed. Today, the tiny structure looks more like a vicarage than a church. Some of the church's contents survived the blast, including silver dating from 1590, which may be the oldest on the island. The Old Devonshire Parish Church is about a 15-minute walk northwest of the "new" Devonshire Parish Church, which dates from 1846.

Middle Rd. ℂ **441/236-3671.** Free admission. Daily 9am–5:30pm. Bus: 2.

Palm Grove HISTORIC HOME   This private estate, 4km (2½ miles) east of the City of Hamilton, is one of the delights of Devonshire Parish. It's famous for its pond, which features a relief map of Bermuda in the middle. On the map, each parish is an immaculately manicured grassy division. The site, which has well-landscaped flower gardens, opens onto a view of the sea.

38 South Rd. No phone. Free admission. Mon–Thurs 8am–5pm. Bus: 1.

SMITH'S PARISH

Even if you're staying in remote Sandys Parish, the 18th-century mansion of Verdmont is worth checking out. If you're in the area, Spittal Pond Nature Reserve also merits some attention.

The Sounds of Silence (& Gregorian Chant)

In crowded Bermuda, finding solitude and tranquility grows increasingly more difficult. But we stumbled upon the 18-hectare (43-acre) **Heydon Trust Estate,** Heydon Drive (© 441/234-1831), in Sandys Parish, open daily dawn to dusk. This setting, which is also a sanctuary for migratory birds, is Bermuda the way it used to be. The grounds are filled with flower gardens, citrus orchards, walkways, and even a tiny chapel dating from 1620. Park benches are positioned throughout the preserve where you can sit and contemplate nature (or your navel).

Spittal Pond Nature Reserve NATURE RESERVE   Follow steep Knapton Hill Road west to South Road, turning at the sign for Spittal Pond, Bermuda's largest wildlife sanctuary. The most important of the National Trust's open spaces, it occupies 24 hectares (59 acres) and attracts about 25 species of waterfowl from November to May. Visitors are asked to stay on the scenic trails and footpaths provided. Bird-watchers especially like to visit in January, when as many as 500 species can be observed wintering on or near the pond.

South Rd. © **441/236-6483.** Free admission. Daily sunrise–sunset. Bus: 1 or 3.

Verdmont ★ HISTORIC HOME   This 18th-century mansion is especially significant to Americans who are interested in colonial and Revolutionary War history. It stands on property that was owned in the 17th century by William Sayle, who left Bermuda to found South Carolina and become its first governor. The house was built before 1710 by John Dickinson, a prosperous ship owner who was also speaker of the House of Assembly in Bermuda from 1707 to 1710. Verdmont passed to Mr. Dickinson's granddaughter, Elizabeth, who married the Hon. Thomas Smith, collector of customs. Their oldest daughter, Mary, married Judge John Green, a Loyalist who came to Bermuda in 1765 from Philadelphia. During and after the American Revolution, Green was judge of the Vice-Admiralty Court and had the final say on prizes brought in by privateers. Many American ship owners lost their vessels because of his decisions. The house, which the National Trust now administers, contains many antiques, china, and portraits, along with the finest cedar stair balustrade on Bermuda.

6 Verdmont Lane, Collectors Hill. www.bnt.bm. © **441/236-7369.** Admission $5 adults, $2 ages 6–18, free for children 5 and under. Combination ticket to all 3 Trust Museums (Bermuda National Trust Museum, Tucker House, Verdmont) $10. May–Oct Wed, Thurs, and Fri 10am–4pm; Nov–Apr Wed 10am–4pm. Bus: 1.

HAMILTON PARISH

Even if you have limited sightseeing time, try to budget at least a half-day for Hamilton Parish. It has some of the most intriguing attractions on the island, notably the Bermuda Aquarium, Museum & Zoo; Crystal Caves; and Leamington Caves. If you have time for only one set of caves, we recommend Crystal Caves. However, if you've seen some of the great caves of America or Europe (or beyond), you may find Bermuda's caves less thrilling.

Bermuda Aquarium, Museum & Zoo ★ AQUARIUM/ZOO ☺ This complex is home to a large collection of tropical marine fish, turtles, harbor seals, and other forms of sea life. In the museum, you'll see exhibits ranging from the geological development of Bermuda to deep-sea exploration to humpback whales. The zoo is home to alligators, monkeys, and Galapagos tortoises, along with a collection of birds, including parrots and flamingos.

The **North Rock Exhibit,** a display that's modeled after an actual geological formation off Bermuda's north shore occupies a 529,958-liter (140,000-gal.) tank. It allows visitors to experience a coral reef washed by ocean surge. The tank houses a living coral reef, as well as reef and pelagic fish species. It's the first living coral exhibit on this scale in the world, made possible by the Bermuda Aquarium, Museum & Zoo's success in the science of coral husbandry.

There's parking for cycles and cars across the street from the aquarium.

40 North Shore Rd. (in Flatts Village). www.bamz.org. 🕿 **441/293-2727.** Admission $10 adults, $5 seniors and children 5–12, free for children 4 and under. Daily 9am–5pm. Closed Dec 25. Bus: 10 or 11 from the City of Hamilton or St. George. From the City of Hamilton, follow Middle Rd. or North Shore Rd. east to Flatts Village; from St. George, cross the causeway and follow North Shore Rd. or Harrington Sound Rd. west to Flatts Village.

Crystal Caves ★ ☺ NATURAL ATTRACTION This network of subterranean lakes, caves, and caverns houses translucent formations of stalagmites and stalactites, and includes the crystal-clear Cahow Lake. A sloping path and a few steps lead to Crystal Caves, which was discovered in 1907; at the bottom, about 36m (118 ft.) below the surface, is a floating causeway. It follows the winding cavern, where hidden lights illuminate the interior. In 2001, a second cave was opened to visitors. All tours through Crystal Caves are guided. Using the lighting system, the guides make shadow puppets and are fond of pointing out the similarity to the skyline of Manhattan. If you suffer from claustrophobia, you might find this space too tight. A small cafe and a gift shop are on-site.

8 Crystal Caves Rd., off Wilkinson Ave., Bailey's Bay. www.caves.bm. 🕿 **441/293-0640.** Admission to either Crystal or Fantasy Cave costs $20 adults, $8 children 5–12, free for children 4 and under. For a guided tour that incorporates visits to each of the 2 caves, adults $27 each, children 5–12 $10 each, free for children 4 and under. Daily 9:30am–4:30pm. Closed Jan 1, Good Friday, Dec 24–25, and Boxing Day. Bus: 1, 3, 10, or 11.

ST. GEORGE'S PARISH

A great way to explore this historic town is by following the "The Best of Bermuda in 1 Day" tour in chapter 3.

The Town of St. George ★★★

King's Square, also called Market Square and King's Parade, is the center of life in St. George. It holds the colorful **White Horse Tavern** (p. 142), where you may want to stop for a drink after your tour of the town.

The street names in St. George evoke its history. Petticoat Lane (sometimes called Silk Alley) reputedly got its name when two newly emancipated slaves paraded up and down the lane rustling their colorful new silk petticoats. Barber's Lane is also named for a former slave. It honors Joseph Hayne Rainey, a freedman from the Carolinas who fled to Bermuda during the Civil War aboard a blockade runner and worked as a barber. After the war, he returned to the United States and was elected to

Congress, becoming the first black member of the House of Representatives during Reconstruction.

The St. George branch of the **Visitors Information Centre** is on King's Square (✆ **441/297-1423**); March to October, it's open daily 9am to 5pm.; November to February it's open Wednesday and Saturday 10am to 4pm. Here you can get a map, transportation passes for the bus and ferry, and other information before setting out to explore. The bureau is to the right of the Town Hall, on the waterfront.

If you're pressed for time, don't worry that you're missing out if you skip interior visits to the sights listed below. The entire town of St. George, with its quaint streets and old buildings, is the attraction, not just one particular monument. If you have time to visit only one attraction's interior, make it St. Peter's Church. Otherwise, just wander around, do a little shopping, and soak in the atmosphere.

To reach these attractions, take bus no. 1, 3, 10, or 11 from the City of Hamilton.

The Bermuda National Trust Museum MUSEUM   This was once the Globe Hotel, headquarters of Maj. Norman Walker, the Confederate representative in Bermuda. Today, it houses relics from the island's involvement in the American Civil War—from a Bermudian perspective. St. George was the port from which ships carrying arms and munitions ran the Union blockade. A replica of the Great Seal of the Confederacy is fitted to a Victorian press so that visitors can emboss copies as souvenirs. There's also a video presentation, *Bermuda: Centre of the Atlantic,* tracing the island's early history.

At the Globe Hotel, King's Sq. www.bnt.bm. ✆ **441/297-1423.** Admission $5 adults, $2 children 6–18, free for children 5 and under. Combination ticket to all 3 Trust Museums (Bermuda National Trust Museum, Tucker House, Verdmont) $10. May–Oct Tues–Sat 10am–4pm; Nov–Apr Wed and Sat 10am–4pm. Free admission Fri. Closed Dec 25 and Good Friday.

Bridge House Gallery COMMERCIAL ART GALLERY   This long-established gallery displays antiques and collectibles, old Bermudian items, original paintings, and Bermuda-made crafts The house, constructed in the 1690s, was home to several of the colony's governors. Its most colorful owner was Bridger Goodrich, a Loyalist from Virginia, whose privateers once blockaded Chesapeake Bay. So devoted was he to the king that he sabotaged Bahamian vessels trading with the American colonies.

1 Bridge St. ✆ **441/297-8211.** Free admission. Wed and Sat 10am–6pm.

Carter House (St. David's Island Historical Site) HISTORIC HOME/ MUSEUM   Set on a hillside about 1.5km (1 mile) east of Swing Bridge, Carter House is believed to be the oldest dwelling place on St. David's Island, at least 3½ centuries old. Reopened in September 2001 after a 3-year renovation, it's now a museum dedicated to the life and values of the people of St. David's, one of the most rugged and hardy districts of Bermuda. The museum houses exhibitions on the history of whaling, piloting, fishing, and farming. Various artifacts of Bermudian life are displayed here, including a 4m (13-ft.) Bermuda sailing dinghy, dolls and children's toys crafted from palmetto leaves, and artifacts and paneling crafted from Bermuda cedar.

S. Side Rd. (St. David's). ✆ **441/297-1387.** Free admission (donations accepted). Apr–Sept Tues– Thurs and Sat 10am–4pm; Oct–Mar Sat 10am–4pm.

Deliverance SHIP   Across from St. George's town square and over a bridge is Ordnance Island, where visitors can see a full-scale replica of *Deliverance.* The shipwrecked survivors of the *Sea Venture* built the pinnace (small sailing ship) in 1610 to carry them on to Virginia. The replica of *Deliverance* is still anchored full time at

SPECIAL PLACES WHERE YOU CAN BE alone

Bermuda is both popular and small—but that doesn't mean that you can't escape the crowds and find peace and serenity in a lovely spot, hopefully with someone you love.

Hamilton Parish The Bermuda National Trust (www.bnt.bm. ℂ **441/ 236-6483**) administers 25 hectares (62 acres) of land at Walsingham, along Harrington Sound Road in Hamilton Parish. Bus no. 1 or 3 runs to the site, and hours are daily dawn to dusk, with no admission charged. The site of Walsingham that visitors, especially bird-watchers, find most appealing is called the **Idwal Hughes Nature Reserve,** which takes up only .5 hectare (1¼ acres) of the lush Walsingham wilderness area sometimes called "Tom Moore's Jungle" by islanders. Walking is rather challenging here, but rewarding because of the scenic landscape and the bird life. Access to the Idwal Hughes Nature Reserve is from the road leading down to Tom Moore's Tavern off Harrington Sound Road. Access is also possible through **Blue Hole Park** (take bus no. 1, 3, 10, or 11 to the Grotto Bay Hotel bus stop), which features its own trails for bird-watching and a wooden deck where you can view a water-filled sunken cave.

Sandys Parish Visitors don't seem to spend a lot of time here, but for wandering about, getting lost, and finding enchanting little vistas, Sandys is without equal on Bermuda. Where Daniel's Head Road meets Cambridge Road, paths will take you to **Somerset Long Bay Park,** where you can swim. After that, take one of the unmarked trails to the **Bermuda Audubon Society Nature Reserve,** a gem of nature. The place is often deserted on weekdays. When the white-eyed vireos and the bluebirds call to you from fiddlewood trees, you'll really feel close to nature.

Southampton Parish In this wind-swept, tourist-trodden parish, you'd think there was no place to find solitude. Not so! Signposted from Middle Road, a trail goes 1km (⅔ mile) down to the entrance to **Seymour's Pond Nature Reserve.** Under the management of the Bermuda Audubon Society, this 1-hectare (2½-acre) site attracts the occasional birder as well as romantic couples looking for a little privacy. Just past the pond, you'll spot pepper trees and old cedars that escaped the blight; you might encounter bluebirds and an egret or two as well. After traversing Cross Church Road, you'll come upon the old **Bermuda**

Ordnance Island. It's one of the Disney-style adventure sights associated with the King's Square (St. George's main square). In midsummer, its caretakers are outfitted in 18th-century sailors' garb.

Ordnance Island. ℂ **441/297-1459.** Admission $3 adults, $1 children 11 and under. Apr–Nov daily 9am–5pm. Closed Dec–Mar.

Old Rectory HISTORIC HOME Built by a reformed pirate in 1705, this charming old cottage was later home to Parson Richardson, who was nicknamed "the Little Bishop." Now a private home, it's administered by the Bermuda National Trust.

At the head of Broad Alley, behind St. Peter's Church. www.bnt.bm. ℂ **441/297-4261.** Free admission (donations appreciated). Nov–Mar Wed 1–5pm.

Old State House ARCHITECTURE/GOVERNMENT BUILDING Behind the Town Hall is Bermuda's oldest stone building, constructed with turtle oil and lime mortar in 1620. Unless there's a special event, the landmark building doesn't offer

Railway Trail, where in summer you can see fennel growing wild. In the distance are panoramic views of shipwreck-clogged Black Bay and Five Star Island.

Warwick Parish   With its beautiful pink sand beaches, seaside parklands, natural attractions, and winding country lanes, this is one of the most charming parishes for exploring and escaping the crowds. Even many longtime local residents haven't seen some of Warwick's beauty spots. The place to head is **Warwick Pond,** a sanctuary for several rare species of birds. Administered by the Bermuda National Trust, it's open daily from sunrise to sunset. You can reach it by following the Bermuda Railway Trail until you come to Tribe Road No. 3; climb this road for a few hundred yards before it dips down a hill to the pond. You might spot the occasional birder in search of a kiskadee, blue heron, or cardinal. The pond, fed by a subterranean channel from the sea, reminds us of Thoreau's Walden Pond.

St. David's Island   Part of St. George's Parish, St. David's is Bermuda "the way it was." Virtually unknown to the average visitor, it awaits your discovery. This is real down-home Bermuda—it's said that some St. David's Islanders have never even visited "mainland" Bermuda. You

can begin your walk at **Great Head Park** in the eastern part of St. David's, south-east of the cricket fields. At the end of the parking lot, follow the trail into a wooded area filled with cherry trees and palmettos. After about 225m (738 ft.), bear right at the fork. Eventually you'll spot **St. David's Lighthouse,** an octagonal red-and-white tower in the distance to the southwest. The trail forks left until you come to a ruined garrison with a panoramic sea view. It's one of the remotest, loveliest spots on the island—and, chances are, you'll have it all to yourself.

Devonshire Parish   This parish is off the beaten track but home to some lovely spots—if you're adventurous enough to seek them out. **Old Devonshire Parish Church** on Middle Road is a landmark; almost directly across the road lies Devonshire Marsh, a natural water basin still in an untamed state. You'll also find two nature reserves, **Firefly and Freer Cox Memorial,** on some 4 hectares (10 acres) of marshland. The Bermuda Audubon Society has set aside this protected area as a bird sanctuary for many endangered wild species. You can also see some of the most unusual Bermudian plants, including orchids. The marsh is always open to the public.

much to see—you might settle for a look at the exterior, then continue on with your sightseeing. The Old State House, where meetings of the legislative council once took place, was eventually turned over to the Freemasons of St. George. The government asked the annual rent of one peppercorn and insisted on the right to hold meetings here upon demand. The Masonic Lodge members, in a ceremony filled with pageantry, still turn over one peppercorn in rent to the Bermuda government every April.

The annual **Peppercorn Ceremony,** a 45-minute spectacle, takes place in early to mid-April. The ceremony begins around 11am with the gathering of the Bermuda Regiment on King's Square. Then the premier, mayor, and other dignitaries arrive, amid the bellowing introductions of the town crier. As soon as all the principals have taken their places, a 17-gun salute is fired as the governor and his wife make a grand entrance. His Excellency inspects a military guard of honor while the Bermuda Regiment Band plays. The stage is now set for the presentation of the peppercorn, which sits on a silver plate atop a velvet cushion. Payment is made in a grand and formal

st. george: A WORLD HERITAGE SITE

Historic St. George and its related fortifications are now a World Heritage Site designated by UNESCO. The architecturally rich, 400-year-old town joins such select sites as the Great Wall of China, Statue of Liberty, Taj Mahal, and historic center of Florence.

As the oldest continuously inhabited town of English origin in the Western Hemisphere, St. George and its surrounding buildings, monuments, and structures illustrate the residents' lifestyles through the 17th, 18th, and 19th centuries. Historic St. George remains in authentic condition, featuring unique and diverse examples of Bermudian architecture spanning the past 4 centuries. The town's various forts are like a textbook illustrating British artillery and the changing styles of fort architecture from 1612 to 1956.

manner, after which the Old State House is immediately used for a meeting of Her Majesty's Council.

Princess St. ✆ **441/296-8766** for appointments. Free admission. May–Nov Wed 10am–2pm or by appointment.

Somers Garden PARK/GARDEN   The heart of Sir George Somers was buried here in 1610; a stone column perpetuates the memory of Bermuda's founder. The garden was opened in 1920 by the Prince of Wales (later King Edward VIII, and then the Duke of Windsor). A large fountain has been built in the middle of the garden to enhance its beauty, where visitors may also take pictures, using the foundation for a background.

Duke of York St. ✆ **441/297-1532.** Free admission. Daily 8am–4pm.

St. George's Historical Society Museum MUSEUM   Set in a home built around 1700, this museum contains an original 18th-century Bermuda kitchen, complete with utensils from that period. Other exhibits include a 300-year-old Bible, a letter from George Washington, and Native American ax heads. Some early settlers on St. David's Island were Native Americans, mainly Pequot.

Duke of Kent St. www.stgeorgesfoundation.org. ✆ **441/297-0423.** Admission $5 adults, $2 children 12 and under. Apr–Nov Mon–Thurs and Sat 10am–4pm; Jan–Mar Wed and Sat 10am–4pm Closed Dec.

St. Peter's Church ★ CHURCH   From King's Square, head east to Duke of York Street, where you'll find St. Peter's Church, the oldest Anglican place of worship in the Western Hemisphere. Colonists built the original church in 1612 almost entirely of cedar, with a palmetto-leaf thatched roof. A hurricane in 1712 almost destroyed it completely. Some of the interior, including the original altar from 1615 (still used daily), was salvaged, and the church was rebuilt in 1713. It has been restored many times since, providing excellent examples of the architectural styles of the 17th to the 20th century. The tower was added in 1814. Before the Old State House was built, the colony held public meetings in the church. The first assize (legislative assembly) convened here in 1616, and the first meeting of Parliament was held in 1620. The church holds Sunday and weekday services.

Some of the tombstones in the Graveyard of St. Peter's (entrance opposite Broad Alley) are more than 3 centuries old; many tombs mark the graves of slaves. Here

5

St. George's Parish

SEEING THE SIGHTS

you'll find the grave of Midshipman Richard Dale, an American who was the last victim of the War of 1812. The churchyard also holds the tombs of Gov. Sir Richard Sharples and his aide, Capt. Hugh Sayers, who were assassinated while strolling on the grounds of Government House in 1973.

Duke of York St. www.anglican.bm. ✆ **441/297-8359.** Free admission (donations appreciated). Daily 10am–4:30pm; Sun services 11am; guide available Mon–Sat.

Town Hall GOVERNMENT BUILDING   Officers of the Corporation of St. George's, headed by a mayor, meet in the Town Hall, located near the Visitors Information Centre. There are three aldermen and five common councilors. The Town Hall holds a collection of Bermuda cedar furnishings, along with photographs of previous mayors.

7 King's Sq. ✆ **441/297-1532.** Free admission. Mon–Sat 10am–4pm.

Tucker House Museum MUSEUM   This was the home of the well-known Tucker family of England, Bermuda, and Virginia. It displays a notable collection of Bermudian furniture, portraits, and silver. Also in the Tucker House is the Joseph Rainey Memorial Room, where Joseph Hayne Rainey (mentioned above in the section on "The Town of St. George") practiced barbering. A new exhibit on the ground floor traces the archaeological history of the site. The kitchen, now restored, has become an exhibit for visitors to see.

5 Water St. www.bnt.bm. ✆ **441/297-0545.** Admission $5 adults, $2 children 6–18, free for children 5 and under. Combination ticket to all 3 Trust Museums (Bermuda National Trust Museum, Tucker House, Verdmont) $10. May–Oct Tues–Sat 10am–2pm; Nov–Apr Wed and Sat 10am–2pm.

Unfinished Church CHURCH/RUIN   After leaving Somers Garden, head up the steps to the North Gate, which opens onto Blockade Alley. The structure here is known as the "folly of St. George's." The cathedral, begun in 1874, was intended to replace St. Peter's. But the planners ran into money problems, and a schism within the church developed. As if that weren't enough, a storm swept over the island, causing considerable damage to the structure. Result: the Unfinished Church.

Blockade Alley. www.bnt.bm. No phone. Free admission. Apr–Nov daily 9am–3pm.

Historic Forts That Never Saw Much Action

From its earliest days, St. George has been fortified. Although it never saw much military action, reminders of that history are interesting to explore. Take Circular Drive to reach the forts, on the outskirts of town. As forts go, these two are of relatively minor interest (unless, of course, you're a fort buff—in that case, be our guest). If you have time for only one fort on Bermuda, Fort Hamilton on Happy Valley Road is the most intriguing. See "Iconic Bermuda in 2 Days," in chapter 3, for details.

Along the coast is Building Bay, where the shipwrecked victims of the *Sea Venture* built their vessel, the *Deliverance* (p. 101), in 1610.

Fort St. Catherine ★ HISTORIC SITE   Towering above the beach where the shipwrecked crew of the *Sea Venture* came ashore in 1609 is Fort St. Catherine, completed in 1614 and named for the patron saint of wheelwrights and carpenters. The fortifications have been upgraded over the years. The last major reconstruction took place from 1865 to 1878, so the fort's appearance today is largely the result of work done in the 19th century.

In the museum, visitors first see a series of dioramas, "Highlights in Bermuda's History." Figures depict various activities that took place in the magazine of the fort, restored and refurnished as it was in the 1880s. In the keep, which served as living quarters, you can see information on local and overseas regiments that served in Bermuda. Also here are a fine small-arms exhibit, a cooking-area display, and an exhibit of replicas of England's crown jewels. There's a short audiovisual show on St. George's defense systems and the forts of St. George.

15 Coot Pond Rd. © **441/297-1920.** Admission $7 adults, $3 children 11 and under. Mon–Fri 10am–4pm. Closed Dec 25–26.

Gates Fort HISTORIC SITE   This small-scale, partially ruined two-story watchtower is capped with a cannon that (symbolically) monitors the entrance to St. George's harbor. With an interior of only two square and angular rooms, it was originally built in 1609 by its namesake, Sir Thomas Gates. One of the original band of settlers from the *Sea Venture* who colonized Bermuda, Gates was later the governor-designate for the Colony of Virginia. In midsummer, when cruise ships drop their anchors for short sojourns in St. George, a gatekeeper in 18th-century costume sometimes hails onboard passengers with a "welcome to Bermuda" spate of bell ringing and an occasional cannon blast. There's virtually nothing to see inside—the allure is entirely a byproduct of its isolated charm near the harbor's entrance.

Cut Rd. No phone. Free admission. Daily 10am–4:30pm.

ESPECIALLY FOR KIDS

Bermuda is a great destination for the entire family. Most resorts offer children's activities and special family packages. Most of the larger properties also give Mom and Dad an opportunity to spend some time alone by offering babysitting services for minimal fees.

More importantly, Bermuda offers many activities that will keep kids interested all day long. Kid-friendly activities include sailing, water-skiing, snorkeling, and glass-bottom-boat trips from April to October, plus tennis, visits to museums and caves, and a wide array of walking tours. Here are some of Bermuda's top sights and activities for kids:

Bermuda Aquarium, Museum & Zoo (p. 100)   This complex offers kids a wonderful introduction to the undersea world. Hand-held recordings let you listen to a history of marine life as you visit live exhibits of Bermuda's native fish.

Bermuda National Museum (also known as the Bermuda Maritime Museum) (p. 89)   Everyone in the family takes equal delight in seeing the exhibits of Bermuda's nautical history in this authentic Victorian fortress museum. Although exhibits are scattered around the grounds of a half dozen outbuildings, its centerpiece, the Commissioner's House, is packed with enough references to the historical dramas of yesteryear to keep preteens diverted and amused.

Bermuda Railway Trail   This nature walk, with strolls overlooking the seashore and along quiet tree-lined alleyways, is suitable for the entire family. You can pick up the 34km (21-mile) trail at many points and explore as many sections as you like, according to your stamina and interests. See "Rattle & Shake: The Bermuda Railway Trail" on p. 55.

Crystal Caves (p. 100)   Two boys chasing a runaway ball in 1907 discovered an enormous cavern and an underground lake. Easily navigable walkways and informative guides take parents and kids down into the caverns in Hamilton Parish.

ORGANIZED TOURS

It's relatively easy to explore Bermuda on your own. But if you prefer help from island-born and -bred residents, it's available. See also "Snorkeling," "Scuba Diving," and "Other Outdoor Pursuits," in chapter 4, for other ways to tour the island.

Insider Tours

ART & ARCHITECTURE WALK   A preopening-hours tour starts at the Bermuda National Gallery (p. 96) with a museum curator, then continues into the town of Hamilton. Guests receive a map of art in public places and local galleries and can meet with the gallery owners or artists on their own.

VERDMONT HISTORIC HOUSE MUSEUM   A historian from the National Trust accompanies visitors on a private tour of Verdmont (p. 99). Built in 1710, the house contains Bermuda's most notable collection of antique cedar-wood furniture, portraits, and toys.

Environmental Tours

The not-for-profit **Bermuda Institute of Ocean Sciences** has collected the world's most comprehensive data on the oceanographic absorption of human-released carbon dioxide. It has tracked carbon dioxide levels for more than 40 years over a 21km (13-mile) area southeast of Bermuda. The National Science Foundation awarded the station a $500,000 grant to study climate change, the greenhouse effect, and the carbon cycle. The station has also compiled an extensive record on acid rain in the North American atmosphere.

You can learn firsthand what the station's scientists are studying by taking a free guided tour of the grounds and laboratory in St. George. Guides explain what scientific studies are being conducted in Bermuda and how they relate to the overall world environment. They also discuss the island's natural areas, including the coral reefs, which are protected by strict conservation laws, and how humans have produced changes in the fragile ecological environment.

Trained volunteers and scientists who are carrying out studies conduct the educational tours. Visitors should assemble before 10am in the Biological Station's Hanson Hall. For more information, contact the Bermuda Biological Station for Research, 17 Biological Lane, Ferry Reach, St. George (www.bios.edu; ✆ **441/297-1880**). The tour, offered every Wednesday at 10am year-round, is free. It lasts about an hour.

SIGHTS & ATTRACTIONS BY THEME INDEX

Architecture

Old State House, City of St. George (p. 102)
Perot Post Office, City of Hamilton (p. 97)
Sessions House, City of Hamilton (p. 98)

Aquarium/Zoo

Bermuda Aquarium, Museum & Zoo ★, Hamilton Parish (p. 100)

Art Museums

Bermuda National Gallery, City of Hamilton (p. 96)
The Masterworks Museum of Bermuda Art ★★, Paget Parish (p. 93)

Biking/Hiking Trail

Bermuda Railway Trail, Southampton Parish (p. 55)

Cathedral

Cathedral of the Most Holy Trinity, City of Hamilton (Bermuda Cathedral) (p. 97)

Churches

Christ Church, Warwick Parish (p. 92)
Cobb's Hill Wesleyan Methodist Church, Pembroke Parish (p. 96)
Old Devonshire Parish Church, Devonshire Parish (p. 98)
St. James' Anglican Church, Sandys Parish (p. 88)
Slave Graveyard/St. Peter's Church ★, City of St. George (p. 104)
Unfinished Church, City of St. George (p. 105)

Commercial Art Galleries

Bermuda Arts Centre, Sandys Parish (p. 89)
The Birdsey Studio, Paget Parish (p. 92)
Bridge House Gallery, Town of St. George (p. 101)

Cultural Institution

Hamilton City Hall & Arts Centre, City of Hamilton (p. 97)

Government Buildings

Government House, City of Hamilton (p. 94)
Old State House, City of St. George (p. 102)
Perot Post Office, City of Hamilton (p. 97)
Sessions House, City of Hamilton (p. 98)
Town Hall, City of St. George (p. 105)

Historic Homes

Carter House (St. David's Island Historical Site), St. David's Island (p. 101)
Old Rectory, City of St. George (p. 102)
Palm Grove, Devonshire Parish (p. 98)
Verdmont ★, Smith's Parish (p. 99)
Waterville, Paget Parish (p. 93)

Historic Sites

Black Watch Well, City of Hamilton (p. 94)
Fort Hamilton, City of Hamilton (p. 95)
Fort St. Catherine ★, St. George's Parish (p. 105)
Gates Fort, St. George's Parish (p. 106)
Gibbs Hill Lighthouse ★, Southampton Parish (p. 92)
Royal Naval Dockyard ★★★, Sandys Parish (p. 88)
Scaur Hill Fort Park ★, Sandys Parish (p. 88)
St. David's Lighthouse, St. David's Island (p. 103)

Sights & Attractions by Theme Index

SEEING THE SIGHTS

Icon

Somerset Bridge, Sandys Parish (p. 88)

Market

Bermuda Craft Market, Sandys Parish (p. 89)

Museums

Bermuda Historical Society Museum, City of Hamilton (p. 95)
Bermuda National Museum (Bermuda Maritime Museum), Sandys Parish (p. 89)
Bermuda National Trust Museum, Town of St. George (p. 101)
Bermuda Underwater Exploration Institute (BUEI), City of Hamilton (p. 97)
Carter House (St. David's Island Historical Site), St. David's Island (p. 101)
St. George's Historical Society Museum, City of St. George (p. 104)
Tucker House Museum, City of St. George (p. 105)

Natural Attraction

Crystal Caves ★, Hamilton Parish (p. 100)

Nature Reserves

Bermuda Audubon Society Nature Reserve, Sandys Parish (p. 102)
Firefly Nature Reserve, Devonshire Parish (p. 103)
Freer Cox Memorial Nature Reserve, Devonshire Parish (p. 103)
Gilbert Nature Reserve, Sandys Parish (p. 85)
Heydon Trust Estate, Smith's Parish (p. 99)
Idwal Hughes Nature Reserve, Hamilton Parish (p. 102)
Paget Marsh, Paget Parish (p. 93)
Seymour's Pond Nature Reserve, Southampton Parish (p. 102)
Spittal Pond Nature Reserve, Smith's Parish (p. 99)
Warwick Pond, Warwick Parish (p. 103)

Parks/Gardens

Admiralty House Park, Pembroke Parish (p. 94)
Botanical Gardens ★, Paget Parish (p. 92)
Great Head Park, St. David's Island (p. 103)
Heydon Trust Estate, Sandys Parish (p. 99)
Hog Bay Park, Sandys Parish (p. 89)
Somers Garden, City of St. George (p. 104)

Ship

Deliverance, City of St. George (p. 101)

Square

King's Square/Market /King's Parade, City of St. George (p. 100)

5

SEEING THE SIGHTS | Sights & Attractions by Theme Index

WHERE TO EAT

Wahoo steak, shark hash, mussel pie, fish chowder laced with rum and sherry peppers, Hoppin' John (black-eyed peas and rice), and the succulent spiny Bermuda lobster (called "guinea chick") await you in Bermuda. Of course, you won't find these dishes on all menus, as many resorts and mainstream restaurants specialize in a more Continental or international cuisine. But for a true taste of Bermuda, search the menu for local grub.

Bermudian food has improved in recent years, but dining out is still not a major reason to visit the island. American and British dishes are common. Innovative gourmet fare often isn't—although the prices might suggest you're getting something special. Dining in Bermuda is generally more expensive than it is in the United States and Canada. Because virtually everything except fish must be imported, restaurant prices are closer to those in Europe.

In general, it's not a good idea to order meat very often; it's flown in, and you can't be sure how long it has been in storage. Whenever possible, stick to local food; for a main course, that usually means fish. The seafood, especially Bermuda rockfish, is generally excellent—that is, when local fishers have caught something that day. Sometimes the waters are too rough for fishing. A lot of fish is imported frozen from the United States; you may want to ask before you order. To find the dishes that are truly worthy, you'll have to pick and choose your way carefully through the menu—and that's where we come in.

Most restaurants, at least the better ones, prefer that men wear a jacket and tie after 6pm; women usually wear casual, chic clothing in the evening. Of course, as most of the world dresses more and more casually, Bermuda's dress codes have loosened up a bit—but this is still a more formal destination than many other islands. It's always wise to ask about required dress when you're reserving a table. During the day, no matter what the establishment, be sure to wear a coverup—don't arrive for lunch sporting a bikini.

Because of the absence of inexpensive transportation, many travelers on a budget eat dinner at their hotels. If you like to dine around and you're concerned about cost, find a hotel that offers a variety of dining options, or stay in or near the City of Hamilton.

best RESTAURANT BETS

o **Best for Families: Palm Court** (p. 139) at the Grotto Bay Beach resort, has a staff that's most gracious in welcoming families. Children tend to go for the burgers and well-stuffed sandwiches, and especially the pizzas straight from the oven, instead of the more elaborate fare served in many Bermudian restaurants. By 6:30pm, the tables start filling up with families that find the pricing affordable.

A Note on Reservations

Nearly all major restaurants prefer that you make a reservation; many popular places require that you do so as far in advance as possible. Weekends in summer can be especially crowded. Some repeat visitors make their reservations for the most popular spots before they leave home.

o **Best Bang for Your Buck:** Grab a great sandwich at **Paradiso Cafe** (p. 134) in the City of Hamilton, one of the city's most consistently crowded lunch spots, with big voyeuristic front windows that allow peekaboo views of the passersby.

o **Best Splurge:** The **Waterlot Inn** (p. 116) is one of our all-time favorites for a special night in Bermuda. Over the years, it has attracted such guests as Mark Twain, James Thurber, Eleanor Roosevelt, and Eugene O'Neill. Each of the three dining rooms are filled with captain's and Windsor chairs, oil paintings of old clipper ships, and lots of exposed wood.

o **Most Romantic:** For romance, with touches of Bermudian history thrown in, head for **Tom Moore's Tavern** (p. 138) in Hamilton Parish, which was built as a private home in 1652. It once housed Thomas Moore, the Irish romantic poet, and a sense of tragic romance still lingers in a refined setting with a classic French and Mediterranean menu.

o **Best Service**: **Tamarisk Dining Room** (p. 114), the signature restaurant within the West End's most elegant cottage colony, Cambridge Beaches Resort, is the top dining spot in the parish for classic cuisine and for innovative fare, boasts a formal decor and impeccable service.

o **Best Sushi:** You'll find some of the best sushi at the **Harbourfront Restaurant & Komodaru Sushi Lounge,** in the basement of the Bermuda Underwater Exploration Institute (BUEI) on the outskirts of the City of Hamilton.

o **Best British Pub Grub: Hog Penny** (p. 132) in the City of Hamilton, has paneled rooms decorated with old fishing and farm tools, bentwood chairs, and antique mirrors. Fish and chips and steak-and-kidney pie are the perennial favorites, comparable to what you'd find in a London pub.

o **Best Ice Cream: Bailey's Ice Cream & Food D'Lites Restaurant** (p. 140) in Hamilton Parish, has all-natural, homemade ice cream, ranging from Bermuda banana, coconut, cherries and white chocolate chips, and other exotic flavors.

o **Best Chinese & Thai: Chopsticks Restaurant** (p. 131) in the City of Hamilton where the chef concocts Szechuan, Hunan, Thai, and Cantonese dishes, with an emphasis on fresh vegetables and delicate sauces.

o **Best Bermuda Seafood:** For a wide sampling from local waters, go to the **Bolero Brasserie,** on Front Street in the City of Hamilton. Here you can enjoy the best of the day's catch, preceded by a bowl of Bermuda fish chowder.

SANDYS PARISH

The following restaurants are all on Somerset Island.

Expensive

Breezes ★★ INTERNATIONAL   This pleasant alfresco restaurant is the less formal dining option within the upscale Cambridge Beaches Resort in the west of the

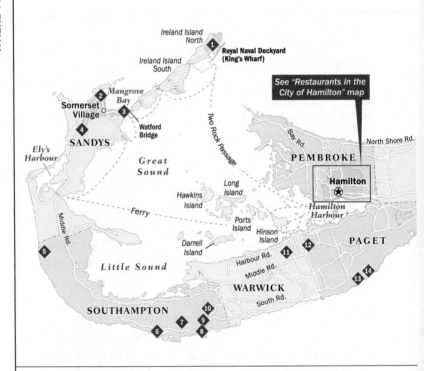

ATLANTIC OCEAN

Ireland Island North

Royal Naval Dockyard (King's Wharf)

Ireland Island South

Mangrove Bay

Somerset Village

Watford Bridge

SANDYS

Ely's Harbour

Great Sound

Two Rock Passage

See "Restaurants in the City of Hamilton" map

Bay Rd.

North Shore Rd.

PEMBROKE

Hamilton

Long Island

Hawkins Island

Ferry

Ports Island

Hinson Island

Darrell Island

Middle Rd.

Little Sound

Hamilton Harbour

PAGET

Harbour Rd.

Middle Rd.

WARWICK

South Rd.

SOUTHAMPTON

0   1 mi
0   1 km

✈ Airport

Bacci **10**
Bailey's Ice Cream & Food D'Lites Restaurant **22**
Beau Rivage **11**
The Bermudiana/The Breakers **15**
Black Horse Tavern **25**
Blû **11**
Bonefish Bar & Grill **1**
Breezes **2**
Café Amici **1**

Café Coco **14**
Coconuts **6**
Dining Room at The Lighthouse Restaurant **7**
Fourways Inn **12**
Freeport Seafood Restaurant **1**
Frog & Onion Pub **1**
Henry VIII **8**
Landfall **20**
The Lido **13**

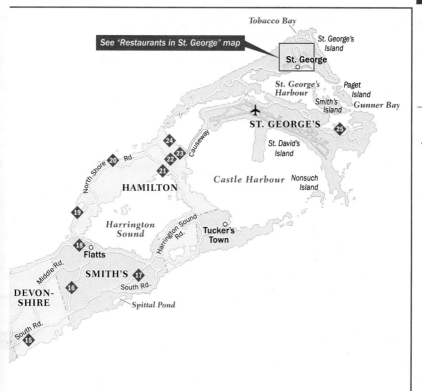

See "Restaurants in St. George" map

Tobacco Bay

St. George's
Island

St. George

St. George's
Harbour

Paget
Island

Smith's
Island

Gunner Bay

ST. GEORGE'S

St. David's
Island

Castle Harbour

Nonsuch
Island

HAMILTON

North Shore Rd.

Harrington
Sound

Harrington Sound Rd.

Tucker's
Town

Flatts

SMITH'S

DEVON-
SHIRE

Middle Rd.

South Rd.

Spittal Pond

South Rd.

ATLANTIC
OCEAN

Mickey's Beach Bistro & Bar 13
North Rock Brewing Company 17
Ocean Club 10
Ocean Echo 6
Ocean Grill & The Cedar Room 5
Palm Court 24
The Point Restaurant 18
Royston's 6
Rustico 19
Salt Rock Grill & Sushi Bar 3

Somerset Country Squire
  Pub & Restaurant 4
Specialty Inn 16
Swizzle Inn Bailey's Bay 23
Tamarisk Dining Room 2
Tio Pepe 9
Tom Moore's Tavern 21
Waterlot Inn 10
Wickets 10

island. Open to breezes and a view of the sea, it lives up to its name. You can dine on the covered veranda attractively positioned beside one of the resort's five beaches, where barbecues are sometimes held. Most diners at lunch opt for freshly made and well-stuffed sandwiches or crisp salads with tantalizing dressings. At night, steaks shipped in from the mainland and seafood (some freshly caught) are offered. The chef features a seafood market concept for dinner: You choose from a wide array of fish options and then you tell the chef to cook it to your taste.

30 King's Point Rd., Somerset. www.cambridgebeaches.com. © **441/234-0331.** Reservations required for dinner. Lunch main courses $12–$22; dinner main courses $24–$52. AE, MC, V. Daily noon–3pm and Wed–Sun 7–9:30pm. Closed Oct–May. Bus: 7 or 8 (each marked "Dockyard").

Tamarisk Dining Room ★★ INTERNATIONAL This, the signature restaurant within the West End's most elegant cottage colony, is the top dining spot in the parish for classic cuisine and also for innovative fare. Tamarisk boasts a formal decor and impeccable service.

The high-ceilinged and very large dining room has the kind of decor you might associate with an extremely sophisticated country club: tones of salmon and lime-green in big-patterned jungle themes, limed wood, and a heavily trussed and beamed ceiling. In warm weather, sliding glass doors extend the dining area onto a rambling, east-facing terrace that overlooks the bay.

At lunch, you're likely to come across platters of chicken-macadamia salad, a signature pita-bread sandwich (stuffed, California-style, with chicken salad, avocado slices, and bean sprouts), and some of the best cheeseburgers in the parish. The dinner menu changes every night, and depending on the season, might include a mousse of foie gras; shrimp cocktail; snails in garlic butter; chargrilled vegetables fashioned into a spicy terrine; grilled lobster tail with drawn butter; tamarind-glazed mahimahi; duck breast roulade; pan-seared sea scallops with mango, pineapple, sweet chile salsa, and saffron oil; and a rack of lamb with mustard and garden-herb crust. Dessert might include a terrine of prunes with vanilla ice cream. Live entertainment is featured April through October.

At Cambridge Beaches Resort, 30 Kings Point Rd. © **441/234-0331.** Reservations required. Jacket optional for men dining inside, not for those dining on terrace. Dinner main courses $25–$55. AE, MC, V. Daily noon–3pm and 7–9pm. Closed at random intervals, depending on business, in winter. Bus: 7 or 8 (each marked "Dockyard").

Moderate

Bonefish Bar & Grill MEDITERRANEAN/SEAFOOD Overlooking a landlocked piazza within the Dockyard Complex, this bar and grill offers a diverse menu that pleases diners who aren't too jaded or too demanding. If you want filling and satisfying food, it's a suitable choice, though it's not quite on par with the **Frog & Onion Pub** (p. 116). There are a limited number of tables inside, a fact that encourages most diners to head for the tables on the large piazza outside. Livio Ferigo, the likable owner, prepares chicken casseroles, rib-eye steaks, lightly braised tuna with black olives, several tempting pastas, and lots of seafood. There's live entertainment, usually presented every Monday and Wednesday from 9 to 11:30pm.

Royal Naval Dockyard. www.bermuda.com/bonefish. © **441/234-5151.** Lunch main courses $8–$26; dinner main courses $16–$29. AE, MC, V. Daily 11:30am–10:30pm (drinks and light fare till 1am in summer). Closed Jan–Mar. Bus: 7 or 8, or ferry from the City of Hamilton.

Café Amici ITALIAN A pub-cum-restaurant, this luncheon eatery lies within the Clocktower Building's shopping mall at the historic Royal Dockyard. The setting is casual and simple—its decor of beige and brown tiles and nondescript furniture doesn't contribute to a setting that's particularly cozy. Nonetheless, it's a worthwhile choice for meals throughout the day, as well as for afternoon tea. An extensive lunch menu includes pastas, pizzas, steaks, fried chicken, burgers, salads, sandwiches, and platters with fish of the day.

Clocktower Bldg., Royal Naval Dockyard. © **441/234-5009.** Reservations recommended for dinner. Smart casual attire required. Main courses $12–$28. AE, MC, V. Daily 9am–5pm (Fri–Sat till 8pm). Bus: 7 or 8, or ferry from the City of Hamilton.

Somerset Country Squire Pub & Restaurant BRITISH/SEAFOOD   You'll pass through a moon-gate arch to reach the raised terrace of this waterside restaurant in the center of the village. Limestone blocks and hedges ring the terrace; inside, the dining room is located downstairs. Steaks are popular here, with lots of them selling as part of meals that often accompany stiff drinks and beer. The bill of fare also includes British pub grub, fresh local fish, and traditional roast beef with Yorkshire pudding. Local Bermudian favorites and the specialties of the day, including curried mussel pie and fresh Bermuda tuna or wahoo, are your best bets. Some months, lobster is a big deal, with much hoopla. Most of the food is fairly routine, but the chef is especially proud of his Bermuda fish chowder, a tomato-based soup that some locals consider the best in the West End.

10 Mangrove Bay Rd., Somerset Village. © **441/234-0105.** Lunch main courses $18–$26; dinner main courses $16–$35. AE, MC, V. Daily 11:30am–4pm and 5:30–10pm. Bus: 7 or 8.

Inexpensive

**Freeport Seafood Restaurant ★ ** STEAK & SEAFOOD   Set within the foreboding walls of the Dockyard complex, and outfitted in tones of Aegean blue and white, this place represents a charming, raffish corner of maritime Italy, thanks to San Remo (Italy)–born owner Valerio Ausenda. Come here for unpretentious locally caught seafood. Somehow this old favorite manages to turn up a fresher catch than its Somerset competitors, and broils it to perfection, a welcome change from the greasy fish and chips served at some other dockyard spots. There is no great presentation or dramatic flourish to the platters served, and some aspects of the place might remind you of a tough maritime bar and grill. But the taste is often delectable, especially the fish platter or one of the broiled Bermuda rockfish dishes, our particular favorite. At least some of the seasonings derive from Signore Ausenda's herb garden, which thrives within an assortment of plastic containers in back. The menu is less formal—and less expensive—at lunch than at dinner. During the day, you get the

---

🔖 Check, Please! A Note on Service Charges

Although a service charge (typically 10%–17%) is added to most restaurant bills, it's customary to leave something extra if the service has been good. However, it isn't necessary—in fact, many diners find 15% too generous. Be on the lookout for this scam: Some restaurants include the basic 15% service charge in the bill, but leave the service charge line blank. Many diners unknowingly add another 10% to 15%, without realizing they've already paid for service. Scrutinize your bill, and don't be shy about asking if you're not sure what's included.

regular chow you'd find almost anywhere, including burgers, salads, pizzas, and steak on the grill. The tasty fish sandwich is usually the star of the lunch menu. In the evening, the fish selection might feature tuna or wahoo. For those who want a good old T-bone, those are on the menu, too. We found the lobster overpriced and over-cooked. This restaurant has a pair of Internet stations for the use of its patrons.

Royal Naval Dockyard. www.freeportseafood.com. © **441/234-1692.** Lunch main courses $10–$25; pizza $11–$15; dinner main courses $15–$27. AE, MC, V. Daily 11:30am–10pm. Bar until around midnight. Bus: 7 or 8.

The Frog & Onion Pub BRITISH   Within the dark and shadowy premises of the former 18th-century cooperage at the Royal Naval Dockyard, the Frog & Onion is the most traditional British pub in Bermuda. It's "named" for the founders, French-born Jean-Paul Magnin (the Frog, who's no longer associated with the place) and Bermuda-born Carol West (the Onion, who is). The place rambles on through at least three rock-sided dining rooms and two outdoor decks, so we recommend that you wander around to find the table that best suits your mood. You might opt to relax with a pint of English lager near the cooperage's cavernous stone fireplace, perhaps pondering the majesty of what used to be the British Empire. At lunch there are standard sandwiches, salads, and tasty bar pies. We like the version with curried mussels for a real taste of Bermuda, although you might opt for the shepherd's pie. The dinner menu includes all the lunchtime choices plus a grilled sirloin steak with mushrooms, Thai-style shrimp or chicken curries, yellowfin tuna sashimi, and melted Brie with walnuts. The food is not spectacular, but it is well prepared and hearty, and no one leaves hungry.

The Cooperage, at the Royal Naval Dockyard. www.frogandonion.bm. © **441/234-2900.** Lunch sandwiches, salads, and platters $13–$19; dinner main courses $17–$29; pub menu platters $11–$24. MC, V. Mon–Sat 11:30am–4pm and 6–9:30pm; Sun noon–4pm and 5:30–9pm. Bar daily 11:30am–midnight. Closed Mon Dec–Feb. Bus: 7 or 8, or ferry from the City of Hamilton.

Salt Rock Grill & Sushi Bar STEAK & SEAFOOD/SUSHI   At the old Loyalty Inn in Somerset, this restaurant has a panoramic terrace overlooking Mangrove Bay. It's a good choice for watching sunsets. The chefs are skilled at cooking Bermuda lobster, locally caught fish, and certified Angus beef. The price of lobster and the Angus beef depends on market conditions. There is also a sushi bar with more than 100 choices. Many locals come here to sit in the bar and watch live sports on the TVs. Daily innova-tive specialties are a regular feature. Some of the best sushi selections include a Tsu-nami Platter containing eight pieces ranging from yellowtail to crab and smoked eel. Another specialty is a Korean barbecue roll with thin slices of prime rib and a sweet potato tempura. Live music is a feature Friday to Sunday from 7:30 to 11pm.

27 Mangrove Bay Rd. www.saltrockgrillbda.com. © **441/234-4502.** Reservations recommended. Lunch main courses $12–$30; dinner main courses $20–$50. AE, MC, V. Daily noon–9:30pm. Bus: 7 or 8.

SOUTHAMPTON PARISH

Very Expensive

Waterlot Inn ★★ STEAK & SEAFOOD   Less formal than the Newport, and with a more spontaneous and less rigid staff, this is one of our all-time favorites for a special night in Bermuda. The service is alert, and the culinary repertoire is inven-tive—doubly impressive given the large number of diners every evening.

About 300 years ago, merchant sailors unloaded their cargo into the basement of this historic inn and warehouse. Over the years, it has attracted such guests as Mark

Twain, James Thurber, Eleanor Roosevelt, and Eugene O'Neill. You can enjoy a drink in an upstairs bar, where a classical pianist entertains. After descending a staircase with a white balustrade, you'll be seated in one of three conservatively nautical dining rooms. Each is filled with captain's or Windsor chairs, oil paintings of old clipper ships, and lots of exposed wood. Menu items include well-prepared steaks and beef dishes, each of them grilled and served according to your wishes. Other tasty dishes include salmon grilled with lobster roe butter, short ribs with ginger sauce, an ultra-upscale burger made with sirloin and savory herbs, seared scallops wrapped in pancetta, oysters Rockefeller, Bermuda onion soup, and breast of duck roasted with maple syrup, lentils, and foie gras. In addition, many kinds of fresh fish can be grilled, broiled, or blackened, according to your request.

At the Fairmont Southampton, 101 South Shore Rd. ✆ **441/238-8000.** Reservations recommended. Jacket required for men. Main courses $30–$85. AE, MC, V. Daily 6–10pm and Sun 11am–2pm. Closed Mon Oct–Mar. Bus: 7.

Expensive

Bacci ★ ITALIAN   On the upper floor of the golf clubhouse, on the manicured grounds of the also-recommended hotel, this restaurant is one of the best for Italian fare. Its staff describes it as "Italian with passion," thanks to excellent food and a decor that incorporates striking tones of red, black, yellow, and pastels; a bar that's busy with espresso and after-dinner-drink lovers late in the evening; and a view that sweeps down over the golf course to the sea. The chef prepares some of the best and most raved-about spaghetti carbonara and lasagna on the island, a tempting version of four-cheese ravioli with cherry tomatoes, black olives, and basil; a sumptuous *osso buco;* several types of simply grilled fresh fish (red snapper in parchment with capers and tomatoes is delicious); acclaimed versions of rib-eye steaks served over beds of risotto; and vegetarian dishes such as risotto with wild mushrooms and truffles. The restaurant's name, translates from the Piemontese dialect as "quick and friendly kisses."

In the golf clubhouse of the Fairmont Southampton, 101 South Shore Rd. ✆ **441/238-8000.** Reservations required. Main courses $12–$39. AE, DC, MC, V. Apr–Oct daily noon–3pm and 6–10pm; Nov–Mar Fri–Sun noon–3pm and Wed–Mon 6–10pm. Bus: 7.

Coconuts ★ 🏠 CARIBBEAN/AMERICAN   We recommend Coconuts not only for its scenic vista, but also for its sense of being tightly woven into the fabric of Bermuda's complicated social pecking order. Enjoying favor among long-time residents of the island, it's set between high cliff rocks and a sandy pink beach on the island's mostly residential south coast. Alfresco dining here is most romantic, although those breezy nights tend to cool your food before you've finished it.

The restaurant is based within an open-sided dining room that's partially paneled with varnished cedar. Lunch is nothing special—burgers, salads, sandwiches, and the like. But at night, the chefs strut their stuff, offering a set menu (which changes daily) full of variety and flavor, and presented with flair. Freshly grown produce is served with Cajun and West Indian spices, for a "taste of the islands." We can't guarantee what you'll get on any given night here, but the scope is wide enough to appeal to most diners—though if you're a picky eater, you'd better call ahead and check.

In the Reefs Hotel, 56 South Rd. ✆ **441/238-0222.** Reservations recommended. Lunch main courses $12–$26; dinner main courses $21–$45. AE, MC, V. Daily noon–3pm (Apr–Oct) and 7–10pm (May–Nov). Bus 7.

Ocean Club ★ ASIAN/SEAFOOD   This oceanfront restaurant, atop a low cliff overlooking rocks and pink sands, is an artfully minimalist, modern venue surrounded with clusters of sea grapes and Norfolk Island pines. The panoramic view through the huge windows is the airy restaurant's most prominent feature.

Expect a roster of Pacific Rim cuisine. Examples include steamed mussels with a coconut curry lemon-grass sauce; tuna tartare with mango; spicy Asian chicken salad; rockfish with smoked paprika, Manila clams, and chorizo sausage; and pan-seared halibut in fennel broth with shiitake mushrooms. There's live entertainment Tuesday through Sunday.

In the Fairmont Southampton, 101 South Rd. © **441/238-8000.** Reservations required. Main courses $25–$39. AE, MC, V. Daily 6–10pm. Closed Oct–Mar. Bus: 7 or 8.

Ocean Echo ★★ BERMUDIAN   This, the most formal and elegant dining room at the Reefs Hotel, enjoys a 180-degree view of the horizon from its perch high on a cliff. Patio seating for 40 diners is slightly less formal. A romantic dining experience, the restaurant has a blue-green decor, inspired by the ocean, and Bermuda cedar beams adorning the ceiling.

You can start with Bermuda classics including a rum-laced fish chowder or a traditional Bermuda fish cake with Asian black plum sauce. For your main course, try a daily fresh Bermudian delicacy, or such classics as rack of lamb crusted with mustard and fresh herbs or grilled beef tenderloin with a smoky bacon sauce and shallots glazed with Bermuda honey. There are always vegetarian options.

In the Reefs Hotel, 56 South Shore Rd. www.thereefs.com. © **441/238-0222.** Reservations required. Jackets recommended for men but not required. Main courses $32–$48. AE, MC, V. Daily 6–10pm. Bus: 7.

The Ocean Grill & The Cedar Room ★★ INTERNATIONAL   Set within the previously recommended Pompano Beach Club, this pair of restaurants offers well-prepared food and big-windowed views over some of the most dramatic seacoast in the Atlantic. The more cutting-edge and "trendy" of the two is the Ocean Grill, offering a double tier of windows with sweeping sea views, and a la carte seafood dishes that evoke a big-city dining enclave. The Cedar Room is more conservative, with furniture crafted from pre-blight cedar. It focuses on traditional North American and Bermudian mainstays. Menu items change with the seasons but are likely to include lamb chops marinated in lavender and pink peppercorns served with a port wine sauce; grilled tiger shrimp with a miso and sake glaze; 10-ounce New York strip steaks with guava-flavored black rum sauce; and a wide array of sinfully rich—and often artfully decorated—desserts such as a dark chocolate pyramid.

In the Pompano Beach Club, 36 Pompano Beach Rd. © **441/234-0222.** Reservations recommended. Set-price dinners (in Cedar Room only) $60; main courses $21–$45. AE, DC, MC, V. Cedar Room daily 6:30–9:30pm; Ocean Grill daily 7–10pm. Bus: 7 or 8.

Royston's ★ CONTINENTAL   As part of 2010's multimillion-dollar expansion of the Reefs Hotel & Club, the owners installed a formal restaurant that's one of the best bets for hotel dining on the island. The cuisine is light, full flavored, and sometimes impertinently inventive. Start with such well-crafted appetizers as beef carpaccio in white truffle oil and perhaps the freshly made cold lobster and melon bisque. Main courses feature the market-fresh catch of the day or else such meat selections as beef Wellington in a truffle sauce. Lobster ravioli is a savory delight, as is the seared halibut with a vegetable ratatouille. One of the chef's specialties is an oven-roasted Cornish hen marinated in Bermuda black rum and served with Italian couscous.

In the Reefs Hotel, 56 South Rd. www.thereefs.com. © **441/238-0222.** Reservations required. Main courses $30–$48. AE, MC, V. Daily 6:30–10pm. Bus: 7.

Putting Together the Perfect Picnic

The kitchens of many major hotels will prepare a picnic lunch for you, but you need to request it at least a day in advance. On Front Street in the City of Hamilton, you can order sandwiches at a cafe and pick up a bottle of wine or mineral water. If it's a weekday, the best place to buy picnic supplies is the **Hickory Stick** (p. 132).

If you enjoy picnicking and biking, you can do both in Sandys Parish. Start by crossing Somerset Bridge (heading in the direction of Somerset Village), and

continue along Somerset Road to **Fort Scaur Park,** where you'll enjoy a panoramic view of Ely's Harbour.

Another ideal location is **Spanish Point Park** in Pembroke, where you will find a series of little coves and beaches. You don't need to go to the trouble of packing a picnic basket—in warm weather, a lunch wagon rolls around every day at noontime. We also love to picnic at one of the island's best beaches, **Warwick Long Bay.**

Moderate

Henry VIII BRITISH/SUSHI   Within a stucco-sided, veranda-ringed building set prominently beside the parish's busiest coastal highway, this restaurant serves a clientele that's about equally divided between local residents and dining-room refugees from the relatively expensive hotels nearby. There's something that's just a bit cloying about the Tudor theme of the place—waitresses, some of them British, in long dresses of royal purple, a menu that makes coy references to Henry VIII's ongoing and oft-changing marriage vows, and a timbered and oak-paneled decor with lots of polished brass. But despite any drawbacks, the food is straightforward and a wee bit less expensive than what you'd find within the more glamorous dining rooms of nearby hotels. The menu is strong on beef dishes, especially steaks and burgers, with some pork and fish choices thrown in for variety. A sushi bar operates in a corner, surprising nearly everybody. Some kind of entertainment, usually a vocalist with a keyboard, begins at 9:30pm and runs until 1am every night of the week except Monday and Tuesday.

52 South Shore Rd. (near the Fairmont Southampton Resort). www.henrys.bm. © **441/238-1977.** Reservations recommended for dinner. Lunch main courses $11–$29; dinner main courses $28–$70; sushi platters $7–$16. Sun brunch $30 per person. AE, DC, MC, V. Daily noon–4:30pm and 6–10pm. Bus: 7.

Tio Pepe ITALIAN/SPANISH   Don't let the Spanish name fool you—the cuisine here is predominantly traditional Italian. A few Spanish dishes do appear on the menu, including roast suckling pig. It's fairly straightforward fare: pizzas, pastas, and classic Italian cuisine in generous portions, all with a bit of Mediterranean pizzazz.

Dress Up for Your Evening Out

As most of the world dresses more and more casually, Bermuda's dress codes have loosened up a bit—but this is still a more formal destination than many other islands. Most restaurants prefer that men wear a jacket and tie after 6pm; women usually

wear casual, chic clothing in the evening. It's always wise to ask about required dress when you're reserving a table. And during the day, no matter what the establishment, be sure to wear a cover-up—don't arrive for lunch sporting a bikini.

One of Bermuda's most delightful traditions is the English ritual of **afternoon tea,** which many local homes and hotels maintain.

In hotels, the typical afternoon tea is served daily from 3 to 5pm. Adding a contemporary touch, it's often served around a pool, with guests partaking in their bathing suits—a tolerated lapse from the usual formal social and dress code.

The usual accompaniments include finger sandwiches made with thinly sliced cucumber or watercress, and scones served with strawberry jam.

The kitchen also prepares local fish, plus salmon and lobster, with subtle Italian flavors. We especially like the huge range of hot appetizers; the clams steamed in white wine, garlic, and parsley; and the chef's *linguine pescatore* with mussels, clams, calamari, shrimp, and fresh tomato sauce. Seating is on a wide garden-view terrace and in three indoor dining rooms. The restaurant is convenient to the Fairmont Southampton and Horseshoe Bay Beach.

117 South Rd., Horseshoe Bay. www.tiopepebermuda.com. *©* **441/238-1897.** Reservations recommended. Dress smart casual. Lunch platters $10–$36; dinner main courses $18–$36. AE, MC, V. May–Sept daily 11:30am–10pm; Oct–Apr daily noon–10pm; lunch served until 5pm. Bus: 7.

Inexpensive

Dining Room at The Lighthouse 👶 ★ ITALIAN/CONTINENTAL If you step inside the local lighthouse, you'll find a contemporary-looking and colorful dining room where they serve Italian cuisine amid views that evoke Bermuda's long maritime traditions. It's a handy place if you're touring the south shore of Southampton Parish. After you've climbed the winding steps leading up to the famous Gibbs Hill Lighthouse, you'll have worked up an appetite. Menu items include pastas such as spaghetti with a lamb-based ragú sauce; a seafood combination platter whose preparation, despite the local fish it contains, evokes what you might have expected in a beach resort in Italy; seared tuna steak with pepper sauce; and a succulent interpretation of rack of lamb. A bar in the corner chugs out impressive numbers of both frozen smoothies and martinis.

Gibbs Hill Lighthouse, 68 St. Anne's Rd. *©* **441/238-8679.** Lunch main courses $16–$22; dinner main courses $22–$38. AE, MC, V. Daily year-round 11:30am–2pm and 6–10pm. Bus: 7 or 8.

Wickets ☺ INTERNATIONAL Outfitted like a British cricket club, this brasserie and bistro features a Sunday morning health-conscious breakfast buffet with low-calorie and low-fat options, as well as one of the most comprehensive lunch menus on the island. It's decent food—nothing more. Standard "family fare" includes deli-style sandwiches, soups, chowders, pastas, salads, and platters such as grilled steaks and veal. The most popular fish dish is codfish with potatoes, which has more flavor than the routine steaks and chops on the menu.

The restaurant, on the lower lobby level of the Fairmont Southampton, overlooks the swimming pool and the ocean beyond. Many Bermudians, with kids in tow, come here for a late lunch or a light supper. The informal but traditional restaurant requests only that guests cover their bathing suits with a shirt. A children's menu is available.

In the Fairmont Southampton, 101 South Rd. *©* **441/238-8000.** Breakfast buffet $25; lunch main courses $13–$24; dinner main courses $16–$38. AE, DC, MC, V. Daily 7am–6pm. Closed Oct–Mar. Ferry from the City of Hamilton.

WARWICK PARISH
Expensive

Blû ★★ AMERICAN/SOUTHWESTERN   Set in the same building that houses the clubhouse and pro shop of the Belmont Hills Golf Course, Blû has a sinuous postmodern decor that evokes a sophisticated corner of Italy, with tones of blue, white, and yellow that reflect the sea views that sweep out from it on all sides. A prominent area is devoted to a bar, and the staff will seem poised on the balls of their feet to make your entrance as theatrical as possible. The restaurant features dishes that may include fresh oysters; Cajun-style fried calamari; shrimp seviche with jalapeño and red onion; roasted pumpkin ginger soup; barbecued chicken quesadillas; firecracker rolls of roasted duck with rice paper noodles, tofu, and mango chili; chili-infused pork loin with mushroom-sausage stuffing and creamy polenta; Spanish meat and seafood paella; organic bourbon-infused chicken; macadamia-crusted wild salmon steaks; or Yankee-style pot roast.

Dressing the Part

Some upscale restaurants in Bermuda ask that men wear a jacket and tie for dinner; some require a jacket but not a tie. When making reservations, always ask what the dress code is. "Casual but elegant" dress is preferred at most Sunday buffets.

In the Clubhouse of the Belmont Hills Golf Course, 97 Middle Rd. ℂ **441/232-2323.** Reservations recommended. Pizzas $12–$17. Main courses $23–$46. Set menus are available for groups. AE, MC, V. Daily 6–10pm. Sun brunch 11:30am–2:30pm. Bus: 7.

PAGET PARISH
Very Expensive

Cafe Coco ★★ BERMUDIAN/INTERNATIONAL   This resort restaurant with a conservative and traditional decor and sweeping ocean views turns out vibrant and innovative cuisine that combines flavor with color. Begin with any of several succulent pastas or vichyssoise with poached lobster and orange oil or grilled ahi tuna and calamari with a chorizo oil and an olive strudel. Some of the best main courses include pan-roasted salmon with creamed spinach and a sherry-laced confit of tomatoes; rib-eye steak with port-flavored gravy; veal marsala, sautéed Gulf shrimp with a timbale of beetroot, or pan-seared Sonoma foie gras with a smoked bacon mousseline and chicken livers with a serving of confit plums.

In Coco Reef Resort, 3 Stonington Circle, Paget Parish. www.cocoreefbermuda.com. ℂ **441/236-5416.** Reservations required. Main courses $18–$36. AE, MC, V. Daily 6:30–8:30pm. Bus: 7.

Expensive

Beau Rivage ★★ FRENCH   Beau Rivage is the most authentically French restaurant on island. Overlooking Hamilton Harbour, it is the domain of award-winning chef Jean Claude Garzia. He not only offers some of the finest dishes on island, but also features tables opening onto a panoramic view.

Using quality ingredients, Garzia gives a modern interpretation to classic French dishes. You'll be served radiantly authentic flavors in fresh shrimp concoctions; tender, well-aged steaks; or succulent veal or lamb chops. Blue crab is often featured, as are vegetarian dishes. Start, perhaps, with a bowl of the velvety lobster bisque, or perhaps an upscale version of Bermuda fish chowder, and follow it with gratin of scallops with duchesse potatoes, Atlantic salmon filet with lemon butter and kumquat marmalade, or chicken breast with a Parmesan crust.

In the Newstead Belmont Hills Golf Resort & Spa, 27 Harbour Rd. ℰ **441/236-6060.** Reservations required. Lunch main courses $13–$28; dinner main courses $26–$50. AE, DC, MC, V. Mon–Sat 11:30am–2:30pm and daily 6:30–9:30pm. Bus: 8.

Fourways Inn ★★★ CONTINENTAL   This elegant restaurant in a restored 17th-century house (now a stylish accommodation; see p. 176 for review) provides a romantic setting for refined cuisine. It's like walking into an English manor house, with prints on the walls and white-clothed tables set with silver and crystal. At dinner, a pianist entertains with soft music.

A classic French cuisine is blended with innovative dishes from the chef, who features locally caught fish and seafood, but also has offerings for vegetarians and for those who are health conscious. The menus change to reflect seasonal ingredients. Classic dishes include chateaubriand for two with a Béarnaise sauce, fresh Maine lobster, veal tenderloin in a lemon and lime butter, or rack of young New Zealand lamb with ratatouille. The dessert specialty is a soufflé with Dark & Stormy rum, coconut, chocolate, strawberry, and a dash of Grand Marnier. It's one of the island's finest dining choices.

1 Middle Rd., Paget Parish. ℰ **441/236-6517.** Reservations required. Main courses $28–$42. AE, MC, V. Mon–Sat 6–8:30pm. Bus: 8.

The Lido ★ MEDITERRANEAN   This well-recommended beachfront restaurant consists of an outdoor terrace and an indoor dining room with big windows that fill the room with light. Come here for the location and convenience to Elbow Beach. Shades of pale yellow and red predominate, the chairs are comfortable enough to linger in, and the menu is one of the most diverse on the island. We recommend the halibut with black-eyed peas, chorizo, and red wine sauce; the seafood casserole with Mediterranean-style red sauce and chili, olives, and capers; Angus rib-eye steak (grilled); or the roasted lamb.

In the Elbow Beach Hotel Sea Terrace, 60 South Rd. ℰ **441/236-9884.** Reservations recommended. Lunch main courses $18–$25; dinner main courses $16–$45. AE, MC, V. Daily noon–2:30 and 6:30–9pm. Bus: 1, 2, or 7.

CITY OF HAMILTON (PEMBROKE PARISH)

Expensive

Ascots ★ MEDITERRANEAN/CONTINENTAL   This restaurant and its tempting Continental menu deserve to be better known. Within a residential neighborhood at the edge of the City of Hamilton, it occupies a spacious house, originally built in 1903, at the end of a country lane. The antique porcelain, Queen Anne armchairs, and Welsh pine evoke a chintz-filled English country house. In the summer, diners sit at candlelit tables on either the front porch or on a rear patio with a view of the garden.

The menu relies on classic techniques and first-rate ingredients. It includes one of the best selections of hot and cold appetizers in the City of Hamilton, ranging from

10

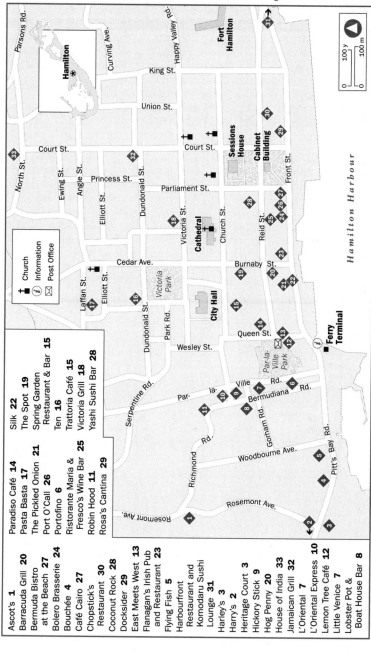

Ascot's **1**
Barracuda Grill **20**
Bermuda Bistro
 at the Beach **27**
Bolero Brasserie **24**
Bouchée **4**
Café Cairo **27**
Chopstick's
 Restaurant **30**
Coconut Rock **28**
Docksider **29**
East Meets West **13**
Flanagan's Irish Pub
 and Restaurant **23**
Flying Fish **5**
Harbourfront
 Restaurant and
 Komodaru Sushi
 Lounge **31**
Harley's **3**
Harry's **2**
Heritage Court **3**
Hickory Stick **9**
Hog Penny **20**
House of India **33**
Jamaican Grill **32**
L'Oriental **7**
L'Oriental Express **10**
Lemon Tree Café **12**
Little Venice **7**
Lobster Pot &
 Boat House Bar **8**

Paradiso Café **14**
Pasta Basta **17**
The Pickled Onion **21**
Port O'Call **26**
Portofino **6**
Ristorante Maria &
 Fresco's Wine Bar **25**
Robin Hood **11**
Rosa's Cantina **29**

Silk **22**
The Spot **19**
Spring Garden
 Restaurant & Bar **15**
Ten **16**
Trattoria Café **15**
Victoria Grill **18**
Yashi Sushi Bar **28**

portobello mushrooms with chicken salad drizzled with herb-flavored bacon/butter/yogurt sauce to fresh homemade ravioli filled with crabmeat and served in smoked-salmon-and-spinach cream sauce. Vegetarian dishes are available. Count on the chef's catch of the day, prepared as you like it, or try blackened mahimahi with tomato, pineapple, and lemon compote. If you prefer more traditional dishes, you might find the grilled sirloin steak with a peppercorn and port wine reduction more to your taste. For dessert, the crepe Garibaldi (warm crepes filled with strawberries and a chocolate-hazelnut sauce, served with fresh berries and crème Chantilly) is a tasty choice. Even more exciting are seasonal berries with Frangelico and chocolate ice cream.

In the Royal Palms Hotel, 24 Rosemont Ave. © **441/295-9644.** Reservations recommended. Lunch main courses $20–$30; dinner main courses $20–$60. AE, MC, V. Mon–Fri noon–2:30pm; Mon–Sat 6:30–10pm. Bus: 1, 2, 10, or 11.

Barracuda Grill ★★ SEAFOOD One of Hamilton's more stylish and contemporary-looking restaurants occupies a pair of dining rooms one floor above street level of a building in downtown Hamilton. Established in April 2002 and focusing on the cuisine of its Canadian chef, Derek Myers, it boasts an ultramodern lighting design, with hanging lamps that shed the kind of light that makes virtually everyone look attractive. Amid walls sheathed with unusual modern paintings, you can order a roster of mostly fish-based dishes that change with whatever comes in from local fishermen on the day of your arrival. The best examples include grilled yellowfin tuna with apple-ginger ravioli; roasted rockfish with a black bean and maple glaze; lobster fettuccine, barracuda crab cake with hazelnut sauce, or the wild Pacific salmon in a hoisin glaze. The most expensive and elegant item on the menu is a "grown-up" grilled cheese sandwich with three kinds of cheese, truffles, andouille sausages, and french fries. Michael Douglas and Catherine Zeta-Jones have been sighted here from time to time.

5 Burnaby Hill. www.barracuda-grill.com. © **441/292-1609.** Reservations recommended. Lunch main courses $15–$42; dinner main courses $24–$42. AE, MC, V. Mon–Fri noon–2:30pm; daily 5:30–10pm. Bus: 1, 2, 10, or 11.

Bolero Brasserie ★★ CONTINENTAL Casual but classy, this is one of the most attractive and appealing restaurants in Bermuda. In the heart of downtown Hamilton, it occupies a large, woodsy-looking dining room with a long bar area, red walls, and lots of mirrors. It does a busy, big-city lunchtime business with the local banking and financial community, with a presentation that's a bit less stressful and more leisurely at night. The venue is that of a typical French or British brasserie, with flavorful menu items inspired by classic Continental cuisine and enough buzz and theatricality to keep virtually anyone amused. Jonny Roberts and his artist wife, Fiona, cook and serve respectively, offering a successful array of dishes that include coq au vin; braised short ribs of beef with lentils braised in red wine; tempura versions of classic French frogs' legs; crepes filled with a confit of chicken with garlic; steak au poivre or rib-eye steak Diane; filet mignon with Yorkshire pudding; and a startlingly varied selection of fresh local fish. Examples include shrimp piri-piri and tuna prepared Niçoise-style, with tomatoes, peppers, and onions. During the midafternoon, there's a tapas menu, any item of which goes well with cocktails.

95 Front St. www.bolerobrasserie.com. © **441/292-4507.** Reservations recommended Fri–Sat. Lunch and dinner main courses $22–$48. AE, DC, MC, V. Mon–Fri 11:30am–2:30pm; Mon–Sat 6–10:30pm. Bus: 1, 2, 10, or 11.

Flying Fish ★ SEAFOOD/SUSHI Established early in 2011, this is a well-received and increasingly popular newcomer on Hamilton's dining scene, host to such local celebs as the Michael Douglas and Catherine Zeta-Jones entourages during some of their forays into the Bermudian night. The venue evokes a watery combination of tones of blue, bubbling holding tanks for lobsters, a simulated waterfall, views over Front Street, and an upscale clientele, many of them from the nearby Fairmont Hamilton Princess. The focus here is on seafood, much of it local, as well as such imported but flavorful dishes as scallops and scampi "innamorati," flambéed with Pernod and smoked hot paprika served over rice noodles. There's sushi and also meat dishes that include rack of lamb roasted with red chilis, oregano, sake, cumin, and garlic. The service is impeccable.

169 Pitts Bay Rd. (btw. Front St. and the Fairmont Hamilton Princess). www.bermuda-dining.com. ⓒ **441/295-2167.** Reservations recommended. Lunch main courses $14–$54; dinner main courses $30–$54. AE, MC, V. Mon–Fri 11:45am–2:30pm and daily 6:30–10:30pm. Bus: 7 or 8.

Harbourfront Restaurant & Komodaru Sushi Lounge ★★ ASIAN/ MEDITERRANEAN/SEAFOOD/SUSHI   This is the most talked about, most fashionable restaurant in Bermuda, with combinations of Asian and European fare that aren't easily available in most other restaurants. Set on the eastern edge of downtown Hamilton, on the ground floor of the Bermuda Underwater Exploration Institute (BUEI), it is an intersecting jumble of sinuous, sun-flooded curves. There's an etched aluminum bar near the entrance, a cozy and woodsy central dining room that evokes a postmodern spin on a traditional British pub, and a high-ceilinged second dining room where the light seems to leap into the room from the yacht-filled piers you'll see through high banks of windows. Menu items are the kind of thing that food and dining magazines like to feature, like rigatoni with chicken, spinach, and cream sauce; lobster salads; blackened codfish; Venetian-style calf's liver; yellowfin tuna with a wasabi-flavored cream sauce; tuna or steak tartare; and charbroiled loin of veal with a shiitake mushroom sauce. Sushi, served Monday to Saturday from 5 to 10pm, is the specialty of the chef, and ranges in price from $6.50 to $15. There is also vegetarian sushi served. Dessert might include *fondant au chocolat*—a warm, partially melted chocolate pudding.

40 Crow Lane, E. Broadway. www.harbourfront.bm. ⓒ **441/295-4207.** Reservations recommended. Lunch main courses $17–$35; dinner main courses $32–$45 (lobster). AE, DC, MC, V. Mon–Sat 11:45am–3pm; daily 6–10pm. Bus: 1, 2, 10, or 11.

Harry's ★★ INTERNATIONAL/STEAK & SEAFOOD   This upscale, solidly entrenched restaurant is the best in Bermuda for steak lovers. In the 1950s, before Harry, its founder, boarded the PanAm Clipper to Bermuda, he stopped in New York to dine at a then-famous steakhouse named Peter's Backyard. His meal was so exceptional he returned to Bermuda with a suitcase full of sirloin, the first unfrozen prime beef that island had ever seen. Decades later, based on that experience, Harry's beef is still full of flavor, aged for 21 days, and impeccably prepared for an audience of businesspersons from the island's financial community. The selection from the grill ranges from filet mignon to boneless rib-eye, from New York hand-cut strip loin to flat iron steak. If you want to go even more upmarket, try the double thick Welsh lamb chops or 14-ounce veal rack chop. All the sides are here, from Bermuda onion rings to a wild mushroom sauté. There's even a raw bar serving oysters on the half shell or yellowfin tuna carpaccio. The classic Old School shrimp cocktail is the most favored appetizer. Harry's still features all sorts of salads from arugula to wild watercress, but the perennial favorite remains the petite iceberg, just as it was back in the '50s.

In high season (Apr–Nov), many resort hotels require guests to take the modified American plan (MAP), or half-board arrangement of breakfast and dinner. To spare guests the routine of eating in the same dining room every night, some hotels offer a "dine around" program that allows you to dine at other hotels on your meal plan or at reduced prices. Ask about dine-around arrangements when booking your room.

96 Pitts Bay Rd. www.harrys.bm. © **441/292-5533.** Reservations required. Lunch main courses $18–$35; dinner main courses $28–$52. MC, V. Mon–Fri 11am–2:30pm and Mon–Sat 6–10pm. Bus: 7 or 8.

Little Venice ★ CONTINENTAL/ITALIAN   This is one of the most prominent Italian restaurants in Bermuda, a staple that has been here as long as anyone can remember. An enduring specialty is a savory *casseruola di pesce dello chef,* which consists of a medley of local seafood—including lobster, shrimp, mussels, clams, and several kinds of fish—cooked with white wine, herbs, and tomatoes. Other choices include flavorful fish chowder, spaghetti with seafood, several veal dishes, and an array of pastas, including superb homemade ravioli stuffed with tomatoes and ricotta. Italian wines are featured, in bottles and (less expensively) in carafes. An abbreviated menu is offered at lunchtime.

32 Bermudiana Rd. (btw. Par-la-Ville Rd. and Woodbourne Ave.). www.littlevenice.bm. © **441/295-3503.** Reservations recommended. Lunch main courses $19–$30, dinner main courses $25–$42. AE, MC, V. Mon–Fri noon–2:15pm; Mon–Sat 6:30–10pm. Bus: 1, 2, 10, or 11.

The Pickled Onion ★★ INTERNATIONAL   Originally built as a liquor warehouse overlooking Hamilton Harbour, this is a popular, reasonably priced dining choice, pickup bar, and after-dark venue, with a dining menu that's recently been the focus of a more aggressive effort by management and chefs. You might begin with Caribbean seafood salad, loaded with calamari, shrimp, fresh mussels, and other local fish, all in a basil vinaigrette. Angus beef, cut and trimmed in-house, is the chef's signature dish; it's tender and cooked to your specifications, accompanied by steak-cut potatoes and zesty peppercorn sauce. Prime rib, sizzling pizza, chicken, pastas, fish, and some of the island's best fish chowder are regularly featured.

The balcony opens onto Front Street. On Wednesday—Harbor Night, the busiest night of the week—the street is closed off and the scene becomes a festive minicelebration, with street performers and vendors setting the tone (May–Oct). Expect a DJ several nights a week here, usually on Friday and Saturday, beginning around 11pm, and occasional stabs at live entertainment, depending on the availability of the singers.

53 Front St. www.thepickledonion.com. © **441/295-2263.** Reservations recommended Wed and Fri–Sat. Lunch main courses $143–$26; dinner main courses $15–$36. AE, DC, MC, V. Sun–Thurs 11am–1am; Fri–Sat 11am–2am; Sun brunch 11am–5pm. Bar open till 1am (Fri–Sat till 2am). Bus: 1, 2, 10, or 11.

Moderate

Bermuda Bistro at the Beach INTERNATIONAL   Despite the promise of a beachfront within this restaurant's name, it occupies the ground floor of a commercial building in the center of "downtown" Hamilton with nary a grain of sand in sight.

But despite that, there's a sense of vacation fun from the cheerful staff here, and an ambience that's one of the closest things to spring break (whatever the season) in town. Come here for big-screen presentation of sporting events, stiff, party-colored drinks, an evening ambience that suggests an uninhibited singles bar with the DJ, and uncomplicated bar food that never pretends to even approach fine cuisine. As the menu promises, the cuisine will "fill your belly" more than adequately with items that include burgers, pizzas, pastas, steaks, and simple preparations of fresh fish. A patio in front offers a safe place for people-watching, and although the full menu stops at 10pm, bar snacks are offered until midnight every night. In synch with this place's role as a jumping late-night singles bar a DJ spins tunes nightly from 10pm till closing.

103 Front St. at Parliament St. © **441/292-0219**. Reservations not needed. Full breakfasts $17; burgers, sandwiches, and pizzas $13–$23; main courses $19–$35. Daily 10am–10pm; bar menu until midnight. Bar 9am–3am: Bus: 1, 2, 10, or 11.

Bouchée FRENCH   Set on the western edge of Front Street, near the corner of Woodbourne Avenue, this place's most recent manifestation (it used to be called Monty's) is as a French-inspired bistro whose venue was rapidly evolving at press time. Food items include croque-monsieurs, fish sandwiches, the catch of the day, strip loin steaks, stuffed breast of chicken, meal-size salads, and a roster of pastas such as fettuccine Alfredo with chunks of lobster, or spaghetti with butternut squash and fresh herbs. The venue is warm, the ambience casual, and classic staples of French cuisine are served. Profiting from its location in the business heart of Hamilton, it does a thriving business at breakfast, churning out sit-down platters of French toast, waffles, omelets, and gallons of fresh coffee.

In the Outerbridge Bldg., 75 Pitts Bay Rd. © **441/295-5759.** Reservations not needed. Full breakfasts $10–$14; lunch main courses $14–$21; dinner main courses $18–$30. MC, V. Daily 7:30am–2:30pm and Mon–Sat 6–10pm. Bus: 1, 2, 10, or 11.

Café Cairo MIDDLE EAST   If you develop a yearning for the cuisines of Morocco, Egypt, or Syria, head for this bastion of Middle Eastern flavors and accents. After 10pm, the place is transformed into a popular singles bar and dance emporium. Amid a decor vaguely reminiscent of Hedy Lamarr in the Casbah, you can order dishes that include a Moroccan-inspired almond-crusted rockfish cooked in a Parmesan shell; chicken *shawerma* that's wrapped and stuffed with onions and peppers and served with chickpea salad; shish kabobs, hummus, and slow-cooked medley of *tagines* (clay pots) filled with vegetables, chicken, fish, and (our favorite) aromatic lamb. Begin a meal here with a sampler platter of either hot or cold appetizers, an assemblage that brings together an assortment of salads, beignets, and appetizers from throughout the Middle East.

93 Front St. near Parliament St. © **441/295-5155.** Reservations not needed. Main courses $22–$35. AE, MC, V. Daily 5pm–3am. Closed Sun–Mon in midwinter. Bus: 1, 2, 10, or 11.

East Meets West ★ CHINESE/INDIAN/MEDITERRANEAN   At this restaurant, bistro, and low-end takeout joint, culinary influences range from Asia to California. About half its business derives from takeout orders, but it maintains tables and chairs for anyone who wants to dine in. An appetizer such as cold Mediterranean tuna with potato salad sounds simple but is a well-flavored entry into a meal. From the Bayou country of Louisiana comes a savory jambalaya served atop Cajun rice. The kettle of spicy rice noodles, with a Malaysian accent, is stir-fried. Indian rotis are filled with lamb curry, and chicken breast is well seasoned and served with fresh broccoli. The chef relies on such ingredients as lime juice, coconut milk, jalapeños, coriander, garlic, and lemon grass. This restaurant can be many things to many people, from a moderately priced and conventional sit-down restaurant, to a slapdash takeout joint.

27 Bermudiana Arcade, off Queen St. (btw. Reid and Church sts.). ☎ **441/295-8580.** Reservations recommended. Main courses for sit-down clients $14–$21; main courses for takeout clients $10–$15. MC, V. Mon–Sat 7:30am–10pm. Bus: 2, 8, 10, or 11.

Flanagan's Irish Pub & Restaurant BERMUDIAN/BRITISH Flanagan's occupies a prime position on Front Street, immediately across the street from the spot where cruise ships float at anchor during their Bermuda sojourns. Don't judge the place by what you'll find on the street level, where you'll find pool tables, big-screen TVs broadcasting up to three different international sporting events at a time, and pinball and automated poker games blaring away in the corners. Try to get a seat in the upstairs dining room or on the panoramic veranda (your best chance to achieve that is to make reservations).

Flanagan's is not known for culinary distinction except in one category: It serves the best fish chowder in Bermuda. Fish chowder is sometimes a bland dish, tasting like boiled fish in milk, but at Flanagan's, the dish has zest and flavor. Their charbroiled 8-ounce sirloin tastes even more delectable when served with a zesty peppercorn sauce. If you prefer lighter fare, opt for the daily changing menu of fresh fish.

In the Emporium Bldg., 69 Front St. www.flanagans.bm. ☎ **441/295-8299.** Lunch main courses $11–$29; dinner main courses $13–$39. AE, MC, V. Daily 11am–4:30pm and 5–11pm; bar Mon–Fri 11am–1am, Sat–Sun 9am–1am (happy hour daily 5–7pm). Bus: 7 or 11.

Harley's MEDITERRANEAN The food at this popular hotel restaurant exhibits some flair, making it a worthwhile choice even if you aren't a Fairmont Hamilton Princess hotel guest. In warm weather, you can dine alfresco near the pool. People who are shopping in the City of Hamilton for the day often drop by for lunch, when there's a large selection of salads. Our favorite is the classic Caesar with grilled *goujons* (slices) of grouper. The catch of the day is available grilled, and there are burgers galore. They also have pizzas and a kids' menu. The dinner menu is significantly better, with a choice of pastas—the best is grilled salmon filets on linguine. We also recommend the prime rib, tuna, salmon, and rockfish. Many of the main dishes conjure up thoughts of sunny Italy. Also delicious are the beef tenderloin with shrimp, stuffed chicken breast served with shiitake mushrooms, and rack of lamb.

In the Fairmont Hamilton Princess, 76 Pitts Bay Rd. ☎ **441/295-3000.** Reservations recommended. Lunch main courses $17–$30; dinner main courses $30–$52. AE, MC, V. Apr–Sept daily 7–10:30pm; Mon–Sat noon–10pm; Sun 12:30–3:30pm and 6–10pm. Closed Oct–Mar. Bus: 7 or 8.

Heritage Court AMERICAN/BERMUDIAN Inside the Fairmont Hamilton Princess, this is a safe and somewhat staid choice for breakfast or lunch. It gets a bit more festive in the evening, however, when live piano music is featured (daily 4:30–6:30pm) and the skilled bartender cranks out rum punches. There's also an excellent selection of single-malt whiskies along with both wine and champagne sold by the glass.

Most people come here for the food, however, which includes such specialties as charbroiled filet of beef with a sweet butter and chipotle glaze with arugula-stuffed potatoes. Perhaps you'll opt for the chef's daily pasta special, or else pan-roasted salmon with a tomato mushroom ragout with a lobster and brandy reduction. Appetizers are tangy and tasty, especially the Bloody Mary prawn cocktail or the sweet chili- and garlic-flavored pork ribs. Every day a different special is featured at lunch, perhaps tandoori rockfish with saffron Basmati rice and banana chutney. At lunch you can also enjoy Bermuda fish chowder, delicious club sandwiches, and even spiny lobster burgers. If you venture inside between May and October on any Friday night between 5:30 and 10pm, there might not be room to sit thanks to the hordes of singles who gather at the bar and on the nearby verandas of the hotel.

76 Pitts Bay Rd. ⓒ **441/295-3000.** Breakfast $16; salads and sandwiches $12–$20; afternoon teas $8–$14; dinner main courses $18–$30. AE, DC, MC, V. Daily 10:30am–1am. Bus: 7 or 8.

Lobster Pot & Boat House Bar ★★ SEAFOOD   For standard island dishes, this traditional favorite one-ups its neighbor **Hog Penny** (p. 132). Near the Hamilton Princess Hotel, within a 5-minute drive of the heart of the City of Hamilton, this is one of the most consistently popular restaurants on the island—a fixture since 1973. The Lobster Pot's rustic cedar plank walls sport big windows, brass trim, and thick wooden tables. There's a bar near the entrance if you want a before-dinner drink, and a dining room behind it. Menu items include both Maine and spiny Caribbean lobster, each prepared six different ways. Fish sandwiches and platters of hogfish, wahoo, tuna, and rockfish are prepared any way you want; we prefer them grilled with amandine, banana, or lemon-butter sauce. The best starter is a cup or bowl of steaming Bermuda fish chowder, enhanced with sherry peppers and shots of black rum. If you like it, you won't be alone—visitors haul quarts of the stuff (frozen) back to North America.

6 Bermudiana Rd. www.lobsterpot.bm. ⓒ **441/292-6898.** Reservations recommended. Lunch main courses $10–$46; dinner main courses $24–$72. AE, MC, V. Mon–Fri 11:30am–3:30pm; daily 6–11pm. Bus: 1, 2, 10, or 11.

L'Oriental ★ ASIAN   In the same building as **Little Venice** (p. 126), L'Oriental is a Pan-Asian restaurant with a penchant for gracefully mixing cuisines as diverse as those of China, Malaysia, Thailand, and Japan. The restaurant is situated in a mahogany- and stone-lined room with bridges, a pagoda, and lots of Asian art. Within the efficiently organized space, you'll find an oyster, salmon, and sushi bar, and a *teppanyaki* table where a team of Japan-trained chefs prepares food on a super-hot grill in front of you. Since L'Oriental prides itself on the variety of its all-Asian cuisine, no one will mind if you "fuse" a meal from the far corners of the world's biggest continent. The cuisine is reliable without ever rising to the ranks of sublime. L'Oriental is a good choice for vegetarians and the health conscious. Most dishes are at the lower end of the price range listed below.

32 Bermudiana Rd. (above Little Venice restaurant). www.diningbermuda.com. ⓒ **441/296-4477.** Reservations recommended. Lunch main courses $16–$36; dinner main courses $19–$38. AE, MC, V. Mon–Fri 11:30–2:15pm; Mon–Sat 6–10pm. Bus: 7 or 11.

Port O' Call SEAFOOD/INTERNATIONAL   In the heart of Hamilton, this warm and elegant bistro is popular with visitors and locals alike, the patrons dining either inside or alfresco on the harbor-view terrace. The emphasis is on fresh Bermuda seafood. The chefs entice with such classic dishes as Bermuda spiny lobster with a lemon risotto, pan-roasted scallops with chorizo sausage and golden raisin vinaigrette, and seared grilled lemon sole in a chive-flavored *beurre blanc*. They also prepare meat and poultry extremely well, including roast rack of lamb with a fresh herb crust or a seared New York strip steak with braised beef short rib. For appetizers, opt for the beef carpaccio with an arugula salad, or perhaps the salt-and-pepper tempura-fried oysters.

Front St. www.portocall.bm. ℂ **441/295-5373.** Reservations recommended. Lunch main courses $18–$26; dinner main courses $21–$45. AE, MC, V. Mon–Fri noon–2:30pm; daily 6–10pm. Bus: 1, 2, 10, or 11.

Ristorante Maria & Fresco's Wine Bar ITALIAN   Italian food like what the owner, Claudio Vigilante, remembers from his childhood is the venue at this understated and cozy restaurant named after his mother, Maria. We find dining and drinking wine here to be less boisterous and more satisfying than at the **Hog Penny** (p. 136) or the **Pickled Onion** (p. 126). Look for the place in an early-19th-century building on a narrow alleyway evocative of Bermuda's old maritime days, when the stone-walled interior functioned as a warehouse. Upstairs, there's a venue inspired by a wine bar you might have expected in Italy, with dozens of Italian and international wines by the glass and an outdoor deck which, weather permitting, grants visitors a back-alley respite from the congestion and bustle of nearby Front Street. Downstairs, in the restaurant section, menu items are a bit less expensive than in some of Hamilton's grander dining rooms, often with a respectful and nostalgic nod to their simple, home-based origins. The menu lists at least a dozen risottos and pastas, antipasti made from fresh vegetables and seafood, fried calamari with herb and garlic stuffing, osso bucco with fresh tagliatelle; and veal cutlets braised with milk and served with strips of cured ham (pancetta). One of the best desserts on Bermuda is a chocolate mousse cake, freshly baked and served with roasted almonds, toffee, marshmallow ice cream, and pistachio crème.

2 Chancery Lane, Hamilton. www.frescosgroup.bm. ℂ **441/295-5058.** Reservations recommended. Main courses $25–$34. AE, MC, V. Mon–Sat noon–2:30pm and 6–10pm. Wine cellar opens at 5pm. Bus: 1, 2, 10, or 11.

Victoria Grill INTERNATIONAL   In the center of Hamilton, this restaurant evokes an urban, big-city bistro with banquettes, a sense of cozy warmth, and a venue that switches throughout the course of a day from a site for business lunches to more relaxed series of evening meals. The food is well partnered with a selection of wines. Lunch might feature a roster of meal-size salads, sandwiches, grills, and a succulent version of an Asian-style tuna pizza with wasabi-flavored mayonnaise, while dinners might include fish cakes, chowders, yellowfin tuna with a soy-ginger glaze, jambalaya, a burger made from Kobe beef, and several kinds of steaks.

29 Victoria St. www.victoria-grill.com. ℂ **441/296-5050.** Reservations recommended. Lunch main courses $11–$23; dinner main courses $17–$35. MC, V. Mon–Fri noon–2:30pm nightly 5:30–10pm (till 11pm Fri–Sat). Bus: 1, 2, 10, or 11.

Silk ★★★ THAI   With an authentic cuisine sometimes based on recipes from the old Kingdom of Siam, a team of chefs from the Shangri-La Hotel in Bangkok dazzle local palates with the stormy flavors of their home country. Evocative aromas and subtle blends of herbs and spices characterize the cuisine. Start with the prawns-and-coconut wrap or the duck-and-mango salad. The curries are exceptional—especially one made with chicken breast in a green curry coconut milk sauce. In addition to a number of spicy rice and noodle dishes, you can order such delights as stir-fried duck breast with baby corn chili and basil sauce or marinated pan-fried quail in a soy sauce laced with cilantro and garlic. Our favorite specialty is the spicy steamed filet of red snapper served on a banana leaf and topped with a ginger-chili sauce.

Masters Bldg., 55 Front St. www.bermudasbestrestaurants.com. ℂ **441/295-0449.** Reservations recommended. Lunch main courses $16–$26; dinner main courses $16–$30. AE, MC, V. Mon–Fri noon–2:30pm; daily 6:30–10:30pm. Bus: 1, 2, 10, or 11.

FAMILY-FRIENDLY restaurants

Bacci (p. 117)   Bacci is one of the only eateries within the Fairmont Southampton Resort that's specifically designated as family-friendly, and it tends to attract goodly numbers of parents with teenage and younger children in tow, especially during early dinner hours.

Bailey's Ice Cream & Food D'Lites Restaurant (p. 140)   Bailey's is a great place to take the kids for some all-natural ice cream on a hot, sunny day. They also serve sandwiches if you're looking for more than just a snack.

Palm Court (p. 139)   The staff here is one of the most gracious in welcoming the family trade. Children tend to go for the burgers and well-stuffed sandwiches,

and especially the piping hot pizzas straight from the oven, instead of the more elaborate fare served in many Bermudian restaurants. By 6:30pm, the tables start filling up with families that find the pricing affordable.

Wahoo's (p. 142)   What kid wouldn't be drawn to this colorful cafe with its selection of seafood and an ice-cream parlor on the premises?

Wickets (p. 120)   The children's menu at this popular spot in the Fairmont Southampton makes this a great place to take the kids. If you arrive before 6:30pm, kids can order dinner from the lower-priced lunch menu.

Inexpensive

Chopsticks Restaurant ★ CHINESE/THAI   It's off the beaten track at the eastern end of the City of Hamilton, but Chopsticks offers Bermuda's best Chinese and Thai food, including spicy soup, tangy pork ribs, and seafood. The chef concocts Szechuan, Hunan, Thai, and Cantonese dishes, with an emphasis on fresh vegetables and delicate sauces. Most of the dishes are the standard ones you'd find in any North American Chinese restaurant, including sweet-and-sour chicken, beef in oyster sauce, and shrimp in lobster sauce. But some, including the duck in red curry, have real flair. We also love the excellent jade chicken, with spears of broccoli, mushrooms, and water chestnuts in a mild Peking wine sauce. Peking duck (served only for two) must be ordered 24 hours in advance. The best Thai dish is green curry chicken (chicken breast strips simmered with onions and bamboo shoots and served with fresh basil, coconut milk, and green curry paste).

88 Reid St. www.bermudarestaurants.com. ✆ **441/292-0791.** Reservations recommended. Lunch main courses $9–$15; dinner main courses $12–$40. AE, MC, V. Mon–Fri noon–2:30pm; daily 5–11pm. Closed public holidays. Bus: 1, 2, 10, or 11.

Coconut Rock INTERNATIONAL   This lively, informal eatery in the center of the City of Hamilton is both a drinking and a dining destination. German-born Christian Herzog and his two Bermuda-born partners preside over a main restaurant and two popular bars where music videos play. The place is a bit of a discovery and not likely to be overrun. Your best bet for dinner is the fish of the day, most often pan-seared and served in lemon-butter sauce with potatoes and vegetables. Spicy linguine and Venetian-style calf's liver, quesadillas, chimichangas, and steaks are always popular, and buffalo chicken wings in honey and hot sauce sell briskly.

Williams House, 10 Reid St. http://coconutrock.com. ✆ **441/292-1043.** Reservations recommended Sat–Sun. Lunch main courses $9–$27; dinner main courses $11–$29. AE, MC, V. Mon–Sat 11:30am–2:30pm; daily 6–10:30pm. Bus: 1, 2, 10, or 11.

6

WHERE TO EAT | City of Hamilton (Pembroke Parish)

Docksider PUB GRUB Don't come here expecting grand cuisine, because that simply isn't part of the mentality of a sometimes rowdy drinking den where food is an afterthought to foaming mugs of beer, stiff drinks, and a crowd that roars its approval or disapproval of whatever's happening in the world of international sports. Set on the building's street level, downstairs from the also-recommended Rosa's Cantina, the place advertises upcoming showcases of major-interest British, Australian, U.S., and European sports (football, rugby, and soccer) long in advance of the actual broadcasts. There's also a jukebox playing for moments when the sports action is less intense. If you have a favorite team about to engage in a major game, expect lots of like-minded fans crowding into the place in time for the big event. Menu items focus on fish and chips, platters of bangers and mash (with a side order of beans, if you want them), shrimp and chips, Philly cheese steaks, chicken strips, burgers, sandwiches, and fresh pastas. A full English breakfast is served throughout the day till 10pm for anyone who wants it. **Note:** If there's enough of a fan base associated with any upcoming sports event, and if that sports event is scheduled for early on any Saturday or Sunday morning, this place has often opened its doors as early as 8am for TV broadcasts of major soccer, football, or rugby games from as far away as Australia.

121 Front St. www.dockies.com. ✆ **441/296-3333.** Reservations not needed. Main courses $11–$24. AE, MC, V. Daily 11:30am–9:30pm. Bar closes at 2am. Bus: 1, 2, 10, or 11.

The Hickory Stick DELI/LIGHT BITES Near the Fairmont Hamilton Princess, the Hickory Stick is the most popular delicatessen and takeout restaurant in the city. It serves as many as 750 customers a day, including lots of office workers. Although one section seems like a coffee shop (with scones, doughnuts, and coffee), most customers come here for overstuffed sandwiches and takeout meals. It ain't glamorous: You'll stand in line, order your food, pay, and carry your food to a table. Offerings include steaming portions of chicken Parmesan, sausage rolls, quiche, beef pies, and fish cakes. Even more popular are the salads and overstuffed sandwiches all of which can be wrapped up for a picnic—the staff provides paper napkins and plastic cutlery on request. Advance telephone orders are accepted—a good idea if you don't want to wait.

2 Church St. (at Bermudiana Rd.). ✆ **441/292-1781.** Salads $4–$9; sandwiches and platters $4–$12. No credit cards. Mon–Fri 6:30am–3pm. Bus: 1, 2, 10, or 11.

Hog Penny BERMUDIAN/BRITISH A bit tired these days (it has thrived in this spot since 1957), Hog Penny remains Bermuda's most famous and enduring pub, serving draft beer and ale to each new generation of mainlanders who head here, probably on the advice of their grandparents. The dark paneled rooms are decorated in the British style, with old fishing and farm tools, bentwood chairs, and antique mirrors. At lunch you can order pub specials (including shepherd's pie) or tuna salad and the like. The kitchen prepares a number of passable curries, including chicken and beef. Fish and chips and steak-and-kidney pie are the perennial favorites, and they are comparable to what you'd find in a London pub. Dinner is more elaborate; the menu might include a whole lobster, a fresh fish of the day (perhaps Bermuda yellowfin tuna), and excellent Angus beef. The food is better and more "fussed over" upstairs at the **Barracuda Grill** (p. 124). There's nightly entertainment from 9:30pm to 1am; dress is casual. Even the staff comments from time to time on this establishment's long-standing appeal as everyone's tried-and-true local: "We'll probably never redecorate, and we'll retain the same decor until the place falls down."

5 Burnaby Hill. ✆ **441/292-2534.** Reservations recommended. Lunch main courses $13–$23; dinner main courses $15–$32. AE, MC, V. Daily 11:30am–4:45pm and 5:30–10pm; pub hours daily 11:30am–1am. Bus: 1, 2, 10, or 11.

House of India ★ 🍴 INDIAN   This is one of the few Indian restaurants in Bermuda, and the only one in the City of Hamilton itself. As such, it's viewed as something of a dining oddity, even though its fans insist that the food here can be genuinely wonderful. Within a dining room that's decorated with Indian paintings and woodcarvings, on the northern edge of the City of Hamilton, you'll enjoy a menu that specializes in the slow-cooked, often-spicy cuisine of northern India. There is a wide variety of vegetarian, beef, lamb, and chicken dishes, prepared to whatever degree of spiciness you request. Our favorite dishes on the menu are lamb *madras* (lamb simmered in an array of spices) and beef *rogan josh* (Indian curry with a variety of spices, plus yogurt and tomatoes). The staff cites chicken tikka masala (slow-cooked chicken with sweet cream and spices) as the restaurant's signature dish. A buffet lunch is served weekdays, including a wide selection of vegetarian dishes. The chefs point out that except for breads and pastries, all dishes are free of gluten and wheat.

Park View Plaza, 57 North St. ℰ **441/295-6450.** Lunch buffet $19 per person. Main courses $16–$23. MC, V. Mon–Fri 11:30am–2:30pm; daily 5:30–10pm. Bus: 7 or 8.

Jamaican Grill CARIBBEAN/JAMAICAN   This casual, aggressively local eatery specializes in the spicy cookery of Jamaica and also serves other West Indian specialties. It's geared mostly to the takeout crowd who place their orders downstairs. You can also sit at tables upstairs. Frankly, we don't recommend it for evening meals, as the surrounding neighborhood is unsafe, but at lunchtime, it represents value for simple, local food. No alcohol is offered; customers consume either natural juices or iced tea at their meals. Many of the juices are of the health-bar variety, including mango, carrot, or a ginger-flavored pineapple concoction. The Jamaican national dish, *ackee* and salt fish, is served here with peas and rice. You can also order such classics as jerk chicken, curried goat, or oxtail stew. We are especially fond of the pineapple-glazed chicken, and there are also such old favorites as macaroni and cheese, chicken pies, or roast beef in a mushroom sauce. Most main dishes are priced at the lower end of the range listed below.

32 Court St. ℰ **441/296-6577.** Reservations recommended Sat–Sun. Main courses $13–$29. AE, MC, V. Mon–Thurs 7am–9pm; Fri–Sat 7am–10pm. Bus: 7 or 8.

Lemon Tree Café CONTINENTAL   Right in the center of Hamilton, this upmarket cafe is being discovered by more and more visitors. You can drop in here for breakfast, ordering some unusual concoctions in addition to the standard scrambled eggs and bacon. Try, for example, a Bermuda fish cake served on a raisin bun. For lunch you might opt for one of their freshly made sandwiches, our favorite being the Parma ham with Brie cheese. Ask the staff about the daily specials—perhaps chilled fresh salmon with a garlic blue-cheese dressing, a savory chicken pie, or one of the wraps, such as one filled with crabmeat and avocado. The chicken salad is arguably the best in Hamilton. Between May and October, every Friday beginning at around 5pm it serves drinks until midnight to local office workers, who transform the place into something akin to a convivial singles bar. The place is at its best during clement weather when customers and their tables expand outward into neighboring Par-la-Ville Park.

7 Queen St. ℰ **441/292-0235.** Breakfast main courses $4–$8; sandwiches $7–$12; main courses $11–$20. MC, V. Mon–Fri 7am–4pm; Sat (summer only) 7am–2pm. Bus: 1, 2, 10, or 11.

L'Oriental Express DELI   This is a state-of-the-art deli, popular at breakfast and lunch with local office crowds, and one of the best choices in Hamilton for takeout if you're planning a picnic. You are offered both exotic and traditional dishes, along with sushi, breakfast wraps, fresh salads, and homemade desserts. It opens for breakfast, offering hot dishes and a wide range of pastries. A fresh soup of the day is also sold, along with the widest array of sandwiches in town, including New York roast beef. There is a selection of hot Asian food, sold in Styrofoam containers and weighed, including crispy duck and beef teriyaki.

Maxwell Roberts Bldg., 1 Church St. www.diningbermuda.com. ⓒ **441/296-7475.** Sandwiches $9.50–$11; Asian dishes $11 per pound. AE, MC, V. Mon–Fri 7am–5:30pm. Bus: 7, 8, 9, or 10.

Paradiso Cafe DELI/LIGHT BITES   One of the City of Hamilton's most consistently crowded lunch spots, with big voyeuristic front windows that allow peek-a-boo views of the passersby outside, the Paradiso Cafe serves hundreds of office workers every day. The most popular choices are pastries, sandwiches, and endless cups of tea and very good coffee, and the platters of the day are full meals in themselves. Depending on what's available at the market, daily specials might include lasagna with a side salad, savory breast of chicken with greens, or a platter of "deep-fried rice" with minced beef or pork.

In the Washington Mall, Reid St. (at Queen St.). ⓒ **441/295-3263.** Reservations not accepted. Sandwiches $7–$12; daily specials $9–$11. MC, V. Mon–Fri 7:30am–5pm; Sat 8am–5pm. Bus: 1, 2, 10, or 11.

Pasta Basta ITALIAN   This is an efficient, "assembly-line" restaurant that specializes in mass production of cafeteria-style pasta-and-salad combinations. Pasta Basta's Italian cuisine seems almost utilitarian, ranking far below those restaurants already recommended, and there's virtually no romance associated with the place, but its prices are very low.

In a summery setting, customers are offered two kinds of salad (tossed and Caesar) and about a dozen varieties of pasta. Served in full, medium-size, or small portions, they include three kinds of lasagna (one is meatless), plus a frequently changing array of pastas topped with a choice of meat, seafood, and vegetarian sauces. The daily special is likely to be shells with sausage and onions, in a pink sauce. This restaurant is a great place to fill up on decent food at a reasonable price. *Note:* No wine, beer, or alcohol is served, and local licensing laws do not permit you to bring your own drinks.

1 Elliott St. ⓒ **441/295-9785.** Reservations not accepted. Pastas $9.50 for a small portion of any pasta; $14 for a half portion; or $18 for a large portion. MC, V. Mon–Fri 11:30am–10pm; Sat noon–10pm; Sun 5–10pm. Bus: 1, 2, 10, or 11.

Portofino ITALIAN   The warm and inviting decor of this trattoria, complete with hanging lamps, evokes northern Italy. This place has its devotees, and some locals insist that it's the most romantic-looking Italian restaurant in Bermuda.

You'll find well-prepared, reasonably priced specialties, including classic minestrone; three kinds of spaghetti; freshly made pastas, including lasagna, ravioli, and cannelloni; and many varieties of 9-inch pizzas. There are also familiar Italian dishes such as Venetian-style liver, veal parmigiana, chicken cacciatore, and beefsteak pizzaiola. Some members of the long-lived Italian staff have been here longer than virtually anyone can remember, adding to its sense of stability and charm. Your best bet is one of the freshly made daily specials. There's a limited selection of Italian wines, and if you want to savor your meal in your hotel room or as part of a picnic, anything here can be prepared for takeout.

20 Bermudiana Rd. ⓒ **441/292-2375.** Reservations recommended. Pizzas $13; main courses $12–$25. AE, MC, V. Mon–Fri noon–2:30pm; Sat–Sun 6–10pm. Bus: 1, 2, 10, or 11.

The Robin Hood INTERNATIONAL Woodsy-looking and percolating in a sense of nostalgia for Merrie Olde England, this is a comfortably rustic tavern that has evolved into the local watering hole for many of Pembroke Parish's nearby residents. No one will mind if you drop in just for a drink or two, and many of your fellow elbow-benders traditionally do that many nights until the closing bell. But if you're in the mood for food as well, you'll find the kind of fare (pizzas, burgers, steaks, and curries) that goes well with liquor and suds. Menu items include jalapeño nachos, spicy buffalo wings, surf and turf, strip loin steak, Caesar salads with shrimp or grilled chicken, and pizzas (including a "porker" that's topped with bacon, ham, ground sausage, pepperoni, and hamburger meat). Main-course platters include sweet-and-sour chicken, pastas of the day, and curried versions of chicken, beef, and shrimp.

25 Richmond Rd. © **441/295-3314.** Lunch salads and sandwiches $8–$13, platters $10–$16; dinner pizzas $11–$25, main courses $13–$27. AE, MC, V. Daily noon–11pm. Bar Mon–Sat 11am–1am; Sun noon–1am. Bus: 6 or 7.

Rosa's Cantina TEX-MEX This cheerful hideaway, upstairs from the also-recommended Docksider Pub, offers the only Tex-Mex menu in Hamilton. Within an enclave outfitted with rustic memorabilia you might remember from a weekend in Tijuana during your college days, it offers steaming versions of the spicy, south-of-the-border cuisine that goes well with beer, tequila, and sombreros. Examples include five kinds of fajitas, tacos, burritos, succulent calamari, different preparations of fresh fish, and shrimp (wrapped in bacon) "carnival." Margaritas, about a dozen kinds, make everything a bit more fun.

121 Front St. near Reid St. www.bermudarestaurants.com. © **441/295-1912.** Reservations not needed. Sandwiches, tacos, burritos, and fajitas $10–$21; main courses $25–$33. AE, MC, V. Daily 11:30am–11pm. Bus: 1, 2, 10, or 11.

The Spot Restaurant 🗲 BERMUDIAN/WEST INDIAN Set on a street running downhill into downtown Hamilton's harbor, this local diner offers a welcome alternative to the high prices you're likely to find in many other nearby restaurants. Originally established in the 1930s, it attracts a clientele of off-duty police officers, construction workers, nurses from the local hospital, residents of nearby vacation apartments, and all kinds of local residents who appreciate the low prices and plentiful portions. You'll find breakfast platters that range from international (all kinds of bacon, egg, pancake, French toast, and waffle dishes) to West Indian (codfish with potato fritters). Your best bet involves scheduling lunch here, but not necessarily dinner. Meals focus on burgers, salads, sandwiches, and daily specials such as roast turkey or chicken platters, oxtail stew, lamb or pork chops, or curried chicken. No alcoholic drinks of any kind are served, but since there is no shortage of bars within the neighborhood for a before-dinner drink, no one seems to mind.

6 Burnaby St. © **441/292-6293.** Reservations accepted only for parties of 6 or more. Breakfast platters $7–$12; burgers, sandwiches, and salads $6–$13; main-course platters $8–$19. MC, V. Mon–Sat 6:30am–7pm. Bus: 1, 2, 10, or 11.

Spring Garden Restaurant & Bar CARIBBEAN Bermudians will quickly tell you that their homeland is not part of the Caribbean, a fact which adds a touch of exoticism to the West Indian cuisine, prepared by a Bajan (Barbadian) owner, in the heart of Hamilton. Most of it lies within an open-to-the-sky courtyard, which is pleasant on balmy nights. Food is simple and unpretentious, focusing on island staples such as braised oxtail, rotis (stuffed dumplings), burgers, steaks, and both curried goat and curried chicken. The drink of choice here seems to be shared by virtually everyone: Dark and Stormys ($6 each) made with Bermuda's Black Seal rum. Late at night, the music focuses on reggae, calypso, and the kind of steel drum music you might have expected in Trinidad.

19 Washington Lane, btw. Reid and Church sts. ☎ **441/295-7416.** Reservations not needed. Main courses $8–$33. AE, DC, MC, V. Daily 10am–10pm. Bar open 10am–3am. Closed Sun Nov–Apr. Bus: 1, 2, 10, or 11.

Ten LIGHT BITES   This elegant, arts-conscious cafe occupying the street level of a residential apartment building in the City of Hamilton is a hot spot for home-brewed coffees, freshly made salads, succulent pastas, well-stuffed sandwiches, delicious tapas, homemade desserts, and a daily changing blackboard of house specials. You can complement your meal with a glass of wine or a cocktail made from berries fresh fruit. The place is casual, hypermodern, and trend-conscious, with indoor and outdoor tables and sometimes startling oversized reproductions of baroque paintings.

Some of the best tapas include feta and caramelized onion–stuffed peppers with an arugula pesto or lobster sausage prosciutto wrapped with pear salsa. Sandwiches feature the likes of a Cajun-spiced shrimp wrap or seared wahoo.

10 Dundonald St. www.ten.bm. ☎ **441/295-0857.** Small plates and tapas $8–$15; sandwiches $9–$13. AE, MC, V. Mon–Fri 7am–10:30pm; Sat 8am–3pm. Bus: 1, 2, 10, or 11.

Trattoria Café ITALIAN   This family oriented restaurant is tucked away in a narrow alley 2 blocks north of the City of Hamilton's harborfront. There's not a single cutting-edge or glamorous thing about it, and that's just what the loyal regulars like. The decor is straight out of old Naples, with a wood-burning pizza oven (the only one in Hamilton) and hanging Chianti bottles. The attentive, if somewhat harried, wait-staff serves generous portions of rather standard, well-flavored Italian food. You'll find more than a dozen kinds of pizza, and the kitchen is happy to create variations for you. Pastas include lasagna and spaghetti *pescatore*. Veal can be ordered parmigiana- or Milanese-style, and there's a revolving array of fresh fish. If you're very demanding of your Italian cuisine, you'll fare better at **Little Venice** (p. 126).

23 Washington Lane (in the middle of the block bordered by Reid, Church, Burnaby, and Queen sts.). ☎ **441/295-1877.** Reservations recommended. Pizzas $11–$18; lunch main courses $7–$17; dinner main courses $11–$25. AE, MC, V. Mon–Sat 11:30am–3:30pm and daily 5:30–10pm (to 10:30pm in summer). Bus: 1, 2, 10, or 11.

Yashi Sushi Bar SUSHI   Bermuda's only sushi bar that is not attached to another restaurant, Yashi Sushi lies in Hamilton next to **Coconut Rock** (p. 131). Many food fanciers consider this the best sushi outlet on island. Specialties include sushi, sashimi, or *makimonos* (special rolls or hand rolls), as well as shrimp or scallops tempura and fish dumplings. Appetizers are among the best of their kind in any of the sushi restaurants, including a soft shell crab tempura or deep-fried calamari. Some of the most favored sushi items include peppered tuna or smoked eel (or salmon). Among *makimonos* offerings is "Hot Rock" (spicy tuna, salmon, yellowtail, smoked eel, scallions, cucumber, and sesame seeds).

Reid St. ☎ **441/296-6226.** Main courses $10–$17. Mon–Sat 11:30am–2:30pm and 5:30–10pm. MC, V. Bus: 1, 2, 10, or 11.

SMITH'S PARISH

Expensive

The Bermudiana/The Breakers ★ INTERNATIONAL   Some clients of this hotel define this as two restaurants, others as one, but regardless, a team of skilled chefs works to please you within the dining facilities at **Pink Beach Club & Cottages** (p. 182). At least one, and often both, will be open during the months the hotel is operating, but which of the two appeals to you will depend on the weather and the season (the Bermudiana is an indoor venue, the Breakers is on an outdoor terrace). The chefs take their inspiration from many light and healthy contemporary styles of cooking and prepare traditional dishes with less fat. The aim is to produce appetizing food with first-rate ingredients, light textures, and natural flavors. Many items include fresh herbs from the garden, with an emphasis on local seafood. Appetizers include classics such as Bermuda fish chowder and Caesar salad, as well as more imaginative fare such as carpaccio of beef tenderloin with Parmesan and pine nuts, or wild mushroom strudel. Savory main courses might include glazed tenderloin of pork with Granny Smith apples and a blue cheese crust; or chicken breast stuffed with chive-flavored mousse and smoked bacon.

At the Pink Beach Club & Cottages, South Rd. www.pinkbeach.com. **441/293-1666.** Reservations required for dinner, recommended for lunch. Lunch main courses $13–$28; dinner main courses $25–$45; AE, MC, V. Daily noon–2:30pm and 6:30–9:30pm. Closed mid-Dec to Mar. Bus: 1.

Moderate

North Rock Brewing Company ★ 🏠 BERMUDIAN/BRITISH Although beer is brewed by other enterprises in Bermuda, this is the only brewery on the island that serves most, if not all, of its product on the premises. The setting is a sometimes rowdy replica of an English pub, complete with ceiling beams and paneling, plus a casually upscale dining room which, rebuilt in 2012, is outfitted in shades of blue. Most diners tend to gravitate to the dining room, but dyed-in-the-wool locals sometimes opt to spend their entire time, meal and all, in the pub section. At least five kinds of beer are offered, all of it hauled in fresh from the organization's brewing operations at the Bermuda Dockyards.

If you come here to drink the local brew, that's fine, but we suggest you stick around for the cuisine, too. This is not the typical pub grub dished up at one of those Front Street drinking emporiums in the City of Hamilton. Dishes here have flair, such as the Brewmaster's veal chop, grilled and served with grain and Dijon mustard sauce. You can also order pub classics such as steak-and-ale pie, or perhaps beef and mushrooms simmered in porter ale. The fish and chips aren't bad either, and we like the luscious pork tenderloin and the codfish cakes. Unless you order shellfish, most dishes are inexpensively priced.

10 South Rd. www.northrockbrewing.com. **441/236-6633.** Lunch main courses $15–$27; dinner main courses $19–$37. AE, DC, MC, V. Daily 11:30am–3:45pm and 6–10pm. Pub till midnight. Bus: 1.

Rustico ITALIAN/PIZZERIA This is a local favorite known for its thin-crust pizzas as well as such dishes as pan-seared scallops wrapped in pancetta. It's casual and fun. You can stop in during the day for sandwiches (often made from fish) or else a home-made burger. At night, the pizza oven is going strong, with the Rustico special topping being Parma ham, arugula salad, and shaved Parmesan cheese. Pastas are succulent, especially the rigatoni with a sweet Italian sausage, roasted red pepper, broccoli, and cherry tomatoes in wine sauce. Fish chowder is made fresh daily. Main meat or poultry courses are limited but full of flavor, especially the tenderloin of veal with saffron-flavored risotto, or the roasted lamb chops with a shallot-laced tarragon sauce.

8 N. Shore Rd. (in Flatts Village). **441/295-5212.** Reservations recommended. Lunch main courses $10–$24; dinner main courses $15–$35. AE, MC, V. Daily 11:45am–2:30pm and 6–10pm. Bus: 10 or 11.

Inexpensive

Specialty Inn INTERNATIONAL/SUSHI   This south-shore restaurant's international menu revolves around Bermudian cuisine with Italian zest. Seating 35 to 40 (mostly locals), the inn is known for its value, generous portions, and its sense of fun, unpretentious cooking. Red bean soup, an ideal starter, reflects the island's Portuguese influence, and the Bermuda fish chowder is particularly good. The fresh catch of the day is usually delectable. Pasta dishes, including lasagna, are homemade. Poultry and meat, though frozen, are generally excellent—the roast lamb and barbecued chicken are especially tasty. Many other dishes display influences that run from Chinese and Indian to Mexican, Spanish, and Portuguese. The sushi bar adds a Japanese flavor to the inn, and sushi is served Monday to Saturday 11:30am to 10pm.

Collectors Hill, 4 South Rd. © **441/236-3133.** Lunch main courses $12–$20; dinner main courses $16–$28. MC, V. Mon–Sat 6am–10pm. Bus: 1.

HAMILTON PARISH

Very Expensive

Tom Moore's Tavern ★★ CONTINENTAL/FRENCH   Bermuda's oldest restaurant, built in 1652 as a private home, is on Walsingham Bay, near the Crystal Caves. The Irish romantic poet Thomas Moore visited in 1804 and wrote some verses here; he referred to a calabash tree that still stands some 180m (590 ft.) from the tavern. The most famous dining room in Bermuda has gone through many incarnations. When Bologna-born Bruno Fiocca opened the present tavern in 1985, it became one of the island's most popular and sought-after upscale restaurants. With its four fireplaces and darkened cedar walls, this landmark establishment serves classic French and Italian cuisine. Its fans have referred to this place as one of the most appealing, evocative restaurants in Bermuda.

Seafood is a specialty. During the summer, there's usually a tank of Bermuda lobsters outside. Local fish selections are likely to include rockfish and yellowtail, which may be your best bet. One reader wrote that he found the place "very expensive, but worth the price, as the service and atmosphere are both top-notch." He also noted, "The cuisine is not light, however. Extremely well-prepared meals contain very rich sauces." He's right. But if you're in the mood for a rich dinner, some of the menu items include foie gras or carpaccio of the day; roast quail with mushrooms, bacon, and goat cheese tart; and a platter that combines roasted loin of veal with veal sausage, corn pudding, spinach-stuffed crêpes, and roasted garlic sauce. Desserts are opulent—perhaps try the chef's "soufflé of the day." The table settings (English silver, German crystal, Luxembourg china) and general ambience contribute to a memorable visit.

Walsingham Lane (in Bailey's Bay). www.tommoores.com. © **441/293-8020.** Reservations required. Jackets preferred for men. Main courses $28–$45. AE, V. Daily 6:30–10pm. Closed Jan. Bus: 1 or 3.

Expensive

Mickey's Beach Bistro & Bar ★ STEAK & SEAFOOD   In Bermuda's most famous hotel, the **Elbow Beach Hotel** (p. 174), this terrace dining room under the stars is Bermuda's only bistro on the beach. It's even been suggested that to be in Bermuda anytime between April and November and to not visit this place involves missing part of the "spirit" of the island. Protected by a large custom-made tent, this is one of the island's best venues for summer dining, and it's also ideal for a sundowner cocktail. The cooking is light and inventive and never overdresses the fresh ingredients. For a Caribbean touch, you might opt for a skewer of scallops and pineapple grilled with a light lemon sauce. Salmon is grilled to perfection and comes with a lemon sauce. The crab cakes are well flavored, and Bermuda lobster is featured almost daily. Meat lovers may prefer the grilled Angus sirloin steak with a grainy mustard sauce. For dessert, nothing tops the mango cheesecake with orange sauce.

At the Elbow Beach Hotel, 60 South Rd. (Ⓒ **441/236-3535.** Reservations recommended. Lunch main courses $14–$29; dinner main courses $17–$43. AE, MC, V. Daily noon–4pm and 6–11pm. Bar 10am–1am. Closed Nov–Apr. Bus: 1, 2, or 7.

The Point Restaurant ★★★ MEDITERRANEAN   There's a "land menu" and a "sea menu" here, but whether it swims or walks, Chef Serge Bottelli wants quality products. He is also inventive, because as he claims, "In Bermuda you find yourself eating the same things." Whenever possible, he buys all meat, vegetables, and seafood locally. For example, he gets chicken and lamb from local suppliers (Wadson's Farm). Duck breast might be prepared with a citrus glaze; tenderloin of beef with a pinot noir or sun-dried tomato and herb marmalade, depending on the mood of the chef. The restaurant celebrates Bermuda's maritime heritage with an extraordinary mural of seafaring ships from the mid-1800s. Guests can wine and dine in luxurious surroundings, enjoying the sunset over Harrington Sound alfresco on the terrace. Serious foodies can also enjoy the "chef's table" in a kitchen where a customized tasting menu is available for up to a dozen people. Constantly searching for new taste explosions, the chef promises to invent something different every day.

In Tucker's Point Hotel & Spa, 60 Tucker's Point Club Dr. (Ⓒ **441/298-9800.** Reservations required. Main courses $40–$50; fixed-price menus $82 for 4 courses, $95 for 5 courses. $45 per person supplement includes a wine selection with each course. Daily 6:30–9:30pm. Jan–Mar closed Sun–Mon Bus: 1, 3, 10, or 11.

Moderate

Landfall ★ BERMUDIAN   Landfall has thrived near the airport for almost as long as anyone can remember. It's set within a white-sided antique home that's at least 200 years old, with a view that some locals claim is the best in Bermuda, encompassing large stretches of seacoast as well as faraway St. David's Island. One of the island's best-known chefs, Seab Ming, took over a few years ago. An expert on Bermuda's cuisine, Ming brings many island specialties to the menu, incorporating fresh local foodstuffs whenever he can. Try his rockfish in orange sauce, Bermuda lobster, fish chowder, pumpkin soup, and cassava cake.

At Clearview Suites & Villas, Sandy Lane. (Ⓒ **441/293-1322.** Lunch main courses $13–$20; dinner main courses $20–$35. AE, DC, MC, V. Daily 10am–10pm. Bus: 10 or 11.

Palm Court ★ ☺ CONTINENTAL   Set within the **Grotto Bay Beach Resort** (p. 183), this restaurant is of particular appeal to families, since, according to local wits, there would be absolutely no judgments rendered even if you showed up with an entire boisterous orphanage. Casual and cost conscious, the setting features terra-cotta tiles, mahogany, and decor with a tropical theme. The chefs focus on Bermuda for their culinary inspiration: Oven-roasted salmon is served, along with succulent steaks. You can also dine on light fare in the evening, including a beef dip sandwich or juicy burgers and pizzas. You can arrive early for an island cocktail at the elegant bar.

At the Grotto Bay Beach Resort, 11 Blue Hole Hill. www.grottobay.com. ✆ **441/293-8333.** Reservations recommended. AE, MC, V. Main courses $12–$36. Daily 6:30–9pm. Bus: 1, 3, 10, or 11.

Inexpensive

Bailey's Ice Cream & Food D'Lites Restaurant 🍴 ☺ DELI/LIGHT BITES/ ICE CREAM
This ice-cream parlor near Grotto Bay Resort and the airport occupies a small cottage. For all-natural, homemade ice cream, there's no comparable spot in Bermuda—the staff concocts at least 30 flavors in the shop's 40-quart ice-cream maker. You can enjoy Bermuda banana, coconut, cherries and white chocolate chips, or other exotic flavors at one of the outdoor tables. The popular sandwiches are served on fresh-baked bread. Also featured are fresh fruit ices, frozen yogurt, and bottled juices—perfect on a hot, sunny day.

At Wilkinson Ave. and Blue Hole Hill (in Bailey's Bay). ✆ **441/293-8605.** Sandwiches $6–$10; ice cream $3.85 per scoop. No credit cards. Daily 11am–6pm. Closed Dec–Feb. Bus: 1, 3, 10, or 11.

Swizzle Inn Bailey's Bay BERMUDIAN/BRITISH
The oldest pub in Bermuda— some 300 years old—is also the home of the famous Bermuda rum swizzle drink (made with sugar and citrus juice). The pub lies west of the airport, near the Crystal Caves. Thousands of business cards and reams of graffiti cover the walls. *The Bermudian* magazine voted the meaty Swizzleburger best in Bermuda; other freshly prepared pub favorites include fish and chips, conch fritters, and shepherd's pie. These dishes are at least a notch above typical Bermudian pub grub. At lunch, the Bailey's Bay fish sandwich and onion rings are popular with locals and visitors alike. The larger, more varied dinner menu appeals to many tastes and diets. Pub grub is available for dinner, as is a seafood medley (rockfish, mussels, and shrimp in marinara sauce), the catch of the day, and some tasty Asian curries. Seating is available inside and on the upper and lower patios; upstairs there are also a smoke-free room and a gift shop.

3 Blue Hole Hill (in Bailey's Bay). ✆ **441/293-1854.** Reservations accepted only for parties of 8 or more. Lunch main courses $12–$20; dinner main courses $16–$32. AE, MC, V. Daily 11am–1am. Closed 4 weeks in Jan–Feb. Bus: 1, 3, 10, or 11.

ST. GEORGE'S PARISH

Moderate

Blackbeard's Hideout BERMUDIAN/INTERNATIONAL
At Fort Catherine's, this eatery has become one of the best places in Bermuda to, well, hide out. With a panoramic view of Achilles Bay, it offers appetizing seafood as well as other "grub and grog." For starters, opt for such well-prepared selections as calamari served with a mango garlic aioli dip or fresh oysters on the half shell. You can also begin with a Bermuda fish chowder prepared with black rum and sherry peppers. For your main, the chef prepares a rum-laced tenderloin of pork flambéed with Calvados, or else a 10- or 14-ounce sizzler steak topped with fried onions and garlic butter. A seafood platter is also offered nightly.

5 Coot Pond Rd., Fort St. Catherine's. www.stgeorgesclub.com. ✆ **441/297-1200.** Main courses $22–$48. MC, V. Tues–Sun 11am–11pm. Closed Nov–Mar. Bus: 7.

Black Horse Tavern ★★ BERMUDIAN/INTERNATIONAL
If you should land here, in a section of the island that Bermudians call "the country," you'll dine with the locals, many of whom maintain (with some justification) that this is the best

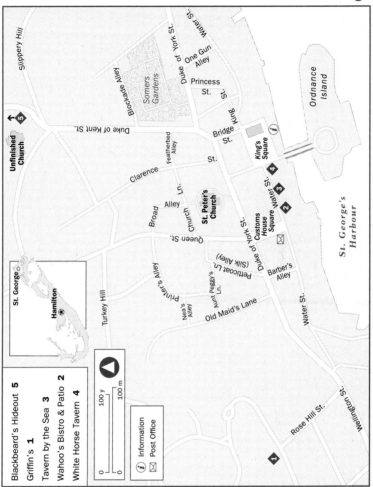

Blackbeard's Hideout **5**

Griffin's **1**

Tavern by the Sea **3**

Wahoo's Bistro & Patio **2**

White Horse Tavern **4**

ⓘ Information

⊠ Post Office

place for "an authentic taste of Bermuda." Black Horse Tavern looks like a private home: It boasts a dusty rose exterior with green shutters and a glassed-in porch in the rear that looks over Smith's Sound. Over the years, the tavern has attracted many celebrities, and some diners arrive in yachts. You can begin your meal with curried conch stew, shark hash (made with minced puppy shark), fish chowder, or curried mussels. Other choices include sandwiches, burgers, and platters of fish and chips. The chef also prepares tempting sirloin steak. If your luck holds, the only Bermuda Triangle you'll encounter is Black Horse's delicious drink—pineapple juice, orange juice, black rum, and Bermuda Gold liqueur.

101 St. David's Rd., on St. David's Island. ⓒ **441/297-1991.** Reservations recommended for parties of 4 or more. Main courses $19–$45. AE, MC, V. Tues–Sun noon–11pm. Bus: 6.

Griffin's ★ STEAK & SEAFOOD Just off York Street, this first-class restaurant opens onto panoramic views of the harbor. Dishes are robust with a strong emphasis on succulent pastas and fresh seafood, including fresh snow crab, Alaskan king crab legs, and scallops in a white-wine sauce. Carnivores will also be pleased by the quality of the lamb and beef dishes—the best in the East End—including T-bone steaks, juicy prime rib, melt-in-your-mouth beef tenderloin, and braised filets of lamb with mint and blueberry sauce. Desserts are usually sumptuous and are prepared fresh daily.

In the St. George's Club, 6 Rose Hill. www.stgeorgesclub.bm. ℂ **441/297-1200.** Reservations recommended. Lunch main courses $13–$22; dinner main courses $20–$33. AE, MC, V. Thurs–Tues noon–2:30pm and 6:30–9:30pm. Bus: 3, 10, or 11.

Tavern by the Sea INTERNATIONAL This restaurant prides itself on its sweeping view of St. George's Harbour. During clement weather, most visitors opt for a seat beneath brightly striped parasols on its wraparound veranda; otherwise, an air-conditioned interior provides nautical nostalgia. The menu here includes pastas, burgers, salads, shepherd's pie, and a short list of German dishes such as Wiener schnitzel and bratwurst. Fish and chips are always reliable, as are the steaks. Pizzas bear names of local monuments, including one known as "The Stocks," made with pepperoni, onions, green peppers, mushrooms, and cheese.

14 Water St. ℂ **441/297-3305.** Reservations strongly recommended. Sandwiches, salads, pastas, and burgers $7–$22; main courses $16–$36. AE, MC, V. Food service daily 11:30am–9:30pm. Bar open daily 11:30am–11pm (Fri–Sat in summer until 2am). Bus: 3, 10, or 11.

Wahoo's Bistro & Patio ☺ ★★ CONTINENTAL One of the most respected and talked-about restaurants in Bermuda occupies a narrow but brightly colored storefront whose rear opens onto an outdoor terrace with a view out over St. George's historic harbor. In 2010, it was acquired by an expatriate Austrian, Alfred Konrad, whose earlier reputation in Bermuda derived from lengthy stints at some of the island's most prestigious restaurants, including Tom Moore's Tavern. Today, in a partnership with German-born Bermudian investor and restaurateur Geza Wolfe, its venue is charming, European/mid-Atlantic, and urbane, focusing on such Continental mainstays as Weinerschnitzel, saltimbocca, upscale pastas, and just about everything succulent that's associated with the game fish, Wahoo. The fish chowder here is superb, as is a signature dish invented by Alfred, "Rockfish Picasso," composed of braised filets of the island's ugliest fish served with artfully arranged citrus fruits and caramelized ginger. Also look for wahoo burgers, wahoo tacos, wahoo nuggets with sweet potato fries and rémoulade sauce; smoked wahoo pâté, and a "Wahoo sampler," which contains a bit of all the other wahoo-derived items mentioned above on one carefully-arranged platter. The vibe here is informal, but there's an undeniable elegance and savvy associated with the place, thanks partly to its European origins and the longstanding culinary experience of its owners. Near the entrance is a display featuring takeout Italian-style gelati (ice creams), which attract a booming business from families with children looking for a midafternoon treat.

36 Water St. www.wahoos.bm. ℂ **441/297-1307.** Reservations recommended. Lunch main courses $12–$30; dinner main courses $22–$45. MC, V. Daily 11:30am–5pm and Tues–Sun 6–10pm. Bus: 3, 10, or 11.

White Horse Tavern BERMUDIAN/SEAFOOD The oldest tavern in St. George is one of the most popular in Bermuda; it's always jammed. This white building with green shutters has a restaurant and cedar bar with a terrace jutting into St. George's Harbour. For years, the most popular item on the menu here was fish and chips, still a favorite lunchtime specialty, served in a seasoned flour batter and some-times overdone, but at dinner, the menu is longer and more elaborate, sometimes with touches of culinary ambition and flair. The fish chowder is good, as are the baby back ribs and a "Bermuda Triangle" composed of three kinds of local fish with mango salsa and lemon and thyme-flavored butter sauce, or the herb-crusted loin of lamb. At lunch, there are burgers, meal-sized salads, pizzas, pastas, and sandwiches. The food is passable, but not special. Another horsy tavern, the Black Horse Tavern (see above), serves a more authentic Bermudian cuisine. Dress is smart casual, and there's often enjoyable entertainment.

8 King's Sq. www.whitehorsebermuda.com. ℰ **441/297-1838.** Reservations accepted only for groups. Breakfast $4–$15; lunch main courses $11–$26; dinner main courses $17–$47. AE, MC, V. Daily 9am–11pm; bar daily 10am–1am. Closed Jan–Feb. Bus: 3, 10, or 11.

RESTAURANTS BY CUISINE

AMERICAN
Blû ★★ ($$$, p. 121)
Coconuts ★ ($$$, p. 117)
Heritage Court ($$, p. 128)

ASIAN
Harbourfront Restaurant & Komodaru Sushi Lounge ★★ ($$$, p. 125)
L'Oriental ★ ($$, p. 129)
Ocean Club ★ ($$$, p. 117)

BERMUDIAN
Blackbeard's Hideout ($$, p. 140)
Black Horse Tavern ★★ ($$, p. 140)
Cafe Coco ★★ ($$$$, p. 121)
Flanagan's Irish Pub & Restaurant ($$, p. 128)
Heritage Court ($$, p. 128)
Hog Penny ($, p. 132)
Landfall ★ ($$, p. 139)
North Rock Brewing Company ★ ($$, p. 137)
Ocean Echo ★★ ($$$, p. 118)
64 Degrees ($$, p. 119)
The Spot Restaurant ($, p. 135)
Swizzle Inn Bailey's Bay ($, p. 140)
White Horse Tavern ($$, p. 142)

BRITISH
Flanagan's Irish Pub & Restaurant ($$, p. 128)
The Frog & Onion Pub ($, p. 116)
Henry VIII ($$, p. 119)
Hog Penny ($, p. 132)

North Rock Brewing Company ★ ($$, p. 137)
Somerset Country Squire Pub & Restaurant ($$, p. 115)
Swizzle Inn Bailey's Bay ($, p. 140)

CARIBBEAN
Coconuts ★ ($$$, p. 117)
Jamaican Grill ($, p. 133)
Spring Garden Restaurant and Bar ($, p. 135).

CHINESE
Chopsticks Restaurant ★ ($, p. 131)
East Meets West ★ ($$, p. 127)

CONTINENTAL
Ascots ★ ($$$, p. 122)
Bolero Brasserie ★★ ($$$, p. 124)
Dining Room at the Lighthouse ($$, p. 120)
Fourways Inn ★★★ ($$$, p. 122)
Lemon Tree Café ($, p. 133)
Little Venice ★ ($$$, p. 126)
Palm Court ($$, p. 139)
Royston's ★ ($$$, p. 118)
Tom Moore's Tavern ★★ ($$$$, p. 138)
Wahoo's Bistro ★★ ($$, p. 142)

DELI/LIGHT BITES
Bailey's Ice Cream & Food D'Lites Restaurant ($, p. 140)
The Hickory Stick ($, p. 132)

KEY TO ABBREVIATIONS:
$$$$** = Very Expensive **$$$** = Expensive **$$** = Moderate **$ = Inexpensive

L'Oriental Express ($, p. 133)
Paradiso Cafe ($, p. 134)
Ten ($, p. 136)

FRENCH
Beau Rivage ★★ ($$$, p. 121)
Bouchée ★★ (p. 127)
Tom Moore's Tavern ★★
   ($$$$, p. 138)

ICE CREAM
Bailey's Ice Cream & Food D'Lites
   Restaurant ($, p. 140)

INDIAN
East Meets West ★ ($$, p. 127)
House of India ★ ($, p. 133)

INTERNATIONAL
Bermuda Bistro at the Beach
   ($, p. 126)
The Bermudiana/The Breakers ★
   ($$$, p. 136)
Blackbeard's Hideout ($$, p. 140)
Black Horse Tavern ★★ ($$, p. 140)
Breezes ★★ (p. 111)
Cafe Coco ★★ ($$$, p. 121)
Harry's ★★ ($$$, p. 125)
The Ocean Grill & The Cedar
   Room ★★ ($$$, p. 118)
The Pickled Onion ★★ ($$$, p. 126)
Port O' Call ($$, p. 129)
The Robin Hood ($, p. 135)
Specialty Inn ($, p. 138)
Tamarisk Dining Room ★★
   ($$$, p. 114)
Tavern by the Sea ($$, p. 142)
Victoria Grill ($, p. 130)
Wickets ($, p. 120)

ITALIAN
Ascots ★ ($$$, p. 122)
Bacci ★ ($$$, p. 117)
Café Amici ($$, p. 114)
Dining Room at The Lighthouse
   ($$, p. 120)
Little Venice ★ ($$$, p. 126)
Pasta Basta ($, p. 134)
Portofino ($, p. 134)
Ristorante Maria & Fresco's Wine Bar
   ($, p. 130)
Rustico ($$, p. 137)

Tio Pepe ($$, p. 120)
Trattoria Café ($, p. 136)

JAMAICAN
Jamaican Grill ($, p. 133)

MEDITERRANEAN
Ascots ★ ($$$, p. 122)
Bonefish Bar & Grill ($$, p. 114)
East Meets West ★ ($$, p. 127)
Harbourfront Restaurant & Komodaru
   Sushi Lounge ★★ ($$$, p. 125)
Harley's ($$, p. 128)
The Lido ★ ($$$, p. 122)
The Point Restaurant ★★★
   ($$$, p. 139)

MIDDLE EAST
Café Cairo ($$, p. 127)

PIZZERIA
Rustico ($$, p. 137)

PUB GRUB
Docksider ($, p. 132)

SEAFOOD
Barracuda Grill ★★ ($$$, p. 124)
Bonefish Bar & Grill ($$, p. 114)
Flying Fish ★ ($$, p. 124)
Harbourfront Restaurant & Komodaru
   Sushi Lounge ★★ ($$$, p. 125)
Lobster Pot & Boat House Bar ★★
   ($$, p. 129)
Ocean Club ★ ($$$, p. 117)
Port O' Call ($$, p. 129)
Somerset Country Squire Pub &
   Restaurant ($$, p. 115)
Wahoo's Bistro ★★ ($$, p. 142)
White Horse Tavern ($$, p. 142)

SOUTHWESTERN
Blû ★★ ($$$, p. 121)

SPANISH
Tio Pepe ($$, p. 120)

STEAK & SEAFOOD
Freeport Seafood Restaurant ★
   (Sandys Parish, $, p. 115)
Griffin's ★ ($$, p. 142)
Harry's ★★ ($$$, p. 125)
Mickey's Beach Bistro & Bar ★
   ($$$, p. 138)

Salt Rock Grill & Sushi Bar ($, p. 116)
Waterlot Inn ★★ ($$$$, p. 116)

SUSHI

Flying Fish ★ ($$, p. 124)
Harbourfront Restaurant & Komodaru
   Sushi Lounge ★★ ($$$, p. 125)
Henry VIII ($$, p. 119)
Salt Rock Grill & Sushi Bar ($, p. 116)
Specialty Inn ($, p. 138)
Yashi Sushi Bar ($, p. 136)

TEX-MEX

Rosa's Cantina ($, p. 135)

THAI

Chopsticks Restaurant ★ ($, p. 131)
Silk ★★★ ($$, p. 130)

WEST INDIAN

The Spot Restaurant ($, p. 135)

SHOPPING

Retailers on less prosperous islands attribute Bermuda's continuing reputation as a shopping mecca not only to the superb climate, but also to many years of skillful marketing. Indeed, no one has ever accused Bermudians of not knowing how to sell their island—or their rich inventories of goods.

Bermuda, once widely hailed as a "showcase of the British Empire," is still that, at least in its variety of goods. The retail scene draws upon its British antecedents: Shopkeepers are generally both polite and discreet, and merchandise is unusual and well made. In addition, most retailers take full advantage of location. Shops usually occupy charming cottages or historically important buildings, making shopping even more fun. Even visitors who intend to do no more than window-shop are likely to break down and make a purchase or two.

In most cases, shopping on Bermuda is about quality, not bargains. Shops face huge import tariffs, plus employee-related taxes, leading to what some view as outrageously high prices. And it rarely pays to comparison shop—the price of a watch in a branch store in St. George is likely to be exactly the same as it is in the main shop in the City of Hamilton.

Bermuda's Best Buys

Most of Bermuda's best shops are along Front Street in the City of Hamilton, where shopping is relaxed and casual. Among the choicest items are imports from Great Britain and Ireland, such as fine china, crystal, and cashmere sweaters and tweed jackets. Many items cost appreciably less than in their country of origin.

Because of a special "colony-like" arrangement with Great Britain, certain British goods are cheaper in Bermuda than in the United States, thanks to lower import tariffs. Some frequent visitors stock up on porcelain, crystal, silverware, jewelry, timepieces, and perfume, perhaps anticipating a wedding gift several months in advance. The island abounds with merchandisers of fine tableware, including Royal Copenhagen, Wedgwood, and Royal Crown Derby. Crystal is also plentiful, with many of the finest manufacturers in Europe and North America providing wide selections of merchandise. For a fee, most items can be shipped.

Liquor is also a good buy in Bermuda. U.S. citizens are allowed to bring back only 1 liter duty-free, but even adding U.S. tax and duty, you can save 35% to 50% on liquor purchases, depending on the brand. Liqueurs offer the largest savings.

The island's wealth of antiques and collectibles is extraordinary. Antiques lovers appreciate Bermuda's fusion of British aesthetic and mid-Atlantic charm. The island has a wealth of antique engravings and

19th-century furniture. Its modern artwork and handmade pottery and crafts are elegant souvenirs. And anyone interested in carrying home a piece of Bermuda's nautical heritage can choose from oversize ship's propellers, captain's bells, brass nameplates, scale models of sailing ships, or maybe even an old-fashioned ship's steering wheel from a salvaged shipwreck.

Other good buys are "Bermudiana"—products made on Bermuda or manufactured elsewhere exclusively for local stores. They include cedar-wood gifts, carriage bells, coins commemorating the anniversary of the island's settlement, flower plates by Spode, pewter tankards, handcrafted gold jewelry, traditional-line handbags with cedar or mahogany handles, miniature cottages in ceramic or limestone, shark's teeth polished and mounted in 14-karat gold, decorative kitchen items, Bermuda shorts (of course), silk scarves, and watches with a map of Bermuda on their faces.

Although some items might be less expensive than they are stateside, be aware that many others are overpriced. You should be familiar with the prices of comparable goods back home before making any big purchases.

THE SHOPPING SCENE
Where to Go
THE CITY OF HAMILTON
The widest range of shopping choices is in the City of Hamilton (see "In the City of Hamilton," below). Most shops are on Front Street, but you should explore the back streets as well, especially if you're an adventurous shopper.

The Emporium on Front Street, a restored building constructed around an atrium, houses a number of shops, including jewelry stores. Windsor Place on Queen Street is another Bermuda-style shopping mall.

HISTORIC ST. GEORGE
The "second city" of St. George also has many shops, stores, and boutiques, including branches of the City of Hamilton's famous Front Street stores. King's Square, the center of St. George, is home to many shops. The other major centers are Somers Wharf and Water Street.

In recent years, this historic port has emerged as a big-time shopping competitor to the City of Hamilton. It's easier to walk around St. George than the City of Hamilton, and St. George is more architecturally interesting, so more and more customers are choosing to do their shopping here. Of course, St. George doesn't have as vast an array of merchandise as the City of Hamilton, so the serious shopper might want to explore both cities.

SANDYS PARISH
Don't overlook the shopping possibilities of the West End. Somerset Village in Sandys Parish has many shops (though quite a few are branches of the City of Hamilton stores). At the Royal Naval Dockyard area on Ireland Island, you can visit the Craft Market, Island Pottery, and the Bermuda Arts Centre at Dockyard, where you'll see local artisans at work.

 The Eternal Search for Bargains

During the off season (autumn and winter), stores often reduce prices to make way for goods for the new season. But sales come and go year-round—keep an eye out for sale signs no matter when you're in Bermuda.

What You Should Know

STORE HOURS

Stores in the City of Hamilton, St. George, and Somerset are generally open Monday through Saturday from 9am to 5:30pm. When large liners are in port, stores may stay open later, and are sometimes open on Sundays. For more information on the local shopping scene, visit **www.experiencebermuda.com/shopping**.

FINDING AN ADDRESS

Some Front Street stores post numbers on their buildings; others don't. Sometimes the number posted or used is the "historic" number of the building, which has nothing to do with the modern number. You can always ask for directions, and most Bermudians are willing to help. Outside the City of Hamilton, don't expect to find numbers on buildings at all—or even street names in some cases.

SALES TAX & DUTY

There's no sales tax in Bermuda, but it's not a duty-free island. Depending on which country you're returning to, you may have to pay duty. See "Customs," in the "Fast Facts" section of chapter 10, for details.

Note: Bermuda is covered by the U.S. law regarding "Generalized System of Preferences" status. That means that if at least 35% of an item has been crafted in Bermuda, you can bring it back duty-free, regardless of how much you spent. If you've gone beyond your $800 allotment, make a separate list of goods made in Bermuda. This will make it easier for the customs officials (and for you).

IN THE CITY OF HAMILTON

Between 7 and 10pm every Wednesday night, **Hamilton Harbour Nights** are staged along Front Street in Bermuda's capital. Late-night shopping becomes a festival, with street performers, horse-and-carriage rides, a variety of live entertainment, and arts and crafts exhibitions. There's a food court and even children's activities.

Department Stores

Generations of Bermuda-bound visitors made Trimingham's and Smith's, headquartered along Front Street, their first stops for shopping. Several years ago, these venerable department stores closed their doors. Although nothing will replace the loss of these emporiums in the hearts of many locals, you can find some of the same type of merchandise at Marks & Spencer, A. S. Cooper & Sons, and to a lesser degree, Gibbons.

A. S. Cooper & Sons   Traditionally, this place has been best known for its selection of crystal and porcelain, but in the wake of the collapse of Trimingham's and Smith's, Cooper has beefed up its cosmetics, perfumes, and men's and women's fashion selections as well. For more on A. S. Cooper, refer to "China & Glassware" below. 59 Front St. www.ascooper.bm. © **441/295-3961.**

Gibbons   Sprawling and cost-efficient, Gibbons isn't the first choice for locals looking for classy, upscale clothing and housewares, but it's a second-tier choice for sundries, the necessities of housekeeping, and that shower curtain you know you needed back home but never had time to buy. Costs are more reasonable than at Marks & Spencer, but the venue is, frankly, a lot less chic. 21 Reid St. www.gibbons.bm. © **441/295-0022.**

Shopping in the City of Hamilton

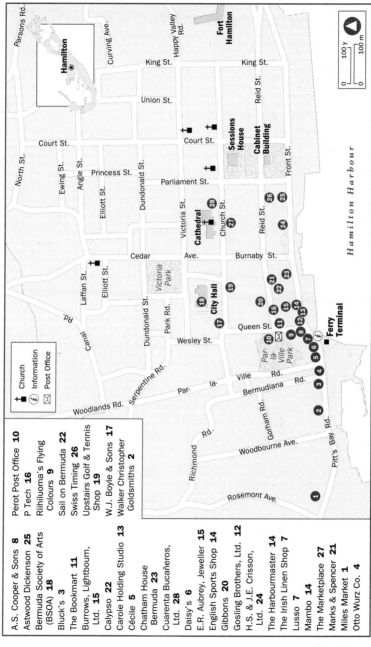

A.S. Cooper & Sons **8**
Astwood Dickenson **25**
Bermuda Society of Arts
(BSOA) **18**
Bluck's **3**
The Bookmart **11**
Burrows, Lightbourn,
Ltd. **15**
Calypso **22**
Carole Holding Studio **13**
Cécile **5**
Chatham House
Bermuda **23**
Cuarenta Bucañeros,
Ltd. **28**
Daisy's **6**
E.R. Aubrey, Jeweller **15**
English Sports Shop **14**
Gibbons **20**
Gosling Brothers, Ltd. **12**
H.S. & J.E. Crisson,
Ltd. **24**
The Harbourmaster **14**
The Irish Linen Shop **7**
Lusso **7**
Mambo **14**
The Marketplace **27**
Marks & Spencer **21**
Miles Market **1**
Otto Wurz Co. **4**

Perot Post Office **10**
P Tech **16**
Riihiluoma's Flying
Colours **9**
Sail on Bermuda **22**
Swiss Timing **26**
Upstairs Golf & Tennis
Shop **19**
W.J. Boyle & Sons **17**
Walker Christopher
Goldsmiths **2**

149

Marks & Spencer   This branch of the famous British chain (sometimes oddly called "St. Michael") carries the same reliable merchandise as its sibling stores in the British Isles. You'll find men's, women's, and children's fashions in everything from resort wear to sleepwear, including lingerie. There are also well-tailored dresses and suits, dress shirts, blazers, and British-tailored trousers, as well as swimwear, toiletries, house and giftware, fabrics sold by the yard or meter, and English sweets and biscuits. 28 Reid St. ✆ **441/295-5516.**

Goods A to Z

ART

Bermuda Society of Arts (BSOA) ★★   Loosely associated with the Bermudian government, this store is devoted to the exhibition of works by Bermuda-based artists and is one of the focal points of the island's arts scene. The West Wing of Hamilton's City Hall (the island's Fine Arts Museum occupies the East Wing) is the permanent home of the oldest arts society on Bermuda. The site contains four separate exhibition areas, where the artwork changes every 3 weeks. Themes range from the moderately avant-garde to the conservative, and every show includes dozens of examples of Bermudian landscapes, seascapes, or architectural renderings, any of which would make worthwhile souvenirs of your stay on the island. All merchandise can be packed for airplane transport. West Wing of City Hall, 17 Church St. www.bsoa.bm. ✆ **441/292-3824.**

BEACHWEAR & SUNGLASSES

Calypso   Calypso carries casual, fun fashions (including unusual garments from Max Mara and Benetton) and the most comprehensive selection of swimwear on Bermuda. The shop also features Italian leather goods, espadrilles, hats, bags, Italian ceramics, beach wraps, and whimsical gift items. It's the exclusive island retailer of Louis Vuitton luggage and accessories. Additional branches can be found at the Fairmont Southampton, Elbow Beach Hotel, Coral Beach Club, and the Dockyard. 23–24 Front St. www.calypsobermuda.com. ✆ **441/295-2112.**

Sail on Bermuda   The locals shop at this store, which carries a unique collection of casual wear, bathing suits, and gifts. A recent poll of shoppers named Sail on Bermuda's T-shirts the best on Bermuda. A small addition, called "Shades of Bermuda," has the finest collection of sunglasses on the island. The store also sells sailing suits. Old Cellar, in the Walker Arcade Front St. (btw. Burnaby and Queen sts.). ✆ **441/295-0808.**

BOOKS

The Bookmart   Administered as a subdivision of the flagship of Bermuda's largest chain of pharmacies, Brown & Co., this is the biggest bookstore on Bermuda. It specializes in bestsellers—mainly from the U.S. market—and carries works by British authors as well. One section is devoted to books about the island. There's also a well-stocked section for the kiddies. In the Phoenix Centre, 3 Reid St. www.bookmart.bm. ✆ **441/279-5443.**

CHINA & GLASSWARE

A. S. Cooper & Sons ★★★   Bermuda's oldest and largest china and glassware store—family owned since 1897—offers a broad range of fine bone china, earthenware, glassware, and jewelry. Among the famous names represented are Minton, Royal Doulton, Belleek, Aynsley, Villeroy & Bosch, Wedgwood, Royal Copenhagen, and Lladró. The Crystal Room displays Orrefors, Waterford, Royal Brierley, and Kosta

Boda. The perfume department offers cosmetics and selections from the world's greatest perfumeries. On the upper floors, there's lots of fashion for men and women, including such labels as Port Marion, Ralph Lauren, Calvin Klein, and Lacoste. 59 Front St. www.ascooper.bm. ℭ **441/295-3961.**

Bluck's ★   Established in 1844, Bluck's is well known for carrying some of the finest names in china, including Royal Worcester, Spode, Royal Doulton, and Herend porcelain from Hungary. The choice in crystal is equally impressive: Kosta Boda, Waterford, Baccarat, Daum, and Lalique (exclusive to Bluck's in Bermuda). 4 Front St. www.blucksbermuda.com. ℭ **441/295-5367.**

FASHION

Also see "Shoes," "Sportswear," and "Woolens," below.

Cécile   Well-stocked Cécile is the center for women's high fashion on Bermuda. Management boasts that visiting Cécile is like calling upon the fashion capitals of the world—you'll find labels such as Basler, Emilio Pucci, Lilly Pulitzer, and Gottex. Its sweater and accessories boutique is also outstanding. 15 Front St. (near the Visitors Information Centre and the Ferry Terminal). ℭ **441/295-1311.**

Daisy's   Established in 2011, this is a small-scale, selective boutique for ladies' clothing, focusing on everything a woman might need if, for instance, she was stranded without luggage over a weekend and had to acquire everything from short shorts to evening gowns. A short list of men's clothing ("The Mac Line") was added in 2012 for holiday-making couples in need of appropriately sporty accessories for long walks on midwinter or midsummer beaches. 11 Front St., Hamilton. ℭ **441/293-7477.**

Mambo   The ambience at this clothing emporium for women, men, and children, is sports and youth oriented. Management describes its offerings as "middle-to-highbrow, trend-centered sportswear," which includes designer jeans (by Diesel, among others) and the kind of windproof garments that look good on a golf course or on a sailboat. 7 Reid St. or 12 Walker Arcade. Front St. (btw. Burnaby and Queen sts.). ℭ **441/295-5698.**

GIFTS

Carole Holding Studio ★   The England-born genius behind this trio of shops has evolved into one of the most famous female entrepreneurs in Bermuda, thanks to hard work and a knack for churning out gift items that instantly evoke happy memories of the island. Her inventories focus on original artworks, as well as hand-painted and/or handcrafted items that include Bermuda scenes painted onto china teapots, bread and cheese boards, porcelain storage containers, coffee mugs, and illuminated recipe books. There's also a scrumptious array of food items that includes rum cakes (the version with lemon and coconut is fabulous), onion marmalades, hot pepper jellies, and "dark and

---

The Right Fit: Finding Your Size in Bermuda

Recognizing that the majority of their customers hail from North America, store managers throughout Bermuda do their best to systematically relabel garments from manufacturers in Europe and the U.K. with sizes that correspond to usage in the U.S. But if for any reason the garment that appeals to you carries a European or British label and hasn't been relabeled, clothing salespersons throughout Bermuda have conversion charts readily available.

stormy" jam with black rum and ginger. Additional locations are in the lower lobby of the Fairmont Southampton Resort (℡ **441/238-7310**) and King's Square in St. George's (℡ **441/297-1833**). 81 Front St., in Hamilton. www.caroleholding.bm. ℡ **441/296-3431**.

Riihiluoma's Flying Colours   This is everybody's favorite catchall emporium for inexpensive, impulse-purchase souvenirs and T-shirts with perky slogans. You'll also find paperweights, beach coverups, sarongs, key chains shaped like Bermuda, and arts and crafts. The establishment's hard-to-spell name comes from the Finnish-born family that established it in 1937 and still manages it today. 5 Queen St. www.flying colours.bm. ℡ **441/295-0890**.

GROCERS

The Marketplace   This is the largest grocery store on the island, catering to locals and vacationers alike. There are various branches scattered across the island, but the chain headquarters is in Hamilton at the address below. Started in 1939, the chain was originally called Piggly Wiggly. If you don't want to cook, you can purchase precooked food to go, including homemade soups, freshly made salads, main courses for dinner, even stir-fries and luscious desserts. Locals often drop in for a hot lunch, and there is a lot of organic foodstuff. The main branch stays open until 10pm, and even keeps Sunday hours from 1 to 5pm. 42 Church St. www.marketplace.bm. ℡ **441/295-6006**.

Miles Market   Visiting New Yorkers call this Balducci's of Bermuda because of its upmarket selection of gourmet food items. On site is the first Godiva coffee bar in the world, and, of course, all Godiva chocolate products are for sale. If you are cooking, you'll find the best selection of meat on the island, including hand-selected and aged beef, along with lamb, pork, poultry, and seafood. Their "World of Cheese" is a special, exotic treat as well. The outlet will also deliver your bag of groceries anywhere on the island. 96 Pitts Bay Rd. (near Fairmont Hamilton Princess), in Hamilton. ℡ **441/295-1234**.

JEWELRY

Astwood Dickinson   Here you'll find a treasure-trove of famous-name watches, including Patek Philippe, Cartier, Tiffany, Tag Heuer, and Omega, plus designer jewelry, all at prices generally below U.S. retail. From the original Bermuda collection, you can select an 18-karat gold memento of the island (jeweled representations of local flora, fauna, and landmarks). There's an additional location in Walker Arcade on Front St. (btw. Burnaby and Queen sts.; ℡ **441/292-4247**). 83–85 Front St. www.astwooddickinson.com. ℡ **441/292-5805**.

E. R. Aubrey, Jewellers   This shop carries an extensive collection of gold chains, rings with precious and semiprecious stones, and charms, including one of the Bermuda longtail bird. 101 Front St. E. ℡ **441/295-3826**.

H. S. & J. E. Crisson Ltd.   Crisson is the exclusive Bermuda agent for Rolex, Ebel, and Seiko watches, and for other well-known makers. It also carries an extensive selection of fine jewelry and gems. 55 and 71 Front St. www.crisson.com. ℡ **441/295-2351**.

Swiss Timing   All the best names in Swiss watchmaking are found here, including Rodania, Certina, Oris, and Zenith, along with a selection of semiprecious jewelry, gold chains, and bracelets. 95 Front St. ℡ **441/295-1376**.

Walker Christopher Goldsmiths ★★   For the past decade or so, the *Bermudian* magazine has cited this goldsmith for selling the finest jewelry on the island. The shop showcases everything from classic diamond bands to strands of South Sea pearls to modern hand-hammered chokers. The store also carries a collection of rare coins—gold doubloons and silver "pieces of eight" salvaged from sunken galleons, as well as Greek and Roman coins that can be mounted and worn as pendants, earrings, and cuff links. Even Egyptian artifacts have been transformed into wearable art. Customers who have their own design in mind can work with a master jeweler to craft a one-of-a-kind piece. The on-site workshop also produces Bermuda-inspired gold jewelry and sterling silver Christmas ornaments. 9 and 69 Front St. www.walkerchristopher.com. © **441/295-1466.**

LEATHER GOODS

The Harbourmaster   This is your best bet for luggage and leather goods. These value items are from Colombia and are often sold at prices that are lower than in the United States. There are more expensive leather goods from Italy (such as handbags), plus an extensive collection of wallets, and nylon and canvas tote bags. The shop also stocks travel accessories, including luggage carts. Washington Mall. © **441/295-5333.**

Lusso   More high-end than many of the other stores selling mostly women's purses, handbags, suitcases, shoes, and perfume, this is a store that causes trend-conscious materialists on Bermuda to actually salivate upon mention of its name. Brands it carries read like a who's who from a recent edition of *Vogue*: Fendi, Prada, Ferragamo, and Jimmy Choo. 49 Front St. in Hamilton. © **441/295-2672.**

LINENS

The Irish Linen Shop   At Heyl's Corner, near the "Birdcage" police officer post, this is the biggest distributor of luxury bed linens in Bermuda. Inventories include pure linen tablecloths from Ireland, and bed sheets and tablecloths from Souleiado of Provence and from other purveyors of luxury bed- and table-linens from around the world. The owners go to Europe twice a year and bring back exceptional items such as Madeira hand embroidery and Belgian lace. You can often save as much as 50% over American prices. 31 Front St. (at Queen St.). © **441/295-4089.**

LIQUOR & LIQUEURS

Alcohol is a good buy in Bermuda. You are allowed to take what U.S. Customs calls a "reasonable amount" of liquor from Bermuda to the United States. There is a duty-free allowance, but you merely pay overage to U.S. Customs at the airport (see "Last-Minute Purchases," at the end of this chapter). Even with the duty, prices are often lower than those in the States.

Burrows, Lightbourn Ltd.   This is the best and most comprehensive liquor store in Bermuda, with a wide array of spirits in various price ranges. You can put together your own package of Bermuda liquors at in-bond or duty-free prices. The store will deliver your packages to the airport or to your ship. Additional locations are located at Harbour Road in Paget Parish ((© **441/236-0355)**, at Water Street in St. George's ((© **441/297-0552)**, and at the airport. E. Broadway in downtown Hamilton. © **441/295-1554.**

Gosling Brothers, Ltd.   The leading competitor of Burrows, Gosling has been selling liquor on Bermuda since 1806. One of their best-sellers is Gosling's Black Seal dark rum, which is viewed as a key ingredient in some Bermuda recipes, including some versions of rum cakes and fish chowder. In addition to their own rum, the store stocks a wide selection of liquors, liqueurs, and wines. If you want to buy liquor to take home under your duty-free allowance, you can arrange to have it sent to the airport. Other locations are at 17 Dundonald St. ((© **441/295-1123)**, in St. George's at the corner of York and Queen streets ((© **441/297-1364)**, and at the airport. Front and Queen sts. www.goslingsrum.com. © **441/298-7337.**

Branching Out

You'll often find branches of the City of Hamilton's stores at major resorts. The prices—even when there's a sale—are the same as those charged by the parent stores in the City of Hamilton.

Although the selection is more limited, resort boutiques remain open on Sunday, when most stores in the City of Hamilton are shuttered.

PHOTOGRAPHIC EQUIPMENT

P-Tech   A leading outlet for photographic and electronic equipment, this outfit stocks cameras, film, and accessories for Canon, Sony, Nikon, Pentax, Fuji, Olympus, and other big names. The store also carries top-of-the-line picture frames and camera bags. Also sold are tapes, tape recorders, and other supplies. 5 Reid St. ☏ **441/295-5496.**

SHOES

W. J. Boyle & Son ★   In business since 1884, this shop offers footwear for men, women, and children. With the best collection in town, it specializes in brand-name footwear from England, Spain, Brazil, and the United States (including Clarks of England, Cole Haan, and Enzo Angiolini). Queen St. at Church St. ☏ **441/295-1887.**

SILVER

Otto Wurz Co.   Otto Wurz is at the western end of Front Street, past the Ferry Terminal and the Bank of Bermuda. It specializes in articles made of silver, including jewelry, charms, and bracelets. One section of the store is devoted to gift items such as pewter ware, cute wooden signs, and glassware. 3–5 Front St. (btw. Par-la-Ville and Bermudiana rds.). ☏ **441/295-1247.**

SPORTSWEAR

Upstairs Golf & Tennis Shop   Everything you'll need for the tennis courts or the golf links is available in this amply stocked store. For golfers, there's merchandise by Ping, Callaway, TaylorMade, Titleist, and Adams. Tennis enthusiasts will recognize products by Wilson, Yonex, and many others. 26 Church St. ☏ **441/295-5161.**

STAMPS

Perot Post Office   Philatelists from all over the world visit this office to buy postage stamps from Bermuda. Highly prized by collectors, the stamps often feature historic figures and the island's flora and fauna. Stamps commemorating the 400th anniversary of Jamestown, Virginia, and the 19th-century sailing sloop *Spirit of Bermuda* are two of the most coveted stamps. Open Monday through Friday from 9am to 5pm. Queen St., at the entrance to Par-la-Ville Park. ☏ **441/297-7865.**

TOBACCO

Many Americans come to Bermuda to enjoy Cuban cigars (which can't be brought back into the United States).

Chatham House Bermuda   Chatham House is a historic retailer of Cuban cigars. Bermuda used to harvest its own tobacco, but now it is imported from Cuba. The store also carries pipes, Swiss Army knives, lighters, and postcards. 63 Front St. ☏ **441/292-8422.**

Cuarenta Bucañeros Ltd.   Licensed by the Cuban government to sell premium, handmade Cuban cigars. and located within a sublimely upscale setting one floor up from street level, this organization sells boxes of the kinds of high-end cigars which go well with public announcements of births, IPO stock buyouts, and corporate mergers. Montecristo, Romeo y Julieta, Trinidad, Cohiba, Partagas and Hoyo de Monterrey are a few of the famous cigars for sale. Since its establishment by Ian Gordon and David Thompson, venture capitalists and real estate developers, they've developed relationships with clients as far away as Dubai, The Philippines, and Russia. In the Continental Bldg., 25 Church St. www.cigarbox.bm. ✆ **441/ 295-4523.**

WOOLENS

English Sports Shop   This shop, established in 1918, is one of the island's leading retailers of quality classic and British woolen goods from Pringles and Marks & Spencer for men, women, and children. Its selection of sweaters, knit golf shirts, and Bermuda shorts is impeccable and, in many cases, appropriately "preppy." 49 Front St., Hamilton. ✆ **441/295-2672.**

AROUND THE ISLAND

As you leave the City of Hamilton and tour the island, you may want to continue looking for typical Bermudian items at the shops listed below.

For other shopping suggestions, consider the **Bermuda Craft Market** (p. 89) and **The Birdsey Studio** (p. 92) in Paget Parish.

Sandys Parish

IRELAND ISLAND

Bermuda Arts Centre at Dockyard   This art gallery specializes in paintings, sculptures, and crafts, mostly by Bermudian artisans. New exhibitions are configured about every 6 weeks. Not to be confused with the nearby Bermuda Crafts Centre, with which it is not associated, it's sponsored by a local foundation and strives for more than a purely commercial approach to art. Prices range from $145 for a reproduction print to as much as $12,000 for an original. Lots of less expensive originals and craft items are also for sale. Some of the staff members here are well versed in the nuances of the local art scene. Maritime Dr., in the Royal Naval Dockyard. www.art bermuda.bm. ✆ **441/234-2809.** Bus: 7 or 8.

The Bermuda Triangle   Most of the gift and fashion items inventoried here are Bermuda inspired and unique. Merchandise includes hand-painted boxes with "Britain in the tropics" designs; island summer clothing; costume jewelry, many pieces made with shells; wind chimes; scented candles; Bermuda Christmas ornaments, and a wide selection of T-shirts. In the Clocktower Mall, Royal Naval Dockyard, Sandys. ✆ **441/234-0837.**

The Dockyard Cakery/The Dockyard Glassworks ★★   Around 1820, the soaring masonry premises of this place were a repair yard for high-masted ships. Today, every inch of the cavernous room is filled with gift items (glassware and baked goods) that are created, displayed, and sold as part of an extraordinarily seamless entrepreneurial process. Somehow, the gift items here taste better and look more valuable because visitors are made aware of how they were made. During peak season, as many as 3,200 people a day wander through this historic factory, marveling at the shimmering beauty of the handblown, handcrafted glass items at one end of the room, and the unctuous flavors and aromas emerging from the "microbakery" at the other. (A microbakery specializes in a high volume of a very limited number of products—in this case, 10 different flavors of rum cakes.) Wendy Avery and Tony Johns are the hardworking owners who sell their cakes for between $13 and $40 depending on the size, and glass objects for between $14 and $900 depending on their complexity and size. 1 Maritime Lane, in the Royal Dockyard, Sandys Parish. www.bermudarumcakes.com and www.dockglass.com. (C) **441/234-4216.**

Southampton Parish

Sharon Wilson Gallery From her private home, just minutes by foot from Horseshoe Beach, and about 3 minutes' drive from the Fairmont Southampton, local artist Sharon Wilson is known for going beyond the picture-postcard view of island life in an attempt to portray Bermuda's spirit in more depth. She explores the scope of Bermudian life and its people through limited and open-edition lithographs and notecards. The gallery is also home to her picture book illustrations, the most well known being the award-winning *The Day Gogo Went to Vote*, published in honor of the end of apartheid in South Africa. Call before you go—Ms. Wilson prefers that appointments be made in advance of your arrival. 2 Turtle Place. (C) **441/238-2583.** Bus: 7.

St. George's Parish

The Bermuda Perfumery This shop carries a roster of perfumes you've seen for sale in other shops, internationally, as well as blends crafted on the island from ingredients which include native frangipani and Bermuda cedar. Someone on-site will explain how the scents are invented and blended. Stewart Hall, 5 Queen St., St. George's. www.lilibermuda.com. (C) **441/293-0627.** Bus: 7

Vera P. Card Established by a Canadian war hero who married the woman (Vera Card) who rescued him from a Nazi POW camp after World War II, this shop is known for its gifts from around the world, including one of the island's largest collections of Lladró and Hummel figurines. There's also a collection of Czech, Austrian, and Bohemian crystal, giftware, and chandeliers; colored gemstones; and 14-karat gold jewelry from "The Bermuda Collection" that will help evoke memories of the island long after your departure. 22 Water St., St. George's (C) **441/295-1729.** Bus: 7

The Book Cellar Built in the 18th century, this small but choice bookshop lies below Tucker House, a National Trust property. It caters to visitors and locals alike, including a lot of "yachties" who stop by to pick up reading material for their time at

Comparison Shopping at Somers Wharf

The best place to begin shopping is at the **Somers Wharf & Branch Stores** along Water Street (bus no. 7), a coterie of shops that includes all the big names from the City of Hamilton, such as A. S. Cooper, the English Sports Shop, and the Crown Colony Shop. Of course, the parent branches in the City of Hamilton tend to be better stocked, but Somers Wharf makes shopping a pleasure because all the island's "name" shops are clustered together, making comparison shopping much easier.

The international airport in Bermuda offers duty-free shops for those last-minute purchases. One shop is in the international departures lounge, and the other lies near the U.S. departures lounge. For that specialty purchase, you should still shop around the island, but now you can buy routine duty-free items such as perfume, cigarettes, and liquor just before boarding the plane. That sure beats the old system of buying duty-free liquor and cigarettes a day or so in advance and having them delivered to the airport.

sea. A lot of people come here for the Cellar's line of books about Bermuda. There's also a wide array of fiction and nonfiction by British and American writers. Parents might be interested in picking up one of the children's books published in Britain—many are quite different from similar editions in America. Water St. © **441/297-0448.** Bus: 7.

Cooper's Frangipani   This is a world of fun, colorful, "dressy casual" fashion for women. You'll find a large selection of comfortable cottons, bright silks, and soft rayons. The store is known for its unusual merchandise, including exclusive island designs. There's also a fine collection of swimwear and unusual accessories. 16 Water St., Somers Wharf. © **441/297-1357.** Bus: 7.

Taylors   Go here for the finest selection of women's and children's kilts and tartans from Scotland. Most of the merchandise is for women, but you'll also find slippers, neckties, and bowties. 30 Water St. © **441/297-1626.** Bus: 7.

BERMUDA AFTER DARK

A s we've mentioned, nightlife is not one of the compelling reasons to go to Bermuda, although there is some after-dark action, mainly in the summer. If you visit during the winter, we trust you'll be content to nurse a drink in a pub.

In the summer, activity seems to float from hotel to hotel, which makes it hard to predict which pub or nightspot will have the best steel-drum or calypso band at any given time. Many pubs feature singalongs at the piano, a popular form of entertainment in Bermuda. Most of the big hotels offer shows after dinner, with combos filling in between shows for couples who like to dance.

The island's visitor centers and most hotels distribute free copies of such publications as *Preview Bermuda, Bermuda Weekly,* and *This Week in Bermuda,* which list the latest scheduled activities and events. There's a calendar of events in the *Bermudian,* sold at most newsstands.

You can also tune in to the local TV station, which constantly broadcasts information for visitors, including details on cultural events and nightlife offerings around the island. From 7am to noon daily, radio station 1160 AM (VSB) broadcasts news of Bermuda's cultural and entertainment events.

THE CLUB & MUSIC SCENE
Pembroke Parish (City of Hamilton)

Coconut Rock   With a name more evocative of the Caribbean than of Bermuda, this restaurant has two of the most active bars in town, both with prices that are relatively reasonable for high-priced Bermuda. It draws locals and visitors (in equal numbers) with background music and videos of the hottest acts in the U.K. and America. Food items from what's technically a separate restaurant, the Yashi Sushi Bar, can be ordered from its location next door if you have the munchies and a hankering for fish. Happy hour is Monday through Friday from 5 to 7pm. Open daily 11:30am to 1am. Williams House, 20 Reid St. *©* **441/292-1043.** Bus: 7 or 8.

LVs Piano Jazz Lounge ★   This custom-built venue is the best place on the island to hear international jazz, often American, which is performed on stage nightly. The bartenders specialize in exotic cocktails, and you can also order "small bites," such as lobster and mango on a skewer with a sweet vanilla chili dressing or scallop ceviche with seaweed salad. There's also a daily dim sum basket. Theme nights are a regular feature Monday to Friday 4 to 8pm, ranging from wines of the week on Monday to champagne night on Friday. Open Monday to Thursday noon to 1am, Friday noon to 3am, and Saturday 8pm to 1am. 12 Bermudiana Rd. www.diningbermuda.com. ✆ **441/296-3330.** Bus: 1, 2, 10, or 11.

Opus It's been described as a wine bar on steroids, drawing clients in their 30s, 40s, and 50s who appreciate the sometimes magnificent vintages that are sold here by the glass. It begins its day as a breakfast cafe, and serves sandwiches, salads, and wraps at lunchtime. But its charms are most visible after 5pm, when it's a preferred after-hours venue for office workers and members of the banking and financial community from nearby Hamilton. The club, open Monday to Saturday 7am to 1am, charges from $7 to $20 for a glass of wine. 4 Bermudiana Rd. www.bermudasbestrestaurants. com. ✆ **441/292-3500.** Bus: 7.

The Spinning Wheel If you'd like to escape from the tourist hordes for a pint of beer with the locals, head to this longtime neighborhood favorite, an institution since its opening in 1970. Named for a song by Blood, Sweat & Tears (remember them?), it's a relaxing joint with an outdoor pool area with a bar, but it sometimes attracts rowdy locals. The place is most crowded with people from outside its immediate neighborhood whenever there's a special event, such as a preannounced performance by a local. An upstairs section for dancing to reggae and more draws a young crowd. Happy hour is noon to 8pm Monday through Friday. Open daily noon to 3am. 33 Court St. ✆ **441/292-7799.** Cover upstairs $17–$22 Fri–Sun. Bus: 7 or 8.

Southampton Parish

Henry VIII This restaurant (p. 119) is also a good bet for music and comedy. Piano tunes and singing are often featured, as are comedians. Performances begin at 9:30pm and last until the restaurant closes at 1am. The stage is visible from the pub and from one of the restaurant's three dining areas. 52 South Shore Rd. www.henrys.bm. ✆ **441/238-1977.** Bus: 7 or 8.

THE BAR SCENE
Hamilton Parish

Swizzle Inn The home of the Bermuda rum swizzle, this bar and restaurant (p. 140) lies west of the airport, near the Crystal Caves. You can order a Swizzleburger and fish and chips throughout the day. There's live entertainment most nights during summer. The tradition is to tack your business card to any place you can find a spot, even the ceiling. The jukebox plays both soft and hard rock. Happy hour is Monday through Friday 5 to 7pm. Food is served from 11am to 10pm. In 2007, based on its roaring success in Hamilton Parish, this place opened a second branch in Warwick Parish, along Bermuda's south shore. Daily 11am to 1am. 3 Blue Hole Hill, Bailey's Bay. www.swizzleinn.com. ✆ **441/293-1854.** Bus: 3 or 11.

Pembroke Parish (City of Hamilton)

Café Cairo For a few years, this Egyptian/Lebanese restaurant was known for the quality of its food and the exotic charm of its Middle Eastern aesthetics. But as business fell away and standards declined, it's now best recommended as a late-night bar where night owls from throughout Bermuda descend for after-hour drinks, dialogues, a flirtation or two, and perhaps a plate of food. Its decor includes elaborately carved doors and window screens imported from the souks of Egypt, copper tables and artifacts hauled in from Cairo, and the kind of diffused lighting that seems to well up from behind the chairs, tables, and chests. Lunch and dinner are served daily from noon to 4pm and from 6pm to midnight, with main courses priced from $23 to around $35, but frankly, the place is most popular among young and nubile Bermudians in its role as a bar and DJ-fueled disco. Within the shadowy world favored by late-night denizens of Bermuda, Café Cairo's main competition derives from the nearby and also-recommended **Square One.** The bar remains open until 3am every night except Sunday. 95 Front St. ✆ **441/295-5155.** Bus: 1, 2, 10, or 11.

Casey's   There's nothing flashy about this long, narrow room, which seems to be a favorite with locals. Look for yellowed photographs of old Bermuda and a carefully preserved, wall-mounted marlin caught by the owner in 1982. Friday nights here are the hands-down winner as the most popular on the island, and the joint overflows. (And frankly, other nights here are a lot less thrilling.) Go here if you like to wander far off-the-beaten tourist trail and want to hang out with local Bermudians. Monday to Saturday 10am to 10pm. 25 Queen St. (btw. Reid and Church sts.). ✆ **441/292-9994.** Bus: 1, 2, 10, or 11.

Docksider   No other bar in Bermuda seems as distinctly controversial and divided into warring camps: Men swear by it, sometimes defining it as their favorite bar, while some of their female peers object to ever even going there. Go figure. Maybe it's the kind of place best reserved for men taking a break from their significant others. At any rate, along its cedar bar you'll find some of the most avid sports fans on Bermuda. There's a phalanx of big-screen TVs broadcasting whatever's happening in the wide world of sports. One section is a wine bar, which is more intimate. You can order pub grub, such as fish and chips or shepherd's pie. On some Fridays, there is a DJ. Happy hour is daily from 5 to 7pm. It's open daily as a restaurant from 11:30am to 9:30pm, and as a bar it stays open till 1am (till 2am Fri–Sat). 121 Front St. www.dockies.com. ✆ **441/296-3333.** Bus: 1, 2, 10, or 11.

Flanagan's   On the second floor of a landmark building in the heart of Hamilton's business district, this restaurant and pub is one of Bermuda's most visible symbols of Irish nationalism and "the 100,000 welcomes" (*cead mile failte*) that often go with it. It's known for some of the town's best music—reggae, Top 40, rock, soca, and what is often called "party music." There are two bars that feature exotic drinks. Happy hour is daily from 5 to 7pm. In the sports bar, you can watch European soccer matches or other sports; there are about a dozen large TV screens. It's open Monday to Friday 11am to 1am, Saturday and Sunday 9am to 1pm. Emporium Bldg., 69 Front St. www.flanagans.bm. ✆ **441/295-8299.** Bus: 7 or 8.

Heritage Court   Most of the time, this pub within the Fairmont Hamilton Princess seems starched, a bit stuffy, and patronized by a clientele preoccupied with whatever sales meeting they're on their way to or from. But whatever you believe to be true about this place will change, perhaps radically, if you venture inside between May and October on any Friday night between 5:30 and 10pm. Then again, thanks to the hordes of singles who gather on the nearby verandas of the hotel, there might not be room to sit. Some islanders insist that it's the hottest and most easy-to-flirt-with-a-stranger venue on the island. We can't confirm that for sure, but with more than a thousand partiers who cram into this place to hear the live entertainment and to see and be seen, the assertion doesn't seem far-fetched. In the Fairmont Princess Hotel, 76 Pitts Bay Rd. ✆ **441/295-3000.** Bus: 7 or 8.

The Pickled Onion ★★   For years, Ye Old Cock & Feather was one of Bermuda's landmark pubs. In 1997, after a multimillion-dollar renovation, it glaringly changed its image (as well as its name), and the once fairly staid pub became a stop on the trend-conscious after-dark circuit. Funky fabrics cover the booths and tables where patrons listen to music that ranges from Top 40 to blues to oldies and hits of the past 50 years. Live music starts at 10pm during the summer season. This place is sometimes cited as one of the few bars in Bermuda that continues to serve snacks and pub grub during the midafternoon, when many of its competitors have locked up their kitchens. Happy hour is Monday to Friday from 5 to 7pm. Open daily from 11am to around 1am (Fri–Sat until 2am). 53 Front St. ✆ **441/295-2263.** Bus: 1, 2, 10, or 11.

The Robin Hood   More than most other drinking spots in Bermuda, this one attracts expatriates from the U.K. who might, if they're in a good mood, satirically describe themselves as "good-natured blokes" and "merry wenches." Set within a 10-minute walk from the offices of downtown Hamilton, it serves foaming pints of lager and hale and hearty pub fare, including some of Bermuda's best pizzas. It's also one of the island's premier sports bars, with big-screen coverage of various U.S. and British league competitions. Some nights, a master of ceremonies conducts trivia quizzes, while other nights focus on reggae and rock 'n' roll. And when it's particularly rowdy, a prize might be awarded to the patron who can drink a pint of ale the fastest. It's open Monday through Saturday 11am to 1am, Sunday noon to 1am. 25 Richmond Rd. ✆ **441/295-3314.** Bus: 6 or 7.

Sandys Parish

The Frog & Onion Pub   Converted from an 18th-century cooperage, or barrel-making factory, this sprawling and perhaps haunted British-style pub (p. 116) is within the solid stone walls of the Royal Naval Dockyard. Sprawling and steeped in a sense of British military history, it serves stiff drinks and bar snacks throughout the afternoon and evening. Established years ago by a "frog" (a Frenchman) and an "Onion" (a Bermudian), the pub is open daily 11:30am to midnight. The Cooperage, Royal Naval Dockyard, Ireland Island. www.frogandonion.bm. ✆ **441/234-2900.** Bus: 7 or 8.

Smith's Parish

North Rock Brewing Company   When this likable pub was first established, it did most of its brewing right on the premises, and as such, did a lot to raise the local community's appreciation for the nuances of fine brew-making. Alas, in 2007, the actual fabrication of the beer was moved to a distant location on the western tip of the island, in the Royal Dockyard. So although you can certainly drink and appreciate the only beer brewed on Bermuda, the actual brewing won't happen, as in days of yore, directly in front of you. Regardless, Bermuda-brewed lagers and ales are king here, and available only for local consumption unless you opt to actually haul a bottle or two back with you. Depending on the day, the inventories, and the season, you'll find brews known respectively as "Whale of a Wheat" and "North Rock Porter." The outdoor roadside patio adds a British flavor (p. 137). Happy hour is Monday through Friday from 5 to 7pm. The pub is open daily from 11am to midnight. 10 South Rd. ✆ **441/236-6633.** Bus: 1.

Southampton Parish

Jasmine   Adjacent to the lobby of the Fairmont Southampton, this elegant, hip, and distinctly urban club has become a popular spot for mixing, mingling, flirting, and greeting an upscale and sometimes nubile collection of locals and short-term visitors to Bermuda. It's also a place to get the quintessential martini. There's a monumental fireplace that roars away during inclement weather, and lots of deeply upholstered sofas that are hard to leave. Light dishes that include salads, sandwiches, and pizza are available as well. The joint really jumps when live entertainment is featured. Drinks begin at $8. It's open daily 11am to 1am. In the Fairmont Southampton, 101 South Rd. ✆ **441/238-8000.** Private ferry to Fairmont Hamilton.

St. George's Parish

The little port of St. George and adjoining St. David's Island are a pub-lover's haven. Our favorite is **Black Horse Tavern** (p. 140), a suitable spot for a congenial evening in good company. It lies on St. David's Island immediately adjoining St. George, and is worth the trek over. If you get hungry, you can always order a plate of shark hash to go with your beer. The oldest pub in St. George, **White Horse Tavern** (p. 142), remains an enduring favorite. It's jammed most evenings with a mixture of locals and visitors. We like the location of this one—at the water's edge, overlooking the harbor. Don't expect speedy service in any of these joints.

THE PERFORMING ARTS

Ballet

The **National Dance Foundation of Bermuda** stages performances, both classical and modern, around the island, featuring both local dancers and major artists imported from venues in Europe and North America. Ask at the tourist office or call the box office at the foundation's headquarters in The Swan Building, 26 Victoria St., Hamilton HM10 (www.dancebermuda.org; ✆ **441/236-3319**). Check the troupe's schedules during your visit. *Note:* Catherine Zeta-Jones, incidentally, has emerged as one of the driving forces and benefactors of this organization since her marriage to Michael Douglas.

Classical Music

The **Bermuda Philharmonic Society,** which maintains strong links to the orchestral scene in the U.K., presents four regular concerts during the season. Special outdoor **"Classical Pops" concerts** are presented on the first weekend in June in St. George and at the Royal Naval Dockyard. Concerts usually feature the Bermuda Philharmonic orchestra, the choir, and guest soloists. You can get tickets and concert schedules by clicking on www.philharmonic.bm, or by visiting the organization's headquarters at 59 Front St., Hamilton, HM 12 (✆ **441/291-6690**). Tickets generally cost $35; seniors and students are often granted discounts, depending on the performance.

Gombey Dancing

Ask at the tourist office or call the box office at the Visitors Information Centre (p. 205) to see whether the **gombey dancers** (p. 29) will be performing during your stay. Gombey (commonly pronounced *goom*-bee or *gom*-bay) is the island's single most important cultural expression of African heritage. Once part of slave culture, the tradition dates from the mid-1700s. The national dance troupe of talented men and women often performs at one of the big hotels in winter (and, on occasion, aboard cruise ships for passengers). On holidays, you'll see the gombeys dancing through the streets of the City of Hamilton in colorful costumes.

The Big Event: The Bermuda Festival

Bermuda's major cultural event is the Bermuda Festival, staged every January and February. Outstanding international classical, jazz, and pop artists perform, and major theatrical and dance companies from around the globe stage productions. During the festival, performances take place on varying nights. Ticket prices start at $55, $20 for children's shows. Some festival tickets are reserved until 48 hours before curtain time for visitors. Visitors who'd like tickets can contact **Bermuda Tickets** (www.bdatix.bm; 𝄢 **800/309-8497** [U.S. and Canada] or 441/232-2255), which holds back a number of tickets that locals cannot access until 48 hours before any given performance, and whose website allows tickets to be preprinted on a conventional printer. Most of the Bermuda Festival's performances are at **City Hall Theatre,** City Hall, Church Street, the City of Hamilton; others are within churches, auditoriums, and gathering places throughout Bermuda, depending on the event. For more information and reservations, contact the **Bermuda Festival,** P.O. Box HM 297, Hamilton HM AX, Bermuda (www.bermudafestival.org; 𝄢 **441/295-1291;** fax 441/295-7403).

Musical Theater

Bermuda and its high percentage of educated consumers is sometimes configured as a presentation venue for theatrical and musical performances from off-island. Harvard University has presented occasional performances of its theater troupe, the **Hasty Pudding Theatricals,** usually during March and April, with tickets priced at around $28 each. Also, the island hosts occasional performances of out-of-town previews for college and professional musical theater, announcements for which are placed on notice boards and in publications such as *ThisWeek in Bermuda* weeks or months in advance and which are widely promoted in the local press. The ticket agency that's most likely to publicize and sell tickets to these performances is **Bermuda Tickets** (www.bdatix.bm; 𝄢 **800/309-8497** [U.S. and Canada] or 441/232-2255), which is more famously associated with the Bermuda Festival (see above).

WHERE TO STAY

Bermuda offers a wide choice of lodgings, ranging from small, casual guesthouses to large, luxurious resorts. Facilities vary greatly in size and amenities within each category. This chapter is organized by the type of available accommodations to help you find your ideal place to stay.

best FOR FAMILIES

- **Elbow Beach Hotel** (Paget Parish; www.mandarinoriental.com/bermuda; ✆ **800/223-7434** or 441/236-3535): This longtime family favorite, on one of the best beaches in Bermuda, allows children 17 and under to stay free when sharing a room with their parents (though be aware that only some rooms are really big enough for an extra person). It also offers a year-round "Family Value Package," which grants very low rates for four people (usually two children and two parents) and includes buffet breakfast, 4 hours of babysitting, 1 hour of paddle-boat rental, 2 hours of tennis, and free passes to the zoo and aquarium. Call the hotel or ask a travel agent for details. See p. 174.

- **Grotto Bay Beach Resort** (Hamilton Parish; www.grottobay.com; ✆ **800/582-3190** in the U.S., or 441/293-8333): With its excellent summer children's program, this hotel attracts many families. It sits on 8.5 tropically landscaped hectares (21 acres), so guests usually don't mind its relative isolation across from the airport. The pool has been blasted out of natural rock, and there are subterranean caves to explore. Beachside barbecues and other activities make this a lively place. See p. 183.

- **Sandpiper Apartments** (Warwick Parish; www.sandpiperbda.com; ✆ **441/236-7093**): This is a viable alternative to the big resort hotels and their high prices. This apartment complex, located a short walk from a beach, attracts self-sufficient families that like to buy their own groceries and cook in their rented apartment to cut down on the lethal dining costs of Bermuda. The accommodations are spacious and suitable for families, but they're far from luxurious. See p. 173.

- **Rosemont** (City of Hamilton, Pembroke Parish; www.rosemont.bm; ✆ **800/367-0040** in the U.S., 800/267-0040 in Canada, or 441/292-1055): It's a 15-minute ride from Elbow Beach, but this complex of cottages is a good choice for families who like to rent units with kitchens to keep dining costs within reason. In a tranquil spot, each cottage opens onto its own veranda. The site offers panoramic views of Hamilton Harbour and the Great Sound. Management can open and lock doors to suit different groups—as many as three rooms can be connected. A grocery store is close at hand, and there is also a coin-operated laundry on-site; babysitting can also be arranged. See p. 180.

best BANG FOR YOUR BUCK

- **The Oxford House** (City of Hamilton, Pembroke Parish; www.oxfordhouse.bm; ℂ **800/548-7758** or 441/295-0503): This is one of the best guesthouses on the island, built in the City of Hamilton in 1938 by a local doctor whose French wife wanted architectural features of her native land. Bedrooms, each named for one of Bermuda's parishes, are handsomely furnished and comfortable. The price is moderate, and quite good for the comfort offered. See p. 181.
- **Salt Kettle House** (Paget Parish; ℂ **441/236-0407**). The name is not the only thing charming about this informal and secluded 2-centuries-old cottage. It's a real discovery, and bargain hunters eagerly seek it out, preferring it to the glitz of the megaresort hotels. You can swim in the nearby cove, retiring to your waterside cottage at night. See p. 178.
- **Granaway Guest House & Cottage** (Warwick Parish; www.granaway.com; ℂ **441/236-3747**): This former private home from 1734 is a near picture-postcard cliché of Bermudian charm, with its pink walls and whitewashed roof. Opening onto views of Great Sound, it has been handsomely converted to receive guests—even the former slave quarters are now comfortable. See p. 174.

best SPLURGE

- **The Fairmont Southampton** (Southampton Parish; www.fairmont.com/southampton; ℂ **866/540-4497** in the U.S. and Canada, or 441/238-8000): The island's most luxurious hotel does everything it can to attract honeymooners seeking lots of activities, from watersports to nighttime diversions (other than those in the honeymoon suite). Its honeymoon packages, which start at 4 days and 3 nights, include breakfast and dinner on a MAP (modified American plan), "dine-around plan" (dinner and breakfast are included in the hotel rate, but you can dine in any of the two Princess resorts' restaurants), a bottle of champagne, a basket of fruit, admission to the exercise club, and even a special-occasion cake, plus a souvenir photo and a watercolor print by a local artist. See p. 167.

best SERVICE

- **Tucker's Point Hotel & Spa** (Hamilton Parish; www.rosewoodtuckerspoint.com; ℂ **866/604-3764** or 441/298-9800): This is the island's most comprehensive, imaginative, and theatrical resort. A uniformed staff guides virtually every aspect of your arrival and well-being. Because the hotel has a huge physical plant but only 88 units, it feels like an intensely personalized boutique resort with big-city amenities. And, you'll find the most comprehensive spa (the Sense Spa) in Bermuda.

most ROMANTIC

- **Cambridge Beaches** (Sandys Parish; www.cambridgebeaches.com; ℂ **800/468-7300** in the U.S. and Canada, or 441/234-0331): Few other resorts in Bermuda boast as loyal a roster of repeat guests, with some elderly clients breaking records for as many as 40 repeat visits. Recognizing the allure of their resort for couples and repeat visitors, in 2008 Cambridge inaugurated an aggressive new self-image

Chances are, you'll take more meals at your hotel in Bermuda (where you can't rent a car) than you would in other destinations. Although you're generally out and about for lunch, many visitors don't care to hire an expensive taxi or take a bike or motorbike along Bermuda's narrow roads at night in search of a spot for dinner. As a result, you're often stuck at your hotel for meals, and therefore you might want to consider food options when deciding where to stay.

as a resort for relationship-building, sexual healing, and romantic "rediscovery." As such, it articulates New Age sensuality with more verve and gusto than any other hotel in Bermuda. Couples in search of self-discovery (or rediscovery) love it. See p. 166.

- **Pompano Beach Club** (Southampton Parish; www.pompanobeachclub.com *℗* **800/343-4155** or 441/234-0222): The first and only American-owned hotel on Bermuda, this hotel appeals to couples in search of privacy, intimacy, and a sense of mystical union with the sea, which seems to roar and foam nearly onto its foundations. And within a cottage colony whose exterior boasts an almost universal shade of pink (they call it pompano pink; lovers refer to it as Valentine pink), how could romance possibly take a back seat? See p. 170.

THE best RESORTS FOR HONEYMOONERS

- **Elbow Beach Hotel** (Paget Parish; www.mandarinoriental.com/bermuda; *℗* **800/223-7434** or 441/236-3535): This hotel promises "marriages made in heaven." Its Romance Packages include a daily breakfast, plus a candlelit dinner for two in your room on the first night. Upon departure, newlyweds receive a copy of the *Elbow Beach Cookbook*. See p. 174.
- **Grotto Bay Beach Resort** (Hamilton Parish; www.grottobay.com; *℗* **800/582-3190** in the U.S., or 441/293-8333): This resort, which actively caters to honeymooners, features everything from midnight swims at a private beach to cozy lovers' nests with balconies overlooking the ocean. The honeymoon packages include romantic dinners and arrangements for cruises and walking tours, as well as optional champagne, fruit, and flowers. See p. 183.

SANDYS PARISH

Cottage Colonies

VERY EXPENSIVE

Cambridge Beaches ★★★ Discreetly but relentlessly upscale, the much-restored Cambridge Beaches attracts rich honeymooners, old-money families, and fashionable couples who seek privacy, pampering, and plenty of facilities. It's one of the most deeply respected resorts in Bermuda, with dozens of clients who return year after year. If you're a first-time visitor, the clubby atmosphere may make you feel like an outsider. Persons 17 and under are in most cases not particularly appreciated, and raucous 20-somethings would probably not fit in.

On a peninsula overlooking Mangrove Bay in Somerset, the colony's 12 hectares (30 acres) of semitropical gardens and green lawns occupy the entire western tip of the island. The colony centers on an old sea captain's house that over the years grew into a compound of lounges, bars, dining rooms, and drawing rooms that give the feeling of a conservative country estate. Scattered throughout the gardens are nicely furnished pink-sided cottages, some of which are nearly 300 years old and much restored. All of the cottages are conservatively furnished—nothing too ostentatious, nothing too flashy—and come with terraces, generally with unobstructed views of the bay and gardens. A cottage can comfortably house four. The less expensive units have land rather than ocean vistas, and balconies and terraces that in some cases are a bit too close to immediate neighbors.

Dining options include the excellent and pricey **Tamarisk Dining Room** (p. 114), as well as some less formal venues. There's also an informal lounge, the **Port O' Call Pub,** whose dark beams and roughly textured plasterwork evoke a 17th-century inn somewhere in the U.K. Live entertainment is presented frequently during the high season. A noted pastime offered to residents involves a rotating series of lectures offering insight into relationship building, sexual healing, and advice on how to enrich a sense of intimacy, either with your significant other or with the world at large. Within a self-contained building on the property is the small but well-equipped **Ocean Spa.** In recent years, the hotel has continued to improve, adding a new pool, a clothing-optional deck, and a beachfront cafe.

30 Kings Point Rd., Sandys Parish MA 02, Bermuda. www.cambridgebeaches.com. ⓒ **800/468-7300** in the U.S., or 441/234-0331. Fax 441/234-3352. 94 units. May–Sept $653–$970 double, $1,035–$1,750 suite; Oct–Apr $355–$590 double, $590–$1,115 suite. Rates include breakfast and afternoon tea. AE, MC, V. Bus: 7 or 8. **Amenities:** 3 restaurants; cafe; 3 bars; babysitting; health club and spa; mopeds; 3 pools (1 indoor, 2 outdoors); room service; 3 tennis courts (1 lit); watersports equipment/rentals; Wi-Fi (free in lobby). *In room:* A/C, TV, fridge, hair dryer.

SOUTHAMPTON PARISH

Resort Hotels

VERY EXPENSIVE

The Fairmont Southampton ★★★ ☺   Sitting atop Bermuda's highest point, this resort is the largest, most comprehensive, and most luxurious property on the island. It overlooks the ocean, the bay, and its own beach, located in front of the hotel. The hotel's beach is sheltered in a jagged cove, flanked by cliffs. The atmosphere is mahogany-trimmed conservatism, glowing and rich-looking and perhaps a little bit uptight and stuffy for some. This mammoth resort stands on 40 gloriously manicured hectares (99 acres).

It's often compared to its sibling, **The Fairmont Hamilton Princess** (p. 178), which is situated in a more urban environment. This hotel is not necessarily the place for travelers looking for a sense of isolation and an intimate, romantic hideaway; in fact, its biggest drawback is that it's a favorite with conventions and tour groups. Nonetheless, along with **Tucker's Point** (p. 182) and **Elbow Beach** (p. 174), it is considered one of the finest choices for the well-heeled family looking for a place with virtually everything on-site.

The Fairmont Southampton is decorated in a tastefully conservative style with rare but usually welcome touches of glitziness and razzmatazz, always with well-upholstered furnishings and a sense of airy spaciousness. The plush guest rooms each have

Hotels in Bermuda

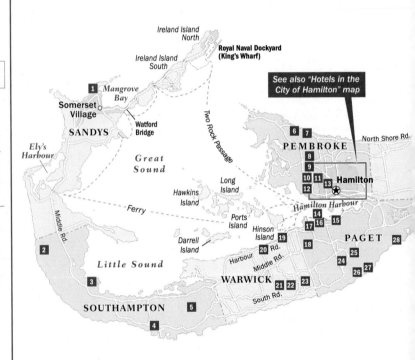

Aunt Nea's Inn at Hillcrest **34**

Cambridge Beaches **1**

Clairfont Apartments **23**

Clear View Suites and Villa **31**

Coco Reef Resort **27**

Dawkins Manor **24**

Edgehill Manor Guest House **9**

Elbow Beach Hotel **26**

Fairmont Hamilton
  Princess **12**

Fairmont Southampton **5**

Fourways Inn **18**

Granaway Guest House
  & Cottage **20**

Grape Bay Cottages **28**

Greenbank Guest House **16**

Greene's Guest House **3**

Grotto Bay
  Beach Resort **32**

Little Pomander
  Guest House **15**

Mazarine by the Sea **7**

Newstead Belmont Hills
  Golf Resort & Spa **17**

Oxford House **13**

Paraquet Guest
  Apartments **25**

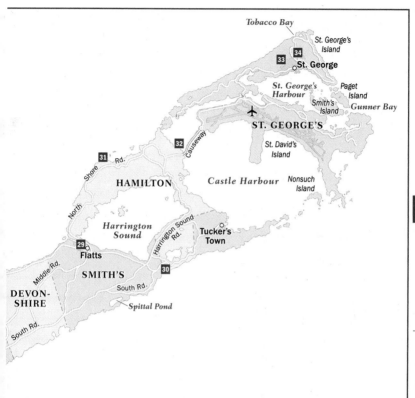

a private veranda with a sweeping view of the water. Rooms are spacious, each with a larger-than-expected balcony. For those who can afford it, the choicest accommodations are on the Fairmont Gold floor, where guests are offered an array of services including private check-ins, complimentary continental breakfast, newspapers, and the use of a fax and VCR.

The cuisine is among the island's finest—we recommend several of the resort's restaurants even if you're not staying here. Choices include **Wickets** (p. 120), the **Ocean Club** (p. 117), the **Waterlot Inn** (p. 116), and **Bacci** (p. 117). Nightlife is a bit staid here, and not every restaurant has a bar that's open to nondiners (the Waterlot Inn does). **Jasmine's Lounge** has an active singles scene, and live music, usually a jazz combo, beginning most evenings at 8pm. On the premises is the vast, Fairmont-owned **Willow Stream Day Spa,** with 20 separate treatment rooms and 31,000 square feet of surface area.

Guests who don't want to leave the premises enjoy a self-contained village of bars, restaurants, shops, and athletic facilities that are among the island's finest. Everyone's favorite pool is an indoor re-creation of a Polynesian waterfall, with streams of heated water spilling from an artificial limestone cliff. You can swim here even during cold weather, thanks to the greenhouse above. A trolley carries guests around the grounds, and a ferry reserved for guests only goes from the Waterlot Inn to the piers of the Fairmont Hamilton Princess.

101 South Rd. (P.O. Box HM 1379), Southampton Parish HM FX, Bermuda. www.fairmont.com/southampton. Ⓒ **866/540-4497** in the U.S. and Canada, or 441/238-8000. Fax 441/238-8968. 593 units. Winter $259–$459 double; from $589 suite; summer $369–$599 double, from $589 suite. Children 17 and under stay free in a room with 1 or 2 adults. AE, DC, DISC, MC, V. Free private ferry to the Fairmont Hamilton Princess. **Amenities:** 7 restaurants; 2 bars; babysitting; beach club; children's programs; concierge; 18-hole golf course; health club and spa; pool (outdoor); room service; watersports equipment/rentals. *In room:* A/C, TV, TV/VCR, hair dryer, Wi-Fi ($14 per day).

Small Hotels
VERY EXPENSIVE
Pompano Beach Club ★ Adjacent to the Port Royal Golf Course, and with a respected pedigree dating back to 1956, this resort is perched on a limestone hill, with a spectacular view of the cove beach fringed with rocky outcroppings. From the beach, waist-deep water covers the clean, sandy bottom for the length of 2½ football fields before the deep water begins. Contained within a low-rise complex of well-maintained buildings, the hotel attracts couples of all ages who want privacy and tranquility; golfers especially like this place, whose public areas were upgraded in 2011.

The hillside villas scattered over the landscaped property have a balcony or terrace to take advantage of the ocean views. If you can afford it, request the deluxe rooms at the top of the price scale, as these accommodations have double sinks and showers near (separate) oversize tubs.

If you don't want to dine around at night, you can order meals in either of its two well-orchestrated restaurants; the **Ocean Grill** and the **Cedar Room** alike are recommended (p. 118). The hotel offers a complimentary shuttle to and from the local Rockaway ferry stop, making it easier for guests to commute back and forth from Hamilton.

36 Pompano Beach Rd., Southampton Parish SB 03, Bermuda. Ⓒ **800/343-4155** in the U.S. and Canada, or 441/234-0222. Fax 441/234-1694. www.pompanobeachclub.com. 74 units. May–Oct $530–$1,100 double; off season $310–$850 double. Rates include MAP (breakfast and dinner). Packages available. AE, MC, V. Rockaway ferry to Hamilton. Bus: 7 or 8. **Amenities:** 2 restaurants; cafe; 3 bars; babysitting; concierge; health club and spa; mopeds; Jacuzzi; pool (outdoor); watersports equipment/rentals; Wi-Fi (free in clubhouse). *In room:* A/C, TV, fridge, hair dryer.

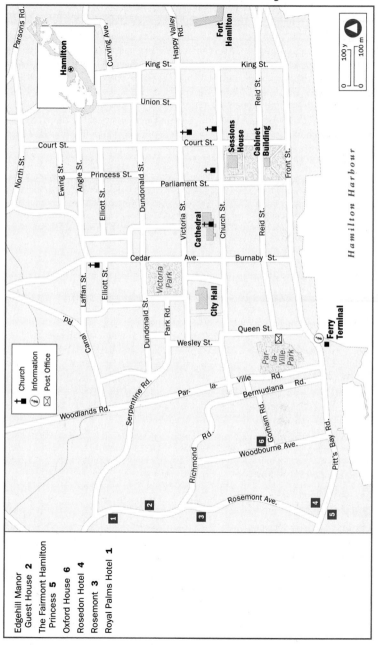

171

The Reefs Hotel & Club ★★   Having benefited from a renovation in 2011, this is one of the island's state-of-the-art inns, opening onto a private beach of pink-flecked sand surrounded by palm trees and jutting rocks.

This inn boasts unmatched ocean views and a somewhat startling loyalty from many island residents, many of whom cite it as their preferred island getaway. With components interconnected with steep and sometimes long flights of concrete stairs, this "lanai colony" of salmon-pink cottages on Christian Bay spreads along the top of a low coral ridge. Each accommodation is cheerfully decorated with comfortable furnishings and has a private sun deck, moderate-size bathrooms, separate dressing areas, and dual basins. The hotel's "Club Suites by the Reefs" are the most desirable.

If you want to let your hair down a bit, opt for **Coconuts** (p. 117); there's no finer or more romantic spot in Bermuda for an alfresco sunset dinner than this beach terrace. **La Serena spa** offers Thai and other styles of massage, reflexology, facials, and other services.

56 South Shore Rd., Southampton Parish SN 02, Bermuda. www.thereefs.com. © **800/742-2008** in the U.S. and Canada, or 441/238-0222. Fax 441/238-8372. 65 units. Summer $670–$730 double, from $925 suite; off season $410–$575 double, from $615 suite. Rates include breakfast and dinner. AE, MC, V. Bus: 7. **Amenities:** 3 restaurants; 2 bars; babysitting; 3 golf courses nearby; limited health club; mopeds; pool (outdoor); watersports equipment/rentals; Wi-Fi (free in clubhouse). *In room:* A/C, TV/DVD, fridge, hair dryer.

Housekeeping Units
MODERATE
Grape Bay Cottages   Small-scale and folksy, this "resort" consists of two cozy saltbox-style cottages, directly beside the sea, owned and managed by Maria Frith. Each has comfortable, unpretentious furniture and lots of reminders of Bermuda's maritime traditions, as well as a simple bathroom containing a tub/shower combination, a fully equipped kitchen, a wide front veranda, and family-friendly ambience. Maid service is provided at regular (but not necessarily daily) intervals, according to the wishes of residents and the availability of the housecleaning staff. The venue, which is often booked 6 months in advance, is about as laissez-faire as you're likely to find anywhere in Bermuda, but it's well suited to visitors who prefer self-catered holidays in a cottage by the beach.

Grape Bay Dr., off Middle Rd., Southampton Parish (P.O. Box HM 1851), Hamilton HM HX, Bermuda. www.gbcbermuda.com. © **441/236-2515.** Fax 441/236-1662. Two 2-bedroom units. Apr–Oct $345 1–4 persons; Nov–Mar $270 1–4 persons. Extra person $35 year-round. No credit cards. Bus: 7 or 8. *In room:* A/C, TV, kitchen.

Guesthouses
INEXPENSIVE
Greene's Guest House   From the outside, this 70-year-old guesthouse overlooking Great Sound is well maintained, cheerful, and unpretentious. A look on the inside reveals pleasant, conservatively furnished rooms that are more impressive than you might have guessed. A pair of lions on stone columns flanks the entry. Owner Jane Greene welcomes guests to use the spacious, well-furnished living room and the sun-washed terraces in back. Bedrooms are small to medium-size, each comfortably furnished with a tidily kept compact private bathroom.

There's a swimming pool in the back garden, and Whale Bay Beach lies 3 minutes away by bus or 10 minutes by foot. Facing the sea is a cozy lounge. The bus to and from the City of Hamilton stops in front of the house.

Southampton Parish

WHERE TO STAY

71 Middle Rd. (P.O. Box SN 395), Southampton Parish SN BX, Bermuda. www.thegreenesguest house.com. ✆ **441/238-0834.** Fax 441/238-8980. 7 units. Year-round $150 double. Rates include full breakfast. MC, V. Bus: 7 or 8. **Amenities:** Internet (free in lobby); pool (outdoor). *In room:* A/C, TV, fridge, hair dryer.

WARWICK PARISH

Housekeeping Units

EXPENSIVE

Surf Side Beach Club ★ This club occupies a steeply sloping hillside that descends through gardens, a 3-minute walk to the sea. There are many things to recommend about this place, but if immediate access to a pristine strip of sand is important to you, look elsewhere. Flowering trees and panoramic walkways adorn the terraced property. From lookout points in the garden, visitors can see grouper and other fish swimming near the rocks of the shallow sea.

Accommodations consist of one-bedroom apartments near the terrace pool and other lodgings in hillside buildings. The self-contained units are simple and sunny, outfitted in bright colors with comfortable accessories. Each has a fully equipped kitchen. This is a pet-friendly facility. A local grocery accepts phone orders and will deliver to your unit, with no charge for orders over $20. The apartments also have private balconies or patios; some have sitting rooms as well.

90 South Shore Rd. (P.O. Box WK 101), Warwick Parish WK BX, Bermuda. www.surfsidebermuda. com. ✆ **800/553-9990** in the U.S., or 441/236-7100. Fax 441/236-9765. 36 units. Summer $325 double, $385–$550 suite; off season $180 double, from $225–$350 suite. Rates include breakfast and dinner. AE, MC, V. **Amenities:** Babysitting; pool (outdoor); room service; Wi-Fi (free in lobby). *In room:* A/C, TV, hair dryer, kitchen (in suites).

MODERATE

Sandpiper Apartments ☺ Built in 1979 and frequently upgraded, this apartment complex is a bargain. Nine units are studios for one or two people, with two double beds, a small tiled bathroom, and a fully equipped kitchenette that's sufficient for simple meals. Five units contain a bedroom (with king-size or twin beds), a kitchen, and a living/dining area with two double pullout sofa beds. Every apartment has a balcony, and there's daily maid service. The Sandpiper is minutes away from restaurants and the supermarket. The closest beach is about 450m (1,500 ft.) away, and the property has gardens for lounging.

South Shore Rd., Warwick Parish (P.O. Box HM 685), Hamilton HM CX, Bermuda. www.sandpiper bda.com. ✆ **441/236-7093.** Fax 441/236-3898. 14 units. Apr–Oct $155 double, $195 suite for 3 or 4; off season $115 double, $160 suite for 3 or 4. Extra adults in any unit pay $35 each per night. Children 11 and under stay free in parent's room; for children 12 and older, add $20 per child. AE, MC, V. Bus: 7. **Amenities:** Babysitting; Jacuzzi; pool (outdoor); Wi-Fi (free by pool). *In room:* A/C, TV, hair dryer, kitchenette, minibar.

Watercolours ★ 🛍 England-born entrepreneur Carole Holding—owner of the **Carole Holding Studio** (p. 151) gift shops—rents two of the most charming bedrooms on record within her private home. They lie within an unconventional and extraordinary house: Built to her specifications in 1996, it occupies land once devoted to a boatbuilding yard directly at waterside on the channel leading in and out of Hamilton's harbor; each unit has ocean views. The design of the house allows guests to have virtually the entire ground floor of the building to themselves. Throughout, the place is gracious, immaculate, and outfitted in color schemes of coral and white. Breakfasts are stylish, and Carole, a gracious hostess with strong points of view about what's good and what's not in Bermuda, is on hand for advice about nearby dining. The pier, where you can catch a ferry to downtown Hamilton, is a 3-minute walk away.

75 Harbour Rd., Warwick Parish PG 01, Bermuda. © **441/535-4001** or 441/236-6002. 2 units. Apr–Oct $295 double; Nov–Mar $195 double. Rates include breakfast. MC, V. 3-night minimum stay required. **Amenities:** Wi-Fi (free). *In room:* A/C, hair dryer.

Guesthouses
INEXPENSIVE

Clairfont Apartments 🏄 It's not on a beachfront, but there are other reasons to recommend this well-run series of accommodations on the South Shore, and price is one of them. Guests meet fellow guests as they relax around the pool. You have a choice of studio units, a large room with a king-size bed and separate kitchen and living area, or else a one-bedroom unit with a better-equipped kitchen and more space with a king-size bed that can be split into twins. Two extra guests can sleep in the living area. This is basically a recommendation for self-service types. The location is a 5-minute walk from pink-sand beaches and just a 3-minute walk to public transportation.

6 Warwickshire Rd., South Shore, Warwick Parish WK 02, Bermuda. www.clairfontapartments.bm. © **441/238-3577.** 8 units. Year-round, $150 double; $175 1-bedroom apt for 2. Extra person $50. AE, MC, V. Bus: 7 or 8. **Amenities:** Pool (outside). *In room:* A/C, phone, TV/DVD, kitchen.

Granaway Guest House & Cottage ★ 🏨 Granaway is a cliché of pink-walled, white-roofed Bermudian charm, with guest rooms and a garden cottage. The property opens onto views of Great Sound.

Once a stately waterfront home, the old cedar beams of the original house are still maintained, although modern conveniences have been added. The bedrooms are handsomely furnished and comfortable, each with a small private bathroom. Four of the rooms are in the main house, although the most romantic retreat is the separate Granaway Cottage, which has a full kitchen, hand-painted Italian floor tiles, and a fireplace. The most scenic way to reach the City of Hamilton is by taking a short walk to Harbour Road, where you can board one of the ferryboats. In fair weather, guests are served breakfast in the garden, by a pool surrounded by lush foliage.

Harbour Rd. (P.O. Box WK 533), Warwick Parish, Bermuda. www.granaway.com. © **441/236-3747.** Fax 441/236-3749. 5 units. Summer $175–$225 double, $250–$325 double with kitchen in cottage; off season $125–$175 double, $150–$225 double with kitchen in cottage. Extra person $25. Rates include continental breakfast (cottage excluded). MC, V. Bus: 8. **Amenities:** Pool (outdoor). *In room:* A/C, TV/DVD, fridge, no phone, Wi-Fi (free).

PAGET PARISH

Resort Hotels
VERY EXPENSIVE

Elbow Beach Hotel ★ This resort has long been a Bermuda legend, but today it has been considerably downsized. Its largest building was closed in 2009, and its current operators, Mandarin Oriental, hawk the far-flung scattering of outbuildings which remain, with some accuracy, as a "downsized, more intimate resort." Buildings are spread across 20 hectares (49 acres) of landscaped gardens, and the resort has its own .5km (⅓-mile) pink-sand beach on the South Shore. Most rooms feature Asian furnishings, hardwood floors, and exposed ceiling beams. The most spacious units are in low-rise buildings on terraces leading down to the sands.

The **Mandarin Oriental Spa** contains six suites—oases where clients can spend hours or even the entire day in total comfort. This is about the most luxurious way to stay in Bermuda if you want complete pampering. The suites, each with an ocean view, are spacious, Zen-like retreats featuring granite soaking tubs, showers lined with river pebbles, and bamboo floors.

The hotel has formal and casual dining options, as well as the **Deep Lounge & Nightclub**.

60 South Rd. (P.O. Box HM 455), Paget Parish HM BX, Bermuda. www.mandarinoriental.com/bermuda. © **800/223-7434** or 441/236-3535. Fax 441/236-8043. 98 units. Summer $695–$895 double, from $1,400 suite; off season $355–$525 double, from $725 suite. Children 17 and under stay free in parent's room (not all rooms are large enough to comfortably fit an extra person). Packages available. AE, DC, MC, V. Bus: 1, 2, or 7. **Amenities:** 3 restaurants; 2 bars; babysitting; children's program; concierge; health club and spa; pool (outdoor); room service; 5 all-weather tennis courts (2 lit); watersports equipment/rentals. *In room:* A/C, TV, hair dryer, minibar, Wi-Fi ($14).

Small Hotels
VERY EXPENSIVE

Coco Reef Resort ★   Pink sands lie a few steps from your room at this hillside reincarnation of the old Stonington Beach Hotel. Opening onto the island's South Shore Beach, this fully restored property is inviting, albeit sleepy, thanks to a somewhat diminished clientele during the tourist industry's recent economic woes. In each room there are original paintings of scenes of Bermudian life, Caribbean-inspired fabrics, and wicker furnishings. Redevelopment of this place early in the millennium included improvements to the atrium-style lobby, better dining options, the refurbishment of all public rooms, and the restoration of all the guest bedrooms, which are midsize and comfortably furnished.

3 Stonington Circle, Paget Parish PG BX, Bermuda. www.cocoreefbermuda.com. © **800/648-0799** in the U.S. and Canada, or 441/236-5416. Fax 441/236-9766. 62 units. Mid-Apr to Oct $399–$499 double; Nov to mid-Apr $119–$139 double. AE, MC, V. Bus: 7. **Amenities:** Restaurant; bar; babysitting; access to nearby health club; pool (outdoor); 2 tennis courts (lit); Wi-Fi (free in lobby). *In room:* A/C, TV, hair dryer.

The Wharf Executive Suites ★   One of Bermuda's most modern accommodations, this boutique hotel caters to the business traveler and the extended-stay visitor. The location is on the harbor overlooking the City of Hamilton, which is reached by taking a 7-minute ferry ride. The management, with some justification, bills its offering as a "home away from home." No hotel can be that, but this one tries admirably. The hotel is in a sand-colored building offering studio suites equipped with kitchenettes and full suites with full kitchens. All bedrooms have executive work centers, including a desk and ergonomic chair, a two-line speakerphone, and a fax machine/printer/copier. Personalized concierge service is also provided. Rooms are spacious, each with a balcony overlooking Hamilton Bay. There is no on-site restaurant, but a continental breakfast is served.

1 Harbour Rd., Paget Parish PG BX, Bermuda. www.wharfexecutivesuites.com. © **441/232-5700.** Fax 441/232-4008. 15 units. Nov to mid-Apr $205 studio for 2, $325 suite; mid-Apr to Oct $285 studio for 2, $399 suite. Rates include continental breakfast. AE, MC, V. **Amenities:** Babysitting. *In room:* A/C, TV, fax, hair dryer, kitchenette (in studios)/full kitchen (in suites), Wi-Fi (free).

Cottage Colonies

VERY EXPENSIVE

Newstead Belmont Hills Golf Resort & Spa ★★ Early in 2008, one of Bermuda's most visible real-estate developments interconnected two separate plots of land within Paget Parish. It involved a "marriage" between a once-lackluster, since-demolished hotel, known since the 1950s as Newstead, and one of the island's most appealing golf courses, Belmont Hills.

With the exception of four preexisting cottages, the entire Newstead hotel was demolished to make room for a new entity. That newcomer now rises in a four-story avant-garde design that includes open-to-the-breeze-on-one-side corridors, a color scheme of moss green and putty, lots of exposed limestone, and ample use of an exotic Brazilian hardwood *(jatoba)* for the interior louvers, doors, and trim. Each of the units is posh, postmodern, boutiquey, and stylish, in a high-style urban-hip way that's rather unusual in understated and conservative Bermuda.

Don't expect a conventional hotel. The resort operates as a time share, and whenever investors don't want access to their units, the resort's management will rent them out to short-term visitors. Hotel guests can opt for studios, one-bedroom units, or two-bedroom units. These lie within a low-rise compound of buildings close to the sea, but within a 10-minute drive of the golf course.

This resort contains a full-service spa, a gym, a pool, a well-recommended restaurant and bar, and water taxi service that makes several runs a day across the Sound to the commercial center of Hamilton.

27 Harbour Rd., Paget Parish PG 02, Bermuda. www.newsteadbelmonthills.com. © **866/706-7801** or 441/236-6060. Fax 441/236-2296. 60 units. Apr–Oct $450–$495 studio for 2; $657 1-bedroom suite for 2; $940 2-bedroom suite for 4. Nov–Mar $355–$373 studio for 2; $468 1-bedroom suite for 2; $657 2-bedroom suite for 4. Rates include breakfast. AE, DC, MC, V. **Amenities:** 2 restaurants; bar; exercise room; spa; 2 tennis courts (lit). *In room:* A/C, TV, CD player, hair dryer, Wi-Fi (free).

Housekeeping Units

EXPENSIVE

Fourways Inn ★ This posh little place feels like a secret hideaway. Pink-sided, airy, and stylish, the Bermudian cottages occupy well-maintained gardens. The sands of Elbow Beach and Mermaid Beach lie within a 15-minute walk or 5-minute scooter ride. The main building is a former private home dating from 1727. Each of the two-bedroom cottages is renovated and contain conservative, comfortable furniture. There's a medium-size grocery store across the road, but the kitchenettes are better suited for sandwich and snack preparation than for making a feast. There's also a well-regarded restaurant on-site.

1 Middle Rd. (P.O. Box PG 294), Paget Parish PG BX, Bermuda. www.fourwaysinn.com. © **800/962-7654** in the U.S. and Canada, or 441/236-6517. Fax 441/236-5528. 10 units within 5 cottages. Apr–Oct $245 double; $295 suite; $495 2-bedroom unit; off season $135 double, $165 suite; $325 2-bedroom unit. Extra person $40. Rates include continental breakfast; MAP (breakfast and dinner) $55 per person. AE, MC, V. Bus: 8. **Amenities:** Restaurant; bar; pool (outdoor); room service. *In room:* A/C, TV, fridge, hair dryer, Wi-Fi (free).

MODERATE

Paraquet Guest Apartments 🍃 If you'll settle for a no-frills type of place, evoking a roadside motel, this is the cheapest option for those who want to lodge only a 5-minute walk from Elbow Beach, one of the island's best. Rooms are well-maintained but furnished in a very basic style. A family-owned business for some 30 years,

Paraquet rents mainly efficiency units, some with two bedrooms accommodating up to five guests. There is also a trio of cottages, each without kitchen facilities, with a spacious bedroom, a small refrigerator, and patio. In the courtyard, guests can lounge under umbrellas or barbecue their dinners. The **Paraquet Restaurant** is nearby, evoking an American diner with family meals offered at moderate prices.

72 South Rd., Paget Parish PG BX, Bermuda. www.paraquetapartments.com. ⓒ **441/236-5842.** Fax 441/236-1665. 12 units. Summer $176–$220 double; winter $154–$186 double. Extra person $50 per day. MC, V. Bus: 1, 2, or 7. **Amenities:** Restaurant. *In room:* Fridge (in some), kitchen (in some), no phone (in some).

Guesthouses

MODERATE

Dawkins Manor In a sleepy residential neighborhood, a 5-minute walk from Elbow Beach, this pink-sided inn offers simple, unpretentious accommodations. Originally built in the 1930s, it has expanded massively since Jamaican-born Celia Dawkins bought the place in the early 1990s. Visiting lecturers conducting classes at nearby Bermuda College sometimes stay here. Even the simplest rooms contain microwaves and coffeemakers; more elaborate ones contain kitchens that are bigger than those in lots of other rental properties, suitable for bona-fide cooking. A grocery store is nearby.

29 St. Michael's Rd. (P.O. Box PG 34), Paget Parish PG BX, Bermuda. www.bermuda-charm.com. ⓒ **441/236-7419.** Fax 441/236-7088. 8 units. Summer $190 double, $250–$275 1-bedroom suite for 2; $380 2-bedroom suite for 4; off season $95 double, $110–$150 1-bedroom suite for 2, $280 2-bedroom suite for 4. Extra person $50 year-round. No credit cards. Bus: 7. **Amenities:** Babysitting; bikes; pool (outdoor). *In room:* A/C, TV, fridge, hair dryer, Internet (free), kitchenette or kitchens (in some).

INEXPENSIVE

Aunt Nea's Inn at Hillcrest ★ ▮▮ This little hotel in St. George's is named after the unrequited love of the Irish poet Tom Moore. Set in formal gardens, the house, much restored, dates from the 1700s. You have a choice of bedrooms, some with four-posters or canopy beds. The Jasmine Rooms are eclectically furnished with four-posters, wrought iron, or sleigh beds. The two elegant and spacious Palm Suites open onto an upstairs veranda with panoramic views of St. George's Harbour.

1 Nea's Alley, St. George's, Bermuda. http://1neasalley.com. ⓒ **888/392-7829** or 441/297-1630. Fax 441/297-1908. 14 units. June–Sept $129–$249 double; Oct–May $99–$199 double. AE, MC, V. **Amenities:** Lounge. *In room:* A/C, TV/DVD (in some), fridge, Wi-Fi (free).

Greenbank Guest House This charming guesthouse stands at the water's edge in Salt Kettle, just across the bay (a 10-min. ferry ride) from the City of Hamilton. It's an old home (the oldest section dates from the 1700s), hidden under pine and palm trees, with shady lawns and flower gardens. There is an antiques-filled drawing room, the atmosphere is relaxed, and the service is personal.

Greenbank offers accommodations with private entrances and kitchens in water-side and garden-view cottages. Rooms vary in size and shape, but most are small, with small bathrooms, each with a shower unit. The furnishings are plain but comfortable. The four units in the main house afford less privacy than the cottages. On the premises is a private dock for swimming. The nearest beach is Elbow Beach, a 15-minute taxi or moped ride away, and one of the departure points for the fast ferry to Hamilton is less than a minute's walk away.

17 Salt Kettle Rd. (P.O. Box PG 201), Paget Parish PG BX, Bermuda. www.greenbankbermuda.com. *C* **441/236-3615.** Fax 441/236-2427. 11 units. Summer $160–$185 double without kitchen, $175–$320 double with kitchen; winter $140–$165 double without kitchen, $155–$210 double with kitchen. Extra person $30 year-round. AE, MC, V. **Amenities:** Wi-Fi (free). *In room:* A/C, kitchen.

Little Pomander Guest House 🎁   The two waterfront Bermuda cottages that form this guesthouse are among the oldest in Bermuda, some 400 years old. The location is on a one-way residential street along an inlet of Hamilton harbor. It's about a 15-minute walk to the City of Hamilton or to the beaches. Guest rooms have a bit of an old-fashioned aura, but they are comfortable, durable, and well maintained, with such extras as microwaves and clock radios. Most of them open onto views of the water, and there is also a well-manicured terrace with lounge chairs where you can sit out and watch harbor traffic. A continental breakfast is served around a large communal table in the dining room.

16 Pomander Rd., Paget Parish, Bermuda. www.bermuda.com/h-p/little-pomander-guest-house. aspx?source=12355. *C* **441/236-7635.** 6 units. Summer $125–$150 double; winter $110–$125 double. AE, MC, V. Bus: 7. **Amenities:** Wi-Fi (free). *In room:* A/C, TV, microwave, fridge.

Salt Kettle House ★★ 🎁   Informal and secluded, with a discreet kind of elegance, this little charmer sits on a narrow peninsula jutting into Hamilton Harbour. You can swim in a cove and watch ships going in and out of the harbor. The core of this guesthouse is a 200-year-old cottage that has been enlarged over the years. Over time, three additional cottages and a "main house," site of three double rooms, were added. Today, the compound is a cheerful architectural hodgepodge that's popular with boaters. Accommodations are generally small, but comfortably furnished. The cottages each have sitting rooms, shaded patios, and kitchens. The Starboard, the best cottage, can comfortably accommodate four guests. Guests in the main house have shared use of a fully equipped kitchen. The outdoor barbecue pits in the garden get frequent use by guests.

10 Salt Kettle Rd., Paget Parish PG 01, Bermuda. *C* **441/236-0407.** Fax 441/236-8639. 7 units. Year-round $180 double, $200 cottage for 2. Rates include full breakfast. No credit cards. Hamilton ferry to Salt Kettle, then 3-min. walk. **Amenities:** Wi-Fi (free). *In room:* A/C, kitchen (cottages). Phone (only in the cottages), pay phone on premises.

PEMBROKE PARISH (CITY OF HAMILTON)

Resort Hotels

VERY EXPENSIVE

The Fairmont Hamilton Princess ★★   This landmark luxury hotel launched Bermuda's tourist industry and, thanks to a healthy demand from business travelers, is still going strong. Its younger larger sibling, the **Fairmont Southampton** (see earlier), has better dining, grander and more comprehensive facilities, and the advantage of being on a beach, but it's somewhat remote; the more "urban" Fairmont Hamilton earns devotees because it is more conveniently positioned for shopping and sightseeing. The hotel, whose pink walls and gingerbread trim evoke a wedding cake, is a short walk from downtown Hamilton, on the edge of Hamilton Harbour. Elbow Beach (the closest beach) is a 20-minute taxi ride or 45-minute bicycle ride from the hotel. The easily accessible ferry delivers guests to the Fairmont Southampton, and sun lovers can get their fill at the sandy stretch there. This is the hotel of choice for movie stars and the yachting set.

Opened in 1884 and named for Princess Louise (Queen Victoria's daughter), this princess is far more staid than the Fairmont Southampton, and with a higher percentage of business clients. It doesn't even attempt to offer the roster of activities available at Elbow Beach, so the young and the restless might want to book elsewhere. This is the oldest and one of the most deeply entrenched members of the Fairmont hotel chain, and it's certainly the one with the most history: British intelligence officers stationed here during World War II worked to crack secret Nazi codes.

Modern wings, pierced with row upon row of balconied loggias, surround the hotel's colonial core. The property was designed around a concrete pier that extends into the harbor, near a Japanese-style floating garden. Many of the spacious rooms have private balconies, and the hotel has a wide array of bars and restaurants, including **Harley's** (p. 128).

76 Pitts Bay Rd., Pembroke Parish HM CX, Bermuda. www.fairmont.com/hamilton. © **866/540-4447** in the U.S., or 441/295-3000. Fax 441/295-1914. 410 units. Winter $329–$409 double, $439–$689 suite; summer $459–$609 double, $579–$819 suite. Children 17 and under stay free in a room with 1 or 2 adults. AE, DC, MC, V. Frequent ferry service to and from the Fairmont Southampton, weather permitting. **Amenities:** 3 restaurants; 2 bars; babysitting; concierge; health club w/saunas; mopeds; 2 pools (outdoor); room service; watersports equipment/rentals. *In room:* A/C, TV, hair dryer, Internet ($14 per day), minibar.

Small Hotels

EXPENSIVE

Rosedon Hotel ★ 🏨 If you'd prefer a small local hotel with charm and character in the City of Hamilton, Rosedon is for you. The staff at this stately 1906 mansion is polite and personable. Although its rates are rather high for what it is—basically, an overblown guesthouse—it has its fans. Business travelers often stay here because of its proximity to the City of Hamilton.

Once occupied by an English family, this was the first house in Bermuda with gaslights. The main house, with the exception of a half-dozen upstairs bedrooms, is mostly used as a reception area and office. Most of the accommodations lie within a rambling two-story contemporary-looking annex that encircles a garden, a flagstone terrace, and a temperature-controlled swimming pool in back.

Regardless of their location, midsize bedrooms are individually decorated. Each was recently renovated, many of them in 2011, and each has a private balcony or patio, along with a small but neat bathroom. The modern, pool-fronting accommodations in the rear are often preferred over rooms in the main house. The colonial-style bedrooms in the main house, however, have more island flavor and character. The honor system prevails at the self-service bar and "pantry" (a repository for ready-made sandwiches and snacks). A tasty, full breakfast, included in the rates, is plentiful. It can also be delivered to your room. There's afternoon tea, but no restaurant.

57 Pitts Bay Rd. (P.O. Box HM 290), City of Hamilton, Pembroke Parish HM AX, Bermuda. www.rosedon.com. © **441/295-1640.** Fax 441/295-5904. 44 units. Apr–Nov $260–$402 double; off season $204–$336 double. Extra person $35–$40. Rates include full breakfast and afternoon tea. AE, MC, V. Free round-trip shuttle service to Elbow Beach, 10 min. away. **Amenities:** Bar; babysitting; pool (outdoor); room service; access to tennis courts at South Shore Beach & Tennis Club. *In room:* A/C, TV/DVD (in some), CD player (in some), iPod Player, hair dryer, Wi-Fi (free).

Housekeeping Units

MODERATE

Mazarine by the Sea   Lying 1.6km (1 mile) from the City of Hamilton, this cluster of apartments stands on the edge of a wild, windswept promontory overlooking the ocean. The special feature of the complex is a private pool set high on a cliff on the island's North Shore. Everything is very laissez-faire—there aren't any hotel services, and the setting is in a residential area, so you'll have to commute by bus to the beaches and into the capital itself.

The apartments, which the owners strictly maintain only for nonsmokers, are furnished in a simple and basic yet comfortable style and are well maintained. Five of the units open onto views of the water. Even though it's not on a beach, you can deep-water swim here and also snorkel.

91 N. Shore Rd., Pembroke Parish HM 13, Bermuda. www.bermuda.com/mazarinebythesea. ℂ **441/292-1690.** Fax 441/292-6891. 7 units. Summer $160–$190 double; winter $120–$150 double. AE, MC, V. Bus: 4 or 10. **Amenities:** Pool (outdoor). *In room:* A/C, kitchenette, phone.

Robin's Nest   Consider Robin's Nest if you'd like a snug and unpretentious little apartment in a sleepy, family-managed compound in a residential neighborhood. It consists of several buildings scattered amid a small but well-maintained garden that's supervised by Milt and Renée Robinson. Units are spacious and have a summery-looking decor that includes lots of wicker. Each unit contains a fully equipped kitchen and a bathroom with a tub/shower combination. The most desirable rooms are eight studios overlooking the pool. Each unit is equipped for full housekeeping, with an excellent modern kitchen, and each comes with a private balcony opening onto a view. Hibachis are available in case you want to expand your cooking into the great outdoors. Two coves, suitable for swimming, lie within a 10-minute walk of the compound.

10 Vale Close, North Shore, Pembroke Parish HM 04, Bermuda. www.robinsnestbda.com. ℂ/fax **441/292-4347.** 12 units. Year-round $175 double; $220 triple. Children 11 and under $10 each. No credit cards. Bus: 4. **Amenities:** Internet (free), pool (outdoor). *In room:* A/C, TV, fridge, hair dryer.

Rosemont ★ ☺   Not to be confused with the more comfortable and more expensive Rosedon Hotel located nearby, Rosemont is a cluster of gray-walled cottages, each with a veranda, on a flowered hillside near the Hamilton Princess. Two of the cottages are former private homes, built in the 1940s; the rest are more modern structures built within the past 2 decades. The harbor is visible from the raised terrace. Business travelers, "subdued" families, and older couples frequent Rosemont, attracted by its peace and tranquility. There is a policy here to "keep it quiet," so the hotel usually doesn't accept college students or large groups.

Rooms are well furnished in a bland, international modern style. As many as three rooms can be joined together to accommodate families. The hotel also has three suites with private entrances and better furnishings. Each room comes with a kitchen and a small but neat private tiled bathroom.

There's no restaurant on the premises; everybody cooks in. A grocery store is close by, downtown City of Hamilton is 10 minutes away, and Elbow Beach is a 15-minute scooter or taxi ride away. Management presents a complimentary buffet of coffee and muffins every morning.

41 Rosemont Ave. (P.O. Box HM 37), City of Hamilton, Pembroke Parish HM AX, Bermuda. www.rosemont.bm. ℂ **800/367-0040** in the U.S., 800/267-0040 in Canada, or 441/292-1055. Fax 441/295-3913. 47 units. Apr–Nov $232–$242 double, $258–$292 suite for 2; Dec–Mar $222–$232 double, $242–$272 suite for 2. For children 2–13, add $20 per child. AE, MC, V. **Amenities:** Babysitting; pool (outdoor); mopeds. *In room:* A/C, TV, fridge, hair dryer, Wi-Fi (free).

Pembroke Parish (City of Hamilton)

WHERE TO STAY

Guesthouses

EXPENSIVE

Royal Palms Hotel ★ ☺   Just a 5-minute walk from the City of Hamilton, the Royal Palms is one of the most sought-after small hotels on the island, thanks to the care and restoration work of owners Susan and her husband, Nick Weare, and their polite, hardworking staff. Built in 1903, it's a fine example of Bermudian architecture, with coral-colored walls, white shutters, a white roof, and a wraparound front porch with rocking chairs and armchairs. The closest beach is Elbow Beach, a 10-minute taxi or scooter ride or a 30-minute walk away.

The guest rooms were once the living rooms, parlors, and bedrooms of the grand private house. All are spacious, sunny, and comfortably furnished, with rich fabrics throughout. Most units have high ceilings and tall windows, and each comes with a small, well-maintained private bathroom. What originally functioned as an outlying cottage ("the mews house) now contains some of the most charming minisuites in the hotel, connected via a brick-paved walkway and a formal courtyard with a fountain to the original (main) house. This guesthouse is an excellent choice for budget-minded families traveling together. Family travelers generally request one of the units that come with kitchen facilities.

Cozy public areas include **Ascots** restaurant (p. 122).

24 Rosemont Ave. (P.O. Box HM 499), City of Hamilton, Pembroke Parish HM CX, Bermuda. www. royalpalms.bm. ✆ **800/678-0783** in the U.S., or 441/292-1854. Fax 441/292-1946. 32 units. Apr–Nov $325–$352 double, $378–$430 suite; off season $293–$317 double, $339–$385 suite. Extra person $40. Children 15 and under $25; children 2 and under stay free in parent's room. Rates include continental breakfast. AE, MC, V. **Amenities:** Restaurant; bar; babysitting; pool (outdoor); Wi-Fi (free). *In room:* A/C, TV, hair dryer, kitchen (in suites).

MODERATE

Edgehill Manor Guest House   Just outside the city limits and a 15-minute walk from the nearest beach, Edgehill Manor is in a quiet residential area that's convenient to the City of Hamilton's restaurants and shopping. It was built around the time of the American Civil War, exudes an old-fashioned, homey quality, and attracts a generally middle-aged clientele. British-born proprietor Bridget Marshall serves English tea in the afternoon. Although each unit has its own style, all have small balconies or patios and come with small tiled bathrooms. The continental breakfast, Ms. Marshall is proud to say, is "all home baked."

36 Rosemont Ave. (P.O. Box HM 1048), City of Hamilton, Pembroke Parish HM EX, Bermuda. www. bermuda.com/c-g/edgehill-manor.aspx. ✆ **441/295-7124.** Fax 441/295-3850. 14 units. Apr–Nov $240–$260 double, $332 triple or quad; off season $200–$220 double, $280 triple or quad. Rates include continental breakfast. AE, DC, MC, V. Bus: 7 or 8. **Amenities:** Babysitting; pool (outdoor); room service. *In room:* A/C, TV, fridge, Internet (free).

The Oxford House ★   The Oxford House is one of the best and most centrally located guesthouses in the City of Hamilton, about a 10-minute scooter ride or a 30-minute walk from Elbow Beach. The only property in Bermuda constructed specifically as a guesthouse, it reeks of a spiffy sense of Britishness thanks to its Welsh-born owner, Ann Smith.

The guesthouse was built in 1938 by a doctor and his French wife, who requested that some of the architectural features follow French designs. Doric columns, corner mullions, and urn-shaped balustrades flank the entrance portico. Inside, spacious, well-furnished guest rooms have high ceilings and dressing areas. Most have been renovated since 2010. There's also a sunny upstairs sitting room. Breakfast might include a fresh fruit salad made with oranges and grapefruit grown in the yard.

20 Woodbourne Ave. (P.O. Box HM 374), City of Hamilton, Pembroke Parish HM BX, Bermuda. www.oxfordhouse.bm. © **800/548-7758** in the U.S., or 441/295-0503. Fax 441/295-0250. 12 units. Mid-Mar to Nov $270 double; off season $222 double. Rates include continental breakfast. AE, MC, V. *In room:* A/C, TV, hair dryer, Wi-Fi (free).

SMITH'S PARISH

Cottage Colonies

VERY EXPENSIVE

Pink Beach Club & Cottages ★★★   Pink Beach remains proudly resistant to the changes that have swept through many of Bermuda's other cottage colonies. Far removed from the congestion of Hamilton, it's the largest cottage colony on Bermuda. Two pretty beaches (Pink Beach and West Beach) flank this complex of pink-sided, white-roofed cottages, and bay grape trees and hibiscus bushes grace its 6.5-hectare (16-acre) oceanfront setting. The staff, among the best on the island, includes people who have been with Pink Beach for decades. Accommodations are among the largest in Bermuda, and are configured as either a junior suite or a suite. All units have a generously proportioned bedroom/sitting area, a fully equipped kitchen, a decent-size bathroom, a patio, and an outdoor terrace or veranda. The most luxurious accommodations include a quartet of oceanfront suites. These are ideal for families seeking spacious accommodations. Management remains faithful to an age-old policy of not furnishing any of its units with a television, although one receiving only the three local Bermuda stations can be brought in without any additional charge.

The heart of the colony is the limestone clubhouse, with a dining room that reflects the service rituals of the Bermuda of many years ago. At least 85% of the clientele here opts for the MAP plan. Vegetables, many of them grown nearby, and fresh seafood go into the international cuisine. Every table provides a view of the ocean, and occasionally of a celebrity diner on a discreet getaway from the madding crowds. During clement weather, an additional outdoor dining terrace, with a separate menu, is available.

116 South Shore Rd., Tucker's Town, Smith's Parish (P.O. Box HM 1017), Hamilton HM DX, Bermuda. www.pinkbeach.com. © **800/355-6161** in the U.S. and Canada, or 441/293-1666. Fax 441/293-8935. 94 units. Summer $575–$1,025 double; off season $460–$675 double. Rates include MAP (breakfast and dinner). AE, MC, V. Bus: 1. **Amenities:** 2 restaurants; bar; babysitting; concierge; access to 2 golf courses; health club and spa; 2 tennis courts (lit); watersports equipment/ rentals. *In room:* A/C, hair dryer, Wi-Fi (free). Closed Jan–Apr.

HAMILTON PARISH

Resort Hotels

VERY EXPENSIVE

Tucker's Point Hotel & Spa ★★★   This resort's inauguration in 2009 signaled the debut of the most opulent and expensive construction in the history of Bermuda (at the time of its opening, construction costs were estimated in excess of $800,000 per guest room). Beginning in 1958, its forerunner, the Castle Harbour Club, welcomed the wintering wealthy of the American and British Empires. In the 1970s, Marriott attempted a renaissance of the place but failed to make a go of it. Recognizing the value of the terrain (81 hectares/200 acres of what some people say is the most beautiful seafront in Bermuda), the need for upscale homes, and the legendary cachet of the old Castle Harbour, the present owners tore most of the infrastructure to the ground. Rising triumphantly from the wreckage is a spectacularly comprehensive resort that proudly asserts its room rates as the most expensive on Bermuda, and its physical plant as the island's most comprehensive, imaginative, and theatrical. In 2011, the resort's management was taken over by the upscale Rosewood chain in a move that entrenched this place as the most upscale and most expensive hotel in Bermuda, with a lot of its business booked as part of uber-upscale corporate conventions for companies involved in the international financial services industries.

Creative styling fairly oozes out of this place. Its centerpiece is a balconied, big-windowed manor house loaded with contemporary art and a combination of antiques and reproductions that evoke a home where items were "collected" over several generations of discerning owners. A uniformed staff guides virtually every aspect of your arrival and well-being. Because the hotel has a huge physical plant but only 88 units, it feels like an intensely personalized boutique resort with big-city amenities. There's a higher percentage of upscale shops within the hotel than within any other competitor on the island, a long beach that's the envy of lesser hotels, and the most comprehensive spa (the Sense Spa) in Bermuda.

60 Tucker's Point Club Dr., Harrington Sound, Hamilton Parish HS 02, Bermuda. www.rosewood tuckerspoint.com. © **866/604-3764** or 441/298-9800. Fax 441/298-4001. 88 units. Summer (May–Aug) $770–$1,020 double, $1,820–$3,600 suite; off season $475–$650 double, $1,000–$2,500 suite. AE, DC, MC, V. **Amenities:** 6 restaurants; bar; concierge; 18-hole golf course; health club and spa; watersports equipment/rentals. *In room:* A/C, TV, hair dryer, MP3 docking station, wet bar (in suites), Wi-Fi (free).

EXPENSIVE

Grotto Bay Beach Resort ★ ☺ This resort (named after its subterranean caves) is lushly planted with tropical fruit trees. The beach is sandy but narrow, with rocky outcroppings, and unfortunately there are not a lot of other decent beaches nearby. However, the nearby coastline is enchanting, with many natural caves and intimate coves. From the seaside, the airy public areas look like a modern version of a mogul's palace, with big windows, thick white, pink, or coral-colored walls, and three peaked roofs with curved eaves.

This restored resort appeals to young couples and families who don't need all the hustle and bustle and central location of a resort such as the Elbow Beach. Although it's unattractively located across from the airport, noise from planes is not a problem. The sprawling, 8.5-hectare (21-acre) property contains 11 three-story buildings with balconies and sea views (but no elevators). All accommodations are well furnished; the bathrooms are well maintained. The children's programs and playground make this a safe bet for families. There are also a lot of activities offered, including nature walks, twice-weekly "cave crawls," daily cave swims, organized activities for teenagers, scavenger hunts, communal croquet near the bar, and fish feeding. The best rooms are directly on the beach, but those with limited mobility should note that they're at the bottom of a serpentine flight of about 30 masonry steps.

The on-site restaurants serve fair if unremarkable Continental cuisine, enlivened by fresh seafood. A multimillion-dollar renovation has perked up the look of all food and beverage outlets, including the **Palm Court** (p. 139). The lounge books live entertainment nightly, and there are a handful of other bars on the property. Afternoon tea is served every day, and there's a daily happy hour. Blasted out of natural rock, the pool has a swim-up bar. Solitude, tranquility, and friendly, personal service are the draws here.

11 Blue Hole Hill, Hamilton Parish CR 04, Bermuda. www.grottobay.com. ℂ **800/582-3190** or 441/293-8333. Fax 441/293-2306. 201 units. May–Oct $373–$425 double; Nov–Apr $203-218 double. Year-round suite for 2 $450. Supplement for all-inclusive (3-day minimum stay required) $99 per person per day. AE, MC, V. Bus: 1, 3, 10, or 11. **Amenities:** 3 restaurants; 2 bars; babysitting; children's programs; exercise room; Jacuzzi; mopeds; pool (outdoor); 4 tennis courts (2 lit); watersports equipment/rentals; Wi-Fi in lobby ($15). *In room:* A/C, TV, fridge, hair dryer.

Cottage Colonies
VERY EXPENSIVE

Clear View Suites & Villas   Adjacent to a grassy, rock-strewn patch of seafront, Clear View offers units that feature kitchenettes and a good deal of privacy. Midway between the City of Hamilton and St. George, it's a cluster of one- and two-story pink concrete buildings, 15 of which were added in 2011. Each holds two to six units decorated with pastel upholstery, tiled surfaces, and big windows. Most rooms have spectacular views of the ocean because of its cliff-side perch.

The centerpiece of the resort is a white-sided farmhouse that holds the restaurant, **Landfall** (p. 139), which offers Bermudian cuisine and a bar. You can swim in the ocean, but there's no beach—most guests head 1.5km (1 mile) west to the sands of Shelly Bay Beach. A small art gallery displays the works of local painters. Residents are welcome to drop in to the on-site working studio of Otto Trout, a widely renowned local painter whose work has been featured in the Bermuda Masterworks Museum.

Sandy Lane, Hamilton Parish CR 02, Bermuda. ℂ **441/293-0484.** Fax 441/293-0267. 54 units. Summer $200–$250 double; off season $150–$200. MAP (breakfast and dinner) $55 per person. AE, DC, MC, V. Bus: 10 or 11. **Amenities:** Restaurant; bar; mopeds; 2 pools (outdoor); tennis court. *In room:* A/C, TV, hair dryer, Internet (in some; free), kitchenette.

ST. GEORGE'S PARISH
Cottage Colonies
VERY EXPENSIVE

St. George's Club ★   A bit less stuffy than the cottage colonies listed above, this resort encompasses 7 hectares (17 acres) atop Rose Hill (off York St.). It features clusters of traditionally designed Bermudian one- and two-bedroom cottages. For a family or for two or three couples traveling together and sharing a cottage, the price is reasonable. A shuttle bus takes guests to the beach club at Achilles Bay, about a 2-minute ride away, where the beach is sandy with some rocky outcroppings. The Atlantic waters are a bit turbulent in autumn and spring, but they're calm during the summer. The complex functions primarily as a time-share property; units are rented to the public when the owners are not using them. Cottages have private balconies or patios, comfortable living and dining areas, fully equipped kitchens, and bathrooms with sunken tubs (and showers) and marble vanities. Views are of the ocean, the pool, or the golf course.

The colony's elegant restaurant, **Griffin's** (p. 142), is open to the public, and is among the finest dining rooms in the area.

6 Rose Hill (P.O. Box GE 92), St. George's Parish GE BX, Bermuda. www.stgeorgesclub.bm. ℂ **441/297-1200.** Fax 441/297-8003. 70 units. Summer $390 1-bedroom cottage, $486 2-bedroom cottage; winter $200 1-bedroom cottage, $240 2-bedroom cottage. AE, DC, MC, V. Bus: 1, 3, 6, 10, or 11. **Amenities:** 2 restaurants; 2 bars; babysitting; 18-hole golf course; 3 pools (outdoor); mopeds; 3 tennis courts (2 lit); watersports equipment/rentals. *In room:* A/C, TV; kitchenette or kitchen; Wi-Fi (in some; free).

PRACTICAL MATTERS: THE LODGING SCENE

Choosing the Place That's Right for You

Accommodations in Bermuda basically fall into five categories:

- **Resort Hotels:** These generally large properties are Bermuda's most lavish, offering many facilities, services, and luxuries—but also charging the highest prices. The lowest rates, usually discounted about 20%, are in effect from mid-November to March. The large resorts usually have their own beaches or beach clubs, along with swimming pools; some have their own golf courses. It's cheaper to choose the modified American plan (MAP) dining option (see "Rates & Reservation Policies," below, for details) than to order all your meals a la carte. However, if you go the MAP route, you'll be confined to the same dining room every night and miss the opportunity to sample different restaurants.

- **Small Hotels:** This option might be just the right fit for those who hate megaresorts. Bermuda's small hotels offer the intimacy of upscale B&Bs, but with more facilities. At a small hotel, you might feel more connected to the island and its people. Another plus? They're often cheaper than the big resorts.

- **Cottage Colonies:** This uniquely Bermudian option consists of a series of bungalows constructed around a clubhouse, which is the center of social life, drinking, and dining. The cottages, usually scenically arranged on landscaped grounds, are designed to provide maximum privacy and are typically equipped with kitchenettes for preparing light meals. In many of the cottage colonies, breakfast isn't available; you can go out, or buy supplies and prepare your own meal. Most colonies have their own beaches or swimming pools.

- **Housekeeping Units:** These cottage or apartment-style accommodations (often called efficiencies in the U.S.) occupy landscaped estates surrounding a main clubhouse. All of them offer kitchen facilities—perhaps not a full, well-equipped kitchen, but a kitchenette at least where you can whip up snacks and breakfast. Most offer minimal daily maid service. Generally, housekeeping units are simpler and less expensive than cottage colonies.

- **Guesthouses:** These are Bermuda's least expensive accommodations. The larger guesthouses are old Bermuda homes in garden settings. Generally, they've been modernized and have comfortable guest rooms. Some have swimming pools. A number are small, modest places, offering breakfast only; you may share a bathroom with other guests, as well as have to "commute" to the beach.

9

WHERE TO STAY

Practical Matters: The Lodging Scene

Your Best Bet May Be a Package

Especially for a destination like Bermuda, where lodging and eating costs can be quite expensive, consider booking a package tour. You can save hundreds over what you would pay by booking your hotel and airfare separately, and some offers include options for airport transfers and activities. Visit your favorite travel-booking website, or the websites of the major airlines that fly to Bermuda. The official Bermuda tourism website, **www.gotobermuda. com**, also offers package deals, as do most large travel agencies.

FAMILY-FRIENDLY accommodations

The Fairmont Southampton (p. 167)   This giant resort offers the best children's program on the island, including parties and reliable babysitting. Children 18 and under stay free in a room with one or two adults.

Grotto Bay Beach Resort (p. 183)   A longtime family favorite, this hotel features a heavily discounted "Family Special" for two adults and two children 15 and under spending at least 4 nights.

Rosemont (p. 180)   Rosemont caters to families, and each of its units contains a kitchen. Some rooms can be joined together to accommodate larger broods. Babysitting can be arranged.

Royal Palms Hotel (p. 181)   Although it can't compete with the big resorts in facilities, this longtime family favorite extends a cordial welcome. It's within walking distance of the City of Hamilton, so families can save on transportation. There's a freshwater pool, but the beach is a 10-minute ride or 30-minute walk away.

Sandpiper Apartments (p. 173)   Families looking for a moderately priced vacation might check in here. Some units have living/dining areas with two double pullout sofa beds. Each unit has a kitchen where Mom and Dad can prepare simple meals to cut down on the high cost of dining out in Bermuda.

Another option is renting a **villa** or vacation home. Villa rentals are like renting someone's home. At some, you're entirely on your own; others provide maid service. Most are on or near a beach. It is generally safe to consider this an expensive option.

Private **apartments** offer fewer frills than villas or condos; the building housing the apartment may not have a swimming pool or even a front desk. Apartments are available with or without maid service.

Cottages, or cabanas, offer the most independent lifestyle in the category of vacation accommodations—they're entirely self-catering. Some open onto a beach, and others surround a communal swimming pool. Most of them are fairly basic, consisting of a simple bedroom plus a small kitchen and bathroom. For the peak summer season, make cabana reservations at least 5 or 6 months in advance.

Several U.S. and Canadian agents can arrange these types of rentals. **Bermuda Realty,** Atlantic House, 11 Par-la-Ville Rd., Hamilton (www.bermudarealty.com; ✆ **441/292-1793**), specializes in condos and villas and can arrange bookings for a week or longer.

Rates & Reservation Policies

The rates that we list throughout this chapter are "rack rates"—the rates you'd be quoted if you walked in off the street. These are helpful for comparison, but almost no one ever pays the rack rate, especially at the big resorts. By booking a package deal that includes airfare, or by asking for packages and discounts at the hotel when you make your reservation, you can usually do much better. At small hotels and guesthouses, the rates quoted here are much more likely to be accurate.

All room rates, regardless of meal plan, are subject to a 7.25% tax, which will be tacked onto your bill. A service charge (10%–15%) is also added to your room rate in lieu of tips. Keep in mind, the service charge does not cover bar tabs. **Note:** The rack rates we list in this chapter include tax and service charge unless otherwise noted. However, we strongly encourage you to confirm what the rates include when you reserve, to avoid any misunderstanding.

Bermuda's high season is spring and summer. Most of Bermuda's hotels charge high-season rates from March (Easter is the peak period) through mid-November. A few hotels have year-round rates, and others charge in-between, or "shoulder," prices in spring and autumn. If business is slow, many smaller places shut down in winter.

For the purposes of grouping hotels in this chapter, any hotel with most rooms costing more than $400 is very expensive, with expensive in general being rooms costing $300 to $400 a night. For the most part, moderate rooms rent for $200 to $300 a night, with anything costing under $200, believe it or not, classified as inexpensive.

Note that some hotels offer a wide range of rooms. For instance, one guest at the Elbow Beach Hotel might be paying a price that can be categorized as "moderate," whereas another might be booked at a "very expensive" rate—it all depends on your room assignment. So even if you can't pay $400 per night, it might be worth a call to see if a cheaper room is available.

You may see some unfamiliar terms and abbreviations used to describe rate plans. **AP** (American plan), sometimes called "full board," includes three meals a day. **MAP** (modified American plan), sometimes called "half-board," includes breakfast and dinner. **BP** (Bermuda plan) includes full American or English breakfast. **CP** (continental plan) includes only continental breakfast (basically bread, jam, and coffee). **EP** (European plan) is always cheapest—it includes only the room, no meals.

Your Own Private Villa

Bermuda Accommodations (www. bermudarentals.com; ☏ **416/232-2243;** fax 416/237-9138) offers more than 80 privately owned cottages, apartments, and villas for rent in Bermuda, at prices beginning at $75 per person per day. Many charming rentals for two guests range from $100 to $200 daily for a well-equipped and fully furnished unit, although some of the large and desirable private houses for rent can go as high as a thousand dollars a day or more, a cost that's easily offset if the rental is divided among eight occupants. Regardless of the price, each has a private garden entrance, kitchen, and bathroom, and many accommodations also have pools on-site as well as easy access to the ocean. The homes are owned by Bermudians for the most part, and are rented when they are not occupied by the owners. Fiona Campbell, a Bermuda-born resident of Canada, is the savvy and well-connected owner of the business and the organization's 20-year veteran director. Her knowledge of her rental pool and her deep involvement in local opinion and politics is awesome.

PLANNING YOUR TRIP TO BERMUDA

S ettling into Bermuda is relatively easy. First-timers soon learn that Bermuda isn't one island, as is commonly thought, but a string of islands linked by causeways and bridges—at least the 20 or so that are inhabited. The other islands can be reached by boat.

In this chapter, you'll find everything you need to plan your trip. Getting to Bermuda is easier than ever, thanks to more frequent flights from such gateway cities as New York, Boston, and Washington, D.C. We also include information on several cruise lines that sail to the island from spring until late autumn.

GETTING THERE

By Plane

The flight from most East Coast destinations—including New York, Raleigh/Durham, Baltimore, and Boston—takes about 2 hours. Flights from Atlanta take 2½ hours; from Toronto, it's less than 3 hours. From London, the trip takes about 7 hours.

American Airlines (www.aa.com; ✆ 800/433-7300) flies nonstop, once or twice a day, from New York's JFK Airport and once daily from Miami. Departures coincide with dozens of connecting flights from elsewhere in North America.

Delta (www.delta.com; ✆ 800/221-1212) offers daily nonstop service from Boston and New York and two flights daily from Atlanta.

Continental Airlines (www.continental.com; ✆ 800/231-0856) offers nonstop service from New Jersey's Newark Airport. Departures are twice daily. The low-cost carrier **JetBlue Airways** (www.jetblue.com; ✆ 800/538-2583) offers two daily nonstop flights between New York and Bermuda. The 2-hour flights originate at Kennedy International Airport.

US Airways (www.usairways.com; ✆ 800/428-4322) offers daily nonstop flights from Philadelphia.

United Airlines (www.united.com; ✆ 800/538-2929) offers daily service from Newark, New Jersey.

Air Canada (www.aircanada.ca; ✆ 888/247-2262) offers one and sometimes two daily nonstop flights from Toronto, with frequent connections into Toronto from virtually every other city in Canada. The airline of choice from the United Kingdom is **British Airways** (www.britishairways.com; ☎ **0844/493-0787**). It flies from London's Gatwick Airport from five to seven times a week, year-round. No other airline flies nonstop between Britain and Bermuda.

Packing Tip

Bermuda is more formal than most resort destinations, so men planning to dine at upscale restaurants should be sure to pack a jacket and tie.

Most airlines offer the best deals on tickets booked at least 14 days in advance, with a stopover in Bermuda of at least 3 days. You might need to stay over on a Saturday night to keep fares down. Airfares fluctuate according to the season, but tend to remain competitive among the companies vying for a piece of the lucrative Bermuda run.

Peak season (summer) is the most expensive time to go; low season (usually from mid-Sept to mid-Mar) sees less expensive fares. The airlines that fly to Bermuda seldom observe a shoulder (intermediate) season.

By Cruise Ship

Cruise ships tie up at three harbors in Bermuda: St. George in the East End, the Royal Naval Dockyard in the West End, and Hamilton Harbour at the City of Hamilton. However, ships coming into the harbor at Hamilton may be on the wane.

While the cruise experience isn't for everyone, it's very appealing to some and is certainly a carefree, all-inclusive vacation. Ships from the East Coast of the United States reach Bermuda in a little over a day. You'll spend a few full days (usually 3) moored at the island, exploring during the day and returning to the ship at night. It's convenient and comfortable—like having a luxury hotel and restaurant that travels with you.

Of course, that's also its major disadvantage. Most cruisers don't get to know the real Bermuda as well as those who stay in hotels ashore. For instance, cruise-ship passengers generally eat all their meals aboard the ship—mainly because they've already paid for the meals as part of their cruise price—so they miss out on sampling Bermuda's cuisine. They also rarely get to meet and interact with Bermudians the way land-based visitors do.

Seven-day cruises out of New York usually include 4 days at sea, with 3 days in port. Cruise lines currently offering regularly scheduled trips to Bermuda include **Celebrity Cruises** (www.celebrity.com; ☎ **800/647-2251**); **Norwegian Cruise Line** (www.ncl.com; ☎ **866/234-7350**); **Princess Cruises** (www.princess.com; ☎ **800/774-6237**); **Royal Caribbean International** (www.royalcaribbean.com; ☎ **866/562-7625**), and, less frequently than its competitors, **Carnival** (www.carnival.com; ☎ **800/764-7419**).

HOW TO GET THE BEST DEAL ON YOUR CRUISE

Cruise lines operate like airlines, setting rates for their cruises and then selling them in a rapid-fire series of discounts, offering almost whatever it takes to fill their ships. Because of this, great deals come and go in the blink of an eye, and most are available only through travel agents.

If you have a travel agent you trust, leave the details to him or her. If not, try contacting a travel agent who specializes in booking cruises. Some of the most likely

10

PLANNING YOUR TRIP TO BERMUDA

Getting There

contenders include the following: **Cruises, Inc.,** 1415 NW 62 St., Ste. 205, Fort Lauderdale, FL 33009 (www.cruiseinc.com; ✆ 888/282-1249); **Cruises Only,** 100 Sylvan Rd., Ste. 600, Woburn, MA 01801 (www.cruisesonly.com; ✆ 800/278-4737); **The Cruise Company,** 10760 Q St., Omaha, NE 68127 (www.thecruisecompany.com; ✆ 800/289-5505); **Hartford Holidays Travel,** 500 Old Country Rd., Suite 110, Garden City, NY 11530 (www.hartfordholidays.com; ✆ 800/828-4813); **Mann Travel & Cruises,** 4400 Park Rd., Charlotte, NC 28209 (www.manntravelandcruises.com; ✆ 800/849-2028 or 704/556-8311); and Direct Line Cruises, 330 Motor Parkway, Hauppage, NY 11788 (www.directlinecruises.com; ✆ 800/352-8088).

GETTING AROUND
Getting into Town from the Airport

Planes arrive at Bermuda's L. F. Wade **International Airport (BDA),** Kindley Field Road, St. George (www.bermudaairport.com; ✆ 441/293-2470), about 15km (9 miles) east of the City of Hamilton and about 27km (17 miles) east of Somerset at the far western end of Bermuda.

After clearing Customs (see "Customs," under "Fast Facts," at the end of this chapter for details), you can pick up tourist information at the airport before heading to your hotel. Because you aren't allowed to rent a car in Bermuda, and buses don't allow passengers to board with luggage, you must rely on a taxi or minivan to reach your hotel.

LEAVING THE AIRPORT BY TAXI OR MINIVAN

More than 600 taxis are available on Bermuda, and cabbies meet all arriving flights. Taxis are allowed to carry a maximum of four passengers. If you and your traveling companion have a lot of luggage, you will need the taxi to yourselves.

Taxis in Bermuda are unduly expensive: They usually move slowly, meters seem to rise alarmingly fast, and taxi fares will inevitably represent a significant percentage of your day-to-day spending money. Regrettably, this situation can't be avoided. Nonresidents are forbidden to drive cars, and your only other option involves either walking (not practical on many of the very narrow roads) or renting either a bicycle or a small-capacity motorcycle (more on that later).

Unless the taxi has been specifically called to pick you up, in which case it will be a bit higher, the meter should read $4.15 when you first get in a cab. After that, expect to pay $4.15 for the first 1.6km (1 mile) and $2.25 for each additional 1.6km (1 mile) for up to four passengers. The following is a sample of taxi fares, including a tip of 10% to 15%, from the airport: To any point within the City of Hamilton, expect a metered fare of around $28 to $35; to points in and around St. George, around $18

Taxi Touring Tip

When a taxi has a blue flag on its hood (locals call the hood the "bonnet"), the driver is qualified to serve as a **tour guide.** The government checks out and tests these drivers, so you should use them if you plan to tour Bermuda by taxi. "Blue-bonnet" drivers charge no more than regular taxi drivers.

to $24; to points near Tucker's Town, around $35; to such south-shore beach hotels as Elbow Beach, around $40 to $54; and to such far-distant points as the West End, around $65. Fares increase by 25% between midnight and 6am, as well as all day on Sundays and holidays. Luggage carries a surcharge of $1 per piece. In almost every case, a meter determines the fare, unless you ask for a general tour of the island.

There are several authorized taxi companies on the island, including **C.O.O.P.** (✆ **441/292-4476**) and **Island Taxi Service** (✆ **441/295-4141**), which tends to pick up and answer its phones more quickly.

It's cheaper for a party of four or more to call a minivan and split the cost than to take two taxis (because usually only two people with luggage can fit into each taxi). Arrange, if it's practical, for a 10-passenger minivan, or if you're conducting a large group, for a bus holding between 20 and 25 passengers, before you arrive in Bermuda by contacting **Bermuda Triangle Tours,** 3 Cahhow Way, St. George CR 04 (www.btt.bm; ✆ **888/308-4687** or 441/293-1334). If you're traveling in a party of only two, consider asking a waiting chartered bus at the airport if it has room to take in two extra passengers. Using that mode of transportation, trips from the airport to such nearby hotels as Grotto Bay will cost as little as $10 per person, trips to the City of Hamilton will cost around $15 per person, and trips to the island's distant West End will cost around $19 per person.

Remember, however, that these fares are imposed on a per-person basis, and taxis charge their rates for a collective carload of up to four passengers, depending on their ability to fit in all their luggage.

Arriving by Cruise Ship

This is the easiest way to arrive in Bermuda. The staff will present you with a list of tour options long before you arrive in port, and almost everything is done for you unless you choose to make your own arrangements (although an independent taxi tour is far more expensive than an organized tour). Most passengers book shore excursions when they reserve their cruise.

Depending on your ship, you will probably arrive in either the City of Hamilton (best for shopaholics) or St. George (best for architecture and history buffs). A few ships dock at the Royal Naval Dockyard on Bermuda's West End. Whichever port you dock at, you can avail yourself of the waiting taxis near your ship, or rent a moped or bicycle and do some touring and shopping on your own. For more information about cruising to Bermuda, see "By Cruise Ship," above.

(But Not) By Car

Bermuda is the only Atlantic island that restricts car ownership to local residents. Part of the reason for this is the notoriously narrow roads, which have small or nonexistent shoulders and hundreds of blind curves. Add the British custom of driving on the left, and there would be traffic chaos if newcomers were allowed to take to the roads in rented cars. You'll rely on taxis, bikes, or motorized bicycles called "putt-putts."

By Taxi

Dozens of taxis roam the island, and virtually every hotel, restaurant, and shop is happy to call one for you. The hourly charge is $55 for one to four passengers. A luxury tour van accommodating up to six passengers costs $60 to $90 an hour. If you want to use one for a sightseeing tour, the minimum is 3 hours.

By Motorbike

Dependence on cabs and rented motor scooters, mopeds, and bicycles is simply a fact of Bermudian life that newcomers quickly accept as part of the island's charm. Although not having a car at your disposal is inconvenient, the island's tourist brochures make it seem just wonderful: a happy couple bicycling or mopeding around Bermuda on a sunny day, slowly putt-putting across the islands.

What the brochures don't tell you is that the roads are too narrow, and Bermudians—who are likely to own cars, and pay dearly for the privilege—feel that the road is theirs. Sometimes it starts raining almost without warning (the skies usually clear rapidly, and the roads dry quickly). During inclement weather, scooter riders are likely to be edged close—sometimes disturbingly close—to the shoulder; after rainstorms, they'll almost certainly be splattered with water or mud. Many accidents occur on slippery roads after it's rained, especially involving those not accustomed to using a motor scooter.

Who should rent a moped or scooter, and who should avoid them altogether? Frankly, the answer depends on your physical fitness and the time of day. Even the most stiffly starched might find a wind-whipped morning ride from the hotel to the beach or tennis courts invigorating and fun. Dressed to the nines for a candlelit dinner, you'd find the experience horrifying. And although the putt-putters can be a lot of fun during a sunny day, the machines can be dangerous and capricious after dark—and, of course, when you've had too many daiquiris. Not everyone is fit enough, either. And visitors on mopeds have a high accident rate, with at least some of the problems related to driving on the left.

Considering the hazards, we usually recommend that reasonably adept sports enthusiasts rent a moped for a day or two. For evening outings, we firmly believe that a taxi is the way to go.

You must be 16 or older to rent a motorbike. Some vehicles are big enough to cozily accommodate two adults. Helmets are required, and rental companies must provide them.

What's the difference between a moped and a motor scooter? Mopeds have larger wheels than scooters, and subject riders to fewer shocks as they traverse bumps in the road. Most (but not all) mopeds are designed for one rider; scooters accommodate either a single passenger or two passengers riding in tandem. Both have similar maximum speeds and horsepower.

There are quite a few gas stations (called "petrol stations"). Once you "tank up" your motorbike, chances are you'll have plenty of gas to get you to your destination; for example, one tank of gas in a motorbike will take you from Somerset in the west to St. George in the east.

Among the rental companies listed below, there's a tendency toward price fixing. Rental fees across the island tend to be roughly equivalent, and shopping around for a better deal is usually a waste of time. On average, mopeds for one rider rent for $48 for the first day, $89 for 2 days, $122 for 3 days, and $173 for 5 days. Scooters for two riders cost about $53 for 1 day, $102 for 2 days, or up to $174 for 4 days. You must pay with a major credit card; it serves as a deposit in case of damage or theft. **Note:** You

Who Are You Talking To?

Police are cracking down on vacationers who use cellphones while riding motorcycles and bicycles—violators are being pulled over by the police and given a fine.

must also purchase a one-time insurance policy for $30 included in the price. The insurance is valid for the length of the rental.

You can rent mopeds and scooters at **Wheels Cycle** (http://web.me.com/dpanchau; ✆ **441/292-2245**), which has five locations scattered throughout Bermuda, two of them in Hamilton. Scooters rent for $45 a day for a single-seater; $50 a day for scooters suitable for two.

Oleander Cycles Ltd., 6 Valley Rd., Paget Parish (www.oleandercycles.bm; ✆ **441/236-5235**), rents only scooters. A first-day rental for a single-seater is $50, $55 for a double. Subsequent days have price reductions depending on the length of rental. There are also locations at 15 Gorham Rd. in the City of Hamilton (✆ **441/295-0919**), 26 York St. in St. George (✆ **441/297-0478**), and King's Wharf Dockyard (✆ **441/234-2764**). Each branch is open daily from 8:30am to 5:30pm.

Eve Cycles Ltd., 114 Middle Rd., Paget Parish (www.evecycles.bm; ✆ **441/236-6247**); 1 Water St., St. George (✆ **441/236-0839**); and at the International Airport (✆ **441/293-6188**), rents a variety of scooters; they cost $48 to $53 for the first day, and $173 to $200 for 5 days, depending on the model, with successively lower prices for each additional day.

A final option for motorbike rentals, with a reputation that goes back to 1947, is **Smatt's Cycle Livery, Ltd.,** 74 Pitts Bay Rd., Hamilton, Pembroke Parish (www.smattscyclelivery.com; ✆ **441/295-1180**). It's adjacent to the Hamilton Princess Hotel. Motorbikes cost $50 for a 1-day rental, $95 for a 2-day rental, and $135 for a 3-day rental. Dual-seaters rent for $75 for 1 day, $127 for 2 days, and $170 for 3 days. Staff will give you instructions on bike safety and protocol.

By Bicycle

Pedaling a bike up Bermuda's steep hills can be a bit of a challenge, but if you're looking for a more natural means of locomotion than a putt-putt, you can rent bikes at most cycle liveries (see above).

Eve Cycles Ltd., 114 Middle Rd., Paget Parish (www.evecycles.bm; ✆ **441/236-6247**), offers one of the best rental deals on the island. Named after the legendary matriarch who founded the company more than 50 years ago, Eve rents men's and women's bicycles (usually 10- to 12-speed mountain bikes, well suited to the island's hilly terrain). Prices for 21-speed mountain bikes are $30 for a 1-day rental, $50 for a 2-day rental, and $65 for a 3-day rental. A $20 one-time fee for an insurance policy is required. The shop is a 10-minute taxi ride (or a leisurely 20-min. cycle) west of the City of Hamilton. As with motorbiking, exercise caution because roads are narrow and often slippery, and scooter riders and left-hand driving can make things confusing. See "Biking," in chapter 4, for more details.

By Bus

Bermuda's bus network covers all major routes, and nearly all hotels, guesthouses, and restaurants have bus stops close by. There's even a do-it-yourself sightseeing tour by bus and ferry. Regularly scheduled buses go to most of the destinations that interest visitors in Bermuda, but be prepared to wait. Some buses don't run on Sundays or holidays, so be sure you know the schedule for the trip you want to make.

Bermuda is divided into 14 zones of about 3km (1¾ miles) each. The regular cash fare for bus travel within up to three zones is $3 if you pay the driver directly (only coins are accepted), and $2.50 if you opt to use a bus token or bus pass (more on these below). For travel through more than three zones, the fare is $4.50 if you pay

PLANNING YOUR TRIP TO BERMUDA

Getting Around

the driver directly, and $4 if you use a bus token or bus pass. Children 5 to 16 pay $2 for all zones; children 4 and under ride free. **Note:** You must have the exact change in either coins or tokens ready to deposit into the fare box as you board the bus. Drivers do not make change or accept bills—to avoid the hassle, especially if you plan to make good use of Bermuda's transportation network during your stay, consider purchasing a ticket booklet or day pass (described below).

You can purchase tokens or passes for either the bus or the ferry at post offices throughout Bermuda or at the **Central Bus Terminal** on Washington Street in the City of Hamilton, where all routes, except Rte. 6, begin and end. Tokens and passes are sold from 7:15am to 5:30pm weekdays, 8:15am to 5:30pm Saturdays and 9:15am to 4:45pm Sundays and holidays.

The terminal is just off Church Street, a few steps east of City Hall. You can get there from Front Street or Reid Street by going up Queen Street or through Walker Arcade and Washington Mall. If you plan to travel a lot, you might want to purchase a booklet of 15 tickets. A booklet of 14-zone tickets costs $30, of three-zone tickets $20. For children, 15 tickets cost $7.50, regardless of the number of zones. Transfers are free when you are traveling from one place to the other as long as you take the next bus in the connecting route. You can buy the booklets at post offices or the central bus terminal. You can also purchase passes that allow travel in all zones for 1 day to 1 month. A 1-day pass costs $12, a 2-day pass costs $20, a 3-day pass costs $28, a 4-day pass is $35, a 1-week pass is $45, and a 1-month pass is $55. For more information on bus service, call ✆ **441/292-3851. Note:** These booklets and passes are also usable on the ferry system (see below), so be sure to factor that in when deciding whether or not to purchase a booklet or pass.

In the east, **St. George's Mini-Bus Service** (✆ **441/297-8492** or 441/297-8199) operates a minibus service around St. George's Parish and St. David's Island. The basic one-way fare is $3. Buses depart from King's Square in the center of St. George, and can be flagged down along the road. In summer, service is daily from 7:30am to midnight. In the off season, service is Monday through Thursday from 7:30am to 10pm, Friday and Saturday from 7:30am to midnight.

Trolleylike **buses** that seat 60 serve the City of Hamilton and the Royal Naval Dockyard. Passengers can get on and off throughout the day for a single fare of $12. The City of Hamilton trolley stops at the major points of interest, including the Botanical Gardens; the dockyard bus calls at the crafts market. Tickets are sold at most hotels, the City of Hamilton train station, and the Oleander cycle shop (see "By Motorbike," above).

By Ferry

One of the most scenic ways of getting around Bermuda is the government-operated ferry service. Ferries crisscross Great Sound between the City of Hamilton and Somerset; the one-way fare is $4. They also take the harbor route, from the City of Hamilton to the hotel-filled parishes of Paget and Warwick. The ride from the City of Hamilton to Paget costs $2.50. On all routes, children 5 to 16 pay $2, and children 4 and under ride free. Motorbikes are allowed on the City of Hamilton to Somerset run for $4,

 Daily Life in Bermuda

Here are some miscellaneous Bermuda survival tips: Know that ATMs dispense only Bermuda dollars, and that buses accept only coins, not bills. Also, don't get caught in the City of Hamilton's rush-hour traffic, which is Monday to Friday 8:30 to 9am and 5 to 6pm.

Getting Around

PLANNING YOUR TRIP TO BERMUDA

with bikes transported free (these rules and fees vary, however, so call ahead if you plan to take a bike or motorbike with you on other routes).

The ferry system also accepts the same ticket booklets and day passes as the bus system. See "By Bus," above, for detailed information on those options.

For ferry service information, call *©* **441/295-4506** in the City of Hamilton. Ferry schedules are posted at each landing and are available at the Ferry Terminal, the Central Bus Terminal in the City of Hamilton, and most hotels.

Note: Like buses, the ferries require exact change. Tickets/tokens/passes are strongly preferred. If you aren't using the aforementioned ticket booklet or pass, be sure you have exact change or tokens.

PLANNING AN ISLAND WEDDING

Getting Married in Bermuda

Couples who would like to get married in Bermuda must file a "Notice of Intended Marriage" with the Registry General, accompanied by a fee of $330 (in the form of a bank draft or money order, not a personal check). Make out the draft to "The Accountant General," and mail or deliver it in person to the **Registry General,** Government Administration Building, 30 Parliament St., Hamilton HM 12, Bermuda (www. bermuda-online.org/marriages.htm; *©* **441/297-7707**). Bermuda Department of Tourism offices in Atlanta and New York (see "Visitor Information," on p. 205) distribute "Notice of Intended Marriage" forms, or you can contact the Bermuda Department of Tourism (*©* **800/BERMUDA** [237-6832]) and a form will be mailed to you. If either of the prospective marriage partners has been married before, that person must attach a photocopy of the final divorce decree to the "Notice of Intended Marriage."

Once the Registry General receives the "Notice of Intended Marriage," it will be published, including names and addresses, in any two of the island's newspapers. Assuming that there is no formal objection, the registry will issue the license 15 days after receiving the notice. There is no requirement that the betrothed couple must reside in Bermuda during the 15-day waiting period. Airmailing your completed notice to Bermuda takes 6 to 10 days, so plan accordingly. The marriage license will be sent to you and will be valid for 3 months. Bermuda's wedding authorities state loudly and very clearly that marriage licenses will not be granted to, or approved for, same-sex couples who want to marry.

Hiring a Wedding Consultant

Many hotels can help make wedding arrangements—reserving the church and clergy, hiring a horse and buggy, ordering the wedding cake, and securing a photographer. Weddings in Bermuda range from simple ceremonies on the beach to large-scale extravaganzas at the Botanical Gardens. Other popular sites include churches and yachts.

The Bridal Suite, 125 North Shore Rd., Pembroke HM 14, East Bermuda (www. bridalsuitebermudaweddings.com; *©* **888/253-5585** or 441/292-2025), arranges wedding packages that range from $2,000 to $30,000.

Some hotels—including the Elbow Beach Hotel and both of the Fairmont hotels—will arrange weddings; see chapter 9 for contact information. If you're staying at a small hotel, it's better to go through a wedding consultant to plan your wedding.

[FastFACTS] BERMUDA

Area Code   The area code for all of Bermuda is **441.**

Banks   The main offices of Bermuda's banks are in the City of Hamilton. All banks and their branches are open Monday to Friday 9am to 4:30pm. Banks are closed Saturdays, Sundays, and public holidays. Many big hotels will cash traveler's checks, and there are ATMs all around the island.

The **HSBC of Bermuda,** 6 Front St., Hamilton (www.hsbc.bm; ✆ **441/299-5959**), has branches on Church Street, Hamilton; on Par-la-Ville Road, Hamilton; and in Somerset.

The **Bank of Butterfield,** 65 Front St., Hamilton (www.butterfieldgroup.com; ✆ **441/295-1111**), has several branches, including locations in St. George and Somerset.

The **Bermuda Commercial Bank** is at 43 Victoria St., Hamilton (www.bermuda-bcb.com; ✆ **441/295-5678**).

Business Hours   Most commercial businesses are open Monday through Friday from 9am to 5pm. Retail shops are generally open Monday through Saturday from 9am to 5pm (or 7pm); several shops open at 9:15am. A few shops are also open in the evening, but usually only when big cruise ships are in port.

Cellphones   See "Mobile Phones," below.

Climate   See "When to Go," in chapter 2.

Crime   See "Safety," later in this section.

Customs   Visitors may bring into Bermuda duty-free apparel and articles for their personal use, including sports equipment, cameras, 200 cigarettes, 1 liter of liquor, and 1 liter of wine, half a kilogram of tobacco, and 50 cigars. Duties are levied if your travel with your pet, even if your pet was acquired, without charge, from an animal shelter Certain foodstuffs may be subject to duties. All imports may be inspected on arrival. Visitors entering Bermuda may also claim a duty-free gift allowance. Be warned that dozens of travelers entering Bermuda have complained bitterly about rude, uncooperative, suspicious, and accusatory customs officials.

Persons who are taking prescription medication must inform Bermuda customs officials at the point of entry. Medicines must be in labeled containers. Travelers should carry a copy of the written prescription and a letter from the physician or pharmacist confirming the reason the medicine is prescribed.

When you're leaving Bermuda (if you're flying back to the U.S.), a customs inspector will ask to see a copy of the incoming Bermuda form that was stamped and given to you as you cleared Bermuda Customs. Make sure that you hold onto it and can produce it on short notice.

For additional information on temporary admission, export and customs regulations, and tariffs, contact **Bermuda Customs** at ✆ **441/295-4816** or visit the Bermuda Customs website at **www.customs.gov.bm**.

Dentists   For dental emergencies, call **King Edward VII Memorial Hospital,** 7 Point Finger Rd., Paget Parish (www.bermudahospitals.bm; ✆ **441/236-2345**), and ask for the emergency department. The hospital maintains lists of dentists on emergency call.

Disabled Travelers   Bermuda is not a great place for persons with disabilities who are not planning to stay on-site at a resort. Getting around the islands is a bit difficult even for the agile, who must rely on motorbikes, bicycles, and buses. It is difficult to walk with a cane outside the town of St. George and the City of Hamilton, because most roads don't have sidewalks or adequate curbs. When two vehicles pass, you are often crowded off the road.

Taking taxis to everything you want to see can be very expensive. Unfortunately, the public buses are not geared for passengers in wheelchairs. However, you can ask your hotel to check on the availability of volunteer buses operated by the Bermuda Physically Handicapped Association (see below). It occasionally runs buses with hydraulic lifts. You can also call the tourist office and request a schedule for such transportation; make arrangements as far in advance as possible.

Before you go, you can seek information from the website of the **Bermuda Physically Handicapped Association** (www.bermuda-online.org/BPHA.htm; *©* **441/293-5035**). Visitors planning to bring a guide dog to Bermuda must obtain a permit in advance from any Bermuda Department of Tourism office; see "Visitor Information," later.

The most accessible hotels in Bermuda are Elbow Beach Hotel, the Fairmont Hamilton Princess, and the Fairmont Southampton (see chapter 9 for listings).

Doctors Finding a doctor or getting a prescription filled on Bermuda is relatively simple. In an emergency, call **King Edward VII Hospital,** 7 Point Finger Rd., Paget Parish (*©* **441/236-2345**), and ask for the emergency department. For less serious medical problems, ask someone at your hotel for a recommendation. See "Drugstores," below, for addresses of pharmacies.

Drinking Laws Bermuda sternly regulates the sale of alcoholic beverages. The legal drinking age is 18, and most bars close at 1am (some close as early as 10pm, and others as late as 3am). Some bars are closed on Sunday, and stores can't sell alcohol on Sunday. You can bring beer or other alcohol to the beach legally, as long as your party doesn't get too rowdy and you generally stay in one spot. The moment you actually walk on the beach or the streets with an open container of liquor, it's illegal.

Driving Rules Visitors cannot rent cars. To operate a motor-assisted cycle, you must be age 16 or over. All cycle drivers and passengers must wear helmets. Driving is on the left side of the road, and the speed limit is 32kmph (20 mph) in the countryside, 24kmph (15 mph) in busy areas.

Drug Laws In Bermuda, there are heavy penalties for the importation of, possession of, or dealing of unlawful drugs (including marijuana). Customs officers, at their discretion, may conduct body searches for drugs or other contraband goods.

Drugstores Try the **Phoenix Drugstore,** 3 Reid St., Hamilton (*©* **441/279-5451**), open Monday through Saturday from 8am to 6pm, Sunday from noon to 6pm.

In Hamilton, **People's Pharmacy,** 62 Victoria St. (*©* **441/292-9261**), is open Monday through Saturday from 8am to 8:30pm, Sunday from 10am to 6pm. The **Somerset Pharmacy,** 49 Mangrove Bay, Somerset Village (*©* **441/234-2484**), is open Monday to Friday 8am to 6pm, and Saturday 8am to 5pm.

Electricity Electricity is 110 volts AC (60 cycles). North American appliances are compatible without converters or adapters. Visitors from the United Kingdom or other parts of Europe need to bring a converter.

Embassies & Consulates For Residents of the U.S.: The American Consulate General is located at Crown Hill, 16 Middle Rd., Devonshire (http://hamilton.usconsulate.gov; *©* **441/295-1342**), and is open Monday through Friday from 8am to 4:30pm.

For Residents of Canada The Canadian Consulate General (Commission to Bermuda) is at 73 Front St., Hamilton (*©* **441/292-2917**).

For Residents of the U.K. As Bermuda is a British territory, Britain does not maintain a consulate in Bermuda. For emergency travel documents, contact the Bermuda Department of Immigration, 30 Parliament Street, Hamilton (www.immigration.gov.bm; *©* **441/295-5151**).

For Residents of Australia The Australian High Commission in Ottawa, Canada (www. canada.embassy.gov.au; ☎ **613/236-0841**) provides consular assistance for Australians traveling in Bermuda.

Emergencies To call the police, report a fire, or summon an ambulance, dial ☎ **911.** The nonemergency police number is ☎ **441/295-0011.** For air-sea rescue, contact the Rescue Coordination Center, ☎ **441/297-1010.**

Etiquette Well-tailored Bermuda shorts are acceptable on almost any occasion, and many men wear them with jackets and ties. On formal occasions, they must be accompanied by navy blue or black knee socks. Aside from that, Bermudians are rather conservative in their attitude toward dress—bikinis, for example, are banned more than 7.5m (25 ft.) from the water. Men are usually encouraged (sometimes strongly) to wear a jacket to dinner.

Family Travel Bermuda is one of the best vacation destinations for the entire family. Toddlers can spend blissful hours in shallow seawater or pools geared just for them, and older children can enjoy boat rides, horseback riding, hiking, and snorkeling. Most resort hotels offer advice for families with kids (including help in finding a babysitter), and many have play directors and supervised activities for various age groups.

Outside the town of St. George and the City of Hamilton, walking with a baby stroller is difficult—most roads don't have sidewalks or adequate curbs. It is extremely dangerous to carry a baby on a motorbike or bike, as baby seats are not provided. Buses, taxis, and ferries are the safest ways to travel around Bermuda with a baby.

For some recommendations on where to stay and eat, refer to "Family-Friendly Accommodations," on p. 186, and "Family-Friendly Restaurants," on p. 131. To locate additional establishments that are particularly kid-friendly, refer to the "Kids" icon throughout this guide.

Gasoline Before you rent a moped, be very clear about what kind of fuel it runs on. Most of the mopeds available for rental by a nonresident of Bermuda have 50cc two-stroke engines that almost always require a mixture of gasoline and oil. Designated locally as "mixed" fuel, it's dispensed directly from specially designated pumps at service stations throughout Bermuda. Larger bikes (including some of the newer models with 80cc engines, and virtually all of the modern-day 100cc engines) require unadulterated gasoline. The octane level of all gasoline in Bermuda is designated as "high test," and all of it, by law, is unleaded.

Health If you suffer from a chronic illness, consult your doctor before your departure. Pack **prescription medications** in your carry-on luggage, and carry them in their original containers, with pharmacy labels—otherwise they won't make it through airport security. Carry the generic name of prescription medicines in case a local pharmacist is unfamiliar with the brand name. Contact the **International Association for Medical Assistance to Travelers (IAMAT;** www.iamat.org; ☎ **716/754-4883,** or 416/652-0137 in Canada) for tips on travel and health concerns in Bermuda, and for lists of local doctors. The United States **Centers for Disease Control and Prevention** (www.cdc.gov; ☎ **800/232-4636**) provides up-to-date information on health hazards by region or country and offers tips on food safety. **Travel Health Online** (www.tripprep.com), sponsored by a consortium of travel medicine practitioners, also offers helpful advice on traveling abroad.

Sunburns & Exposure Limit your exposure to the sun, especially between the hours of 11am and 2pm and during the first few days of your trip. Use a sunscreen with a high protection factor and apply it liberally. Also, as you travel around Bermuda on a scooter, on bike, or on foot, it's always wise to carry along some bottled water to prevent dehydration.

Seasickness A great deal of the population tends toward seasickness. If you've never been out on a boat, or if you've been seasick in the past, make sure you take any seasickness prevention measures that work for you *before* you board; once you set sail, it's generally too late. On the boat, stay as low and near the center of the boat as possible. Stay out in the fresh air and watch the horizon. If you start to feel queasy, drink clear fluids like water, and eat something bland, such as a soda cracker.

Cuts   All cuts obtained in the marine environment must be taken seriously because the high level of bacteria present in the water can quickly cause the cut to become infected. The best way to prevent cuts is to wear a wet suit, gloves, and reef shoes. If you get a coral cut, the book *All Stings Considered* recommends gently pulling the edges of the skin open and removing any embedded coral or grains of sand with tweezers. Next, scrub the cut well with fresh water, and then press a clean cloth against the wound to stop the bleeding.

Hospitals   **King Edward VII Memorial Hospital,** 7 Point Finger Rd., Paget Parish (www.bermudahospitals.bm; ✆ **441/236-2345**), has a highly qualified staff and Canadian accreditation.

Insurance   Although close to the United States, a visit to Bermuda is, in essence, "going abroad." You can encounter all the same problems in Bermuda that you would in going to a more remote foreign destination. Therefore, it's wise to review your insurance coverage, especially concerning lost luggage or medical insurance.

   For information on traveler's insurance, trip-cancellation insurance, and medical insurance while traveling, please visit www.frommers.com/planning.

Internet Access   Most of the larger hotels in Bermuda have some Internet service. If your hotel does not, there are a few places where you can go. The following places will allow you to log on for a fee: **Logic Internet Cafe,** 10–12 Burnaby St. in Hamilton (✆ **441/294-8888**), provides fresh coffee for Internet users who pay $5 per half-hour. Open Monday to Friday 8am to 6pm. **TeleBermuda International Custom Centre,** at the corner of Reid Street and Queen Street in Hamilton (✆ **441/296-9000**), allows you to surf the Web for $2.50 per 15 minutes. Open Monday to Friday 9am to 5pm. **Internet Lane,** the Walkway, 22 Reid St., Hamilton (✆ **441/296-9972**) offers seven computer workstations, any of which can be used for Web browsing at a rate of $2.50 per 15-minute session, Monday to Saturday 9am to 7pm.

Legal Aid   Your consulate will inform you of your limited rights and offer a list of attorneys. (See "Embassies & Consulates," above.) However, the consulate's office cannot interfere with Bermuda's law-enforcement officers.

For Residents of the U.S.   The **Citizens' Emergency Center** of the Office of Special Consular Services, in Washington, D.C. (http://travel.state.gov/travel/tips/emergencies/emergencies_1212.html; ✆ **888/407-4747** or 202/647-5225), operates a hot line that's useful in an emergency for U.S. citizens arrested abroad. The staff can also tell you how to send money to U.S. citizens arrested abroad.

For Residents of Canada   Contact the **Operations Centre of Foreign Affairs** via its 24-hour emergency hot line (✆ **888/949-9993** toll-free in Bermuda or 613/996-8885 collect).

For Residents of the U.K.   Because Bermuda is a British territory, Britain doesn't have an embassy or a consulate in Bermuda; local authorities deal with requests for consular-type assistance.

For Residents of Australia   Australians should contact the **24-hour Consular Emergency Centre** (✆ **2-6261-3305**) or their consulate (see above).

LGBT Travelers   Think twice before planning a vacation in Bermuda. Although many gays live in and visit Bermuda, the island is rather repressive to homosexuals, and for most of its existence, Bermuda had laws making sex between consenting legal-age males a crime subject to imprisonment. That is no longer the case, but displays of affection by same-sex couples will be frowned upon at public beaches and most hotel pools, restaurants, and attractions. If you want really happening gay beaches, bars, and clubs, head for South Miami Beach, Key West, Puerto Rico, or the U.S. Virgin Islands, a series of islands that are much more accepting of homosexual relationships.

Mail Deposit regular mail in the red pillar boxes on the streets. You'll recognize them by the monogram of Queen Elizabeth II. The postage rate for airmail letters up to 10 grams and for postcards is 70¢ to the United States and Canada, 85¢ to the United Kingdom. Airmail letters and postcards to the North American mainland can take 6 to 8 days, to Britain possibly a little longer.

Mobile Phones The three letters that define much of the world's wireless capabilities are GSM (Global System for Mobiles), a big seamless network that makes for easy cross-border cellphone use in dozens of countries, including Bermuda. Chances are high that your existing U.S. or U.K.-based cellphone might work adequately in Bermuda, although the details of your individual calling plan will determine the rate at which you'll pay roaming charges, or if roaming charges will apply at all. Check with your carrier for details, and if you're aboard a cruise ship, be very alert before you begin making onboard cellphone calls from your phone, the rate at which they'll be funneled and factored through your cruise ship's electronic communications system.

Regrettably, because of restrictive government and telecommunications restrictions, the widely competitive options for cellphone service you've come to expect in the U.S. and U.K. aren't usually available in Bermuda. The best cellphone connections in Bermuda are arranged through **rangeRoamer** (www.rangeroamer.com), which provides short-term cellphone service for travelers to Bermuda. You can use your own phone if it uses GSM, if it is "world capable" (dual band international) and if, as mentioned above, your individual calling plan won't drive you into bankruptcy as part of the process of staying in touch. If your individual plan is too expensive, or too restrictive, consider "unlocking" your phone to accept any SIM card from either rangeRoamer or from another carrier. GSM phones have a SIM card slot, which lets you insert the rangeRoamer SIM card in it. Whereas most phones from AT&T and T-Mobile have this slot, a lesser percentage of phones from Verizon or Sprint do.

In most cases, incoming calls to Bermuda through rangeRoamer cost $2 a minute; outgoing calls from Bermuda to the U.S, Canada, or the U.K. are charged $3 a minute. A less expensive, but less convenient, alternative involves buying a prepaid SIM card, before your arrival in Bermuda, from **Telestial Wireless Solutions** (www.telestial.com; ✆ **800/707-0031**) for a flat fee of $59. The insertion of Telestial's SIM card into a compatible phone brings the per-minute cost of calls to or from Bermuda to or from the U.S., Canada, or Europe, down to 75¢ a minute.

Money & Costs Legal tender is the Bermuda dollar (BD$), which is divided into 100 cents. It's pegged through gold to the U.S. dollar on an equal basis—BD$1 equals US$1.

U.S. currency is generally accepted in shops, restaurants, and hotels. Currency from the United Kingdom and other foreign countries is usually not accepted, but can be easily exchanged for Bermuda dollars at banks and hotels. You should exchange enough petty cash to cover airport incidentals, tipping, and transportation to your hotel before you leave home, or withdraw money upon arrival at an airport ATM. For up-to-the-minute currency conversions, visit **www.xe.com/ucc**.

THE VALUE OF THE BERMUDAN DOLLAR VS. OTHER POPULAR CURRENCIES

BD$	Aus$	Can$	Euro (€)	NZ$	UK£	US$
BD$1	A$.96	C$1	€.75	NZ$1.22	£.63	$1

WHAT THINGS COST IN BERMUDA	US$/BD$
Taxi from the airport to center of Hamilton	$28.00
Double room, moderate	$200.00
Double room, inexpensive	$110.00
Three-course dinner for one without wine, moderate	$25.00
Bottle of beer	$4.50
Cup of coffee	$2.75
Admission to most museums	$10.00
Average daily scooter rental	$50.00

ATMs   The easiest and best way to get cash away from home is from an ATM. These machines are plentiful in Bermuda. The **Cirrus** (www.mastercard.com; ☎ **800/424-7787**) and **PLUS** (www.visa.com) networks span the globe; look at the back of your bank card to see which network you're on, and then call or check online for ATM locations at your destination. Be sure you know your personal identification number (PIN) and daily withdrawal limit before you depart. **Note:** Remember that many banks impose a fee every time you use a card at another bank's ATM, and that fee can be higher for international transactions (up to $5 or more) than for domestic ones (where they're rarely more than $2). In addition, the bank from which you withdraw cash may charge its own fee. For international withdrawal fees, ask your bank.

Credit Cards   Credit cards are another safe way to carry money, but their use has become more difficult, especially in Bermuda (see warning below). They also provide a convenient record of all your expenses, and they generally offer relatively good exchange rates. But note that many banks now assess a 1% to 3% "transaction fee" on *all* charges you incur abroad (whether you're using the local currency or your native currency).

There is almost no difference in the acceptance of a debit or a standard credit card.

Note: The Discover Card (popular in the U.S.) is *not* accepted in Bermuda. MasterCard and Visa, however, are generally accepted.

"Chip and PIN" represents a change in the way that credit cards and debit cards are used. The program is designed to cut down on the fraudulent use of credit cards. More and more banks are issuing customers Chip and PIN versions of their debit or credit cards. In the future, it will be common for vendors to ask for a four-digit personal identification number or PIN when you use your credit card.

Warning: A number of places in Bermuda are moving to this new system. In the changeover in technology, some retailers have falsely concluded that they can no longer take swipe cards, or can't take signature cards that don't have PINs. In the interim between traditional swipe credit cards and those with an embedded computer chip, here's what you can do to protect yourself: Get a four-digit PIN from your credit card's issuing bank before leaving home.

For help with currency conversions, tip calculations, and more, download Frommer's convenient Travel Tools app for your mobile device. Go to **www.frommers.com/go/mobile** and click on the Travel Tools icon.

Newspapers & Magazines   Bermuda has one daily newspaper, the *Royal Gazette*, new editions of which appear Monday to Saturday (but not Sunday). Its major competitor provides a tabloid-driven alternative, *Bermuda Sun*, which is issued every Wednesday and Friday. Less comprehensive is a weekly advertising-with-news-and-infomercials circular, *This Week in Bermuda* (www.thisweekbm.com), which is distributed without charge four times a month to hotels, restaurants, bars, shops, and sporting venues across the island. Major

U.S. newspapers, including the *New York Times* and *USA Today*, and magazines such as *Time* and *Newsweek*, are delivered to Bermuda on the day of their publication on the mainland. *This Week in Bermuda* is a weekly guide for tourists.

For your media fix, go to the Washington Mall magazines stand on Reid Street in Hamilton. They carry major U.S. newspapers and magazines.

Passports Since the September 11, 2001 terrorist attacks, passports have been strictly required to get out of and back into your respective country. Another acceptable document is the **U.S. Passport Card,** which is a newer, limited-use travel document that fits into your wallet and costs less than a U.S. passport. But it is only valid for land and sea, not air travel.

Bermuda immigration authorities require **U.S. citizens** to have at least one of the following items in their possession: a birth certificate (or a certified copy of it accompanied by a photo ID), a U.S. naturalization certificate, a valid passport, a U.S. Alien Registration card, or a U.S. reentry permit. Go with the passport, because you will need it to reenter the U.S.

Bermuda Immigration authorities require visitors from **Canada,** the **United Kingdom,** and **Europe** to show a valid passport. All visitors must have a return or onward ticket in addition to their valid passport or original birth certificate.

Any traveler staying in Bermuda longer than 3 weeks must apply to the **Chief Immigration Officer** in person, at the Government Administration Building, 30 Parliament St., Hamilton HM 12, Bermuda (www.immigration.gov.bm; ✆ **441/295-5151**) for an extended stay. You will be asked to fill out an immigration application for an extended stay, which then will or will not be approved by authorities.

The websites listed below provide downloadable passport applications as well as the current fees for processing passport applications.

Australia   Australian Passport Information Service (www.passports.gov.au; ✆ **131-232**).

Canada   Passport Office, Department of Foreign Affairs and International Trade, Ottawa, ON K1A 0G3 (www.ppt.gc.ca; ✆ **800/567-6868**).

Ireland   Passport Office, Setanta Centre, Molesworth Street, Dublin 2 (www.foreign affairs.gov.ie; ✆ **01/671-1633**).

New Zealand   Passports Office, Department of Internal Affairs, 47 Boulcott St., Wellington, 6011 (www.passports.govt.nz; ✆ **0800/225-050** in New Zealand or 04/474-8100).

United Kingdom Visit your nearest passport office, major post office, or travel agency or contact the **Identity and Passport Service (IPS),** 89 Eccleston Sq., London, SW1V 1PN (www.ips.gov.uk; ✆ **0300/222-0000**).

United States To find your regional passport office, check the U.S. State Department website (travel.state.gov/passport) or call the **National Passport Information Center** (✆ **877/487-2778**) for automated information.

Pets To take your pet with you to Bermuda, it must be a minimum of 10 months of age, and if it's a dog, it must not be a member of any of the approximately 20 breeds that local authorities define as dangerous. You'll need a special permit issued by the director of the **Department of Agriculture, Fisheries, and Parks,** P.O. Box HM 834, Hamilton HM CX, Bermuda (www.animals.gov.bm; ✆ **441/236-4201**). The island has no quarantine facilities, so animals arriving without proper documents will be refused entry and will be returned to the point of origin. Some guesthouses and hotels allow you to bring in small animals, but others will not; be sure to inquire in advance. Always check to see what the latest regulations are before attempting to bring a dog or another pet—including Seeing Eye dogs—to Bermuda.

Pharmacies See "Drugstores," earlier.

Police In an emergency, call ✆ **911;** otherwise, call ✆ 441/295-0011.

Post Offices   The **General Post Office,** 56 Church St., Hamilton (✆ **441/297-7866**), is open Monday to Friday from 8am to 5pm, Saturday from 8am to noon. Post office branches and the Perot Post Office, Queen Street, Hamilton, are open Monday to Friday from 8am to 5pm. Some post offices close for lunch from 11:30am to 1pm. Daily airmail service for the United States and Canada closes at 9:30am in Hamilton. See also "Mail," above.

Safety   Bermuda has always been considered a safe destination, especially when compared to countries of the Caribbean such as Jamaica. However, there is some crime here, and the U.S. State Department has an advisory. Criminal activity continues to take place at St. George, a popular cruise-ship destination. Incidents of verbal and physical assault against tourists have been reported. Petty drug use is frequent, and gang activity has been reported in the area as well.

In recent years, the area of Pitts Bay Road from the Hamilton Princess Hotel into the City of Hamilton has been a common setting for muggings. The back streets of Hamilton are often the setting for nighttime assaults, particularly after the bars close.

Valuables left in hotel rooms (occupied and unoccupied) or left unattended on beaches are vulnerable to theft. Criminals often target transportation systems and popular tourist attractions. Examples of common crimes include pickpocketing, theft of unattended baggage and items from rental motorbikes, and purse snatchings (often perpetrated against pedestrians by thieves riding motorbikes).

Travelers should exercise caution when walking after dark or visiting out-of-the-way places on the island, which can be vulnerable to crime, and because narrow and dark roadways can contribute to accidents.

Senior Travel   Though much of the island's sporting and nightlife activity is geared toward more youthful travelers, Bermuda has a lot to offer seniors. The best source of information for seniors is the Bermuda Department of Tourism (see "Visitor Information," on p. 204). If you're staying in a large resort hotel, the activities director or concierge is another excellent source.

Smoking   In the spring of 2006, the government of Bermuda passed a law banning smoking in enclosed public places. Tobacconists and other stores carry a wide array of tobacco products, generally from either the United States or England. Prices vary but tend to be high.

Student Travel   The Bermuda Department of Tourism offers Spring Break programs for sports teams from the mainland, as well as Spring Break Arts Programs. Inquire with the tourism office for details (see "Visitor Information," p. 204).

Taxes   Bermuda charges visitors a Passenger Tax before they depart from the island; it's hidden within the cost of an airline or cruise-ship ticket. Frankly, you might never know that a tax has actually been imposed, but if you're interested, $25 of the cost of your airline ticket, and $60 of the cost of your cruise-ship ticket, goes to the Bermudian government. Children age 2 and younger are exempt from paying this tax.

All room rates, regardless of the category of accommodations or the plan under which you stay, are subject to a government tax of 7.25%.

Taxis   See "Getting Around," earlier in this chapter.

Telephones   Worldwide direct-dial phone, fax, and cable service is available at the headquarters of **Link Bermuda, Ltd.** (formerly known as the **Cable & Wireless Office**), 12 Burnaby St., Hamilton (www.LinkBermuda.com; ✆ **441/497-7000**). Hours are Monday through Friday from 9am to 5pm. Prepaid phone cards may be purchased and used islandwide, and calling cards may be used from selected call boxes.

Cash-card phone booths are available at numerous locations around the island. Making international calls with cash cards can be a lot cheaper than using the phone at your hotel, which might impose stiff surcharges. To make a local call, deposit 20¢ in either Bermudian or U.S. coins. Hotels often charge between 20¢ and $1 for local calls.

Special phones at passenger piers in the City of Hamilton, St. George, and the dockyard will connect you directly with an AT&T, Sprint, or MCI operator in the United States, permitting you to make collect or calling-card calls.

To call Bermuda:

1. Dial the international access code: 00 from the U.K., Ireland, or New Zealand; or 0011 from Australia. From North America, no international access code is necessary; just dial 1.
2. Dial country code 441.
3. Dial the local number.

To make international calls: To make international calls from Bermuda to North America, simply dial 1. For countries besides the U.S. and Canada, first dial 00 and then the country code (U.K. 44, Ireland 353, Australia 61, New Zealand 64). Next, dial the city or area code and local number.

For directory assistance: Dial 411 if you're looking for a number inside Bermuda, and dial 0 for numbers to all other countries.

For operator assistance: If you need operator assistance in making a call, dial 0.

Toll-free numbers: There are no toll-free numbers in Bermuda. Calling an 800 or 888 number in North America from Bermuda costs the same as an overseas call.

Time   Bermuda is 1 hour ahead of Eastern Standard Time (EST). Daylight saving time is in effect from the second Sunday in March until November 1.

Tipping   In most cases, a service charge is added to hotel and restaurant bills. In hotels, the charge is in lieu of tipping various individuals, such as bellhops, maids, and restaurant staffers (for meals included in a package or in the daily rate). Check for this carefully to avoid double tipping. Otherwise, a 15% tip for service is customary. Taxi drivers usually get 10% to 15%.

Toilets   The City of Hamilton and St. George provide public facilities, but only during business hours. In the City of Hamilton, toilets are at City Hall, in Par-la-Ville Gardens, and at Albouy's Point. In St. George, facilities are available at Town Hall, Somers Garden, and Market Wharf. Outside of these towns, you'll find restrooms at the public beaches, at the Botanical Gardens, in several of the forts, at the airport, and at service stations. Often you'll have to use the facilities in hotels, restaurants, and wherever else you can find them.

Transit Information   For information about ferry service, call ✆ **441/295-4506.** For bus information, call ✆ **441/292-3854** or 441/292-3851.

Useful Telephone Numbers   On Bermuda, for **time and temperature,** call ✆ **909.** To learn **"What's On in Bermuda,"** dial ✆ **974.** For **medical emergencies** or the **police,** dial ✆ **911.** If in doubt during any other emergency, dial ✆ **0** (zero), which will connect you with your hotel's switchboard or the Bermuda telephone operator.

Visas   Americans who plan to be in Bermuda less than 90 days don't need a visa. Likewise, for the same stays, British citizens, as well as Canadians, Australians, South Africans, New Zealanders, and Irish nationals, don't need a visa. For travelers from other nations, passport and visa requirements are liable to change at short notice. Before planning a trip to Bermuda, check with your local embassy or consulate.

Visitor Information   The Department of Tourism's websites, **www.bermudatourism. com** and **www.gotoBermuda.com** feature comprehensive information broken down into user-friendly categories for vacationers, weddings, travel agents, and media. An interactive map of the island lets visitors see exactly where they'll be going on their Bermuda vacation as well as information on weather, entry requirements, and travel packages, and it also features a state-of-the-art booking device.

The Bermuda government offers a personalized Bermuda mini-guidebook for potential visitors. Within minutes of hanging up the phone, Internet-connected **800/BERMUDA** [237-6832] callers in the U.S. and Canada receive a personalized "weblet" that gives specific, detailed information on hotels and activities based on information supplied by the caller. Your weblet's search engines allow you to supply personal criteria and receive a selection of hotels and restaurants designed to appeal to your taste and pocketbook. Special-interest buttons can be pressed for data on golf, honeymoon packages, nightlife, and sports facilities. U.K. residents should call ℂ **0800/883-0857** to use this service, and residents of other countries will need to consult a travel agent in their particular area.

To speak to a travel representative, contact the **Bermuda Department of Tourism,** 675 Third Ave., New York, NY 10017 (ℂ **212/818-9800**).

In the **United Kingdom,** contact the Bermuda Department of Tourism, 6 Arlington St., London SW1A 1RE, at ℂ **0800/883-0857** or 020/7096-4246.

In Bermuda, you can get answers to most of your questions at the Visitors Information Centre locations at the **Ferry Terminal,** 8 Front St., City of Hamilton (ℂ **441/295-1480**), open Monday to Saturday 9am to 5pm; and at the **Royal Naval Dockyard** (ℂ **441/234-3824**), open daily 9am to 5pm.

Water   Tap water is generally safe to drink.

Weather   Call ℂ **977** at any time for a forecast covering the next 24-hour period or go to www.weather.bm. For average temperatures in Bermuda, see "When to Go," in chapter 2.

Index

See also Accommodations and
Restaurant indexes, below.

General Index

Accommodations

Restaurants